Deconstructing developmental psychology

Deconstructing Developmental Psychology analyses both the knowledge base and the cultural practices associated with developmental psychology. It provides a critical overview of modern developmental psychology, and is designed to accompany and comment on the standard textbooks. Erica Burman explores what is missing in these accounts as a consequence of their primary focus on 'the child', and argues that the selection of the child as the unit of development abstracts development from historical and socio-political conditions.

Current developmental models are seen as fundamentally asocial, with the result that developmental psychology pathologises those individuals and groups who fail to meet its idealised models. The author shows how developmental psychology is a normalising discipline which presents homogenised descriptions of development and is unable to recognise or theorise differences except as inferiorities. Finally, *Deconstructing Developmental Psychology* draws attention to the functions of developmental psychological knowledge in policies and professional practices in education, welfare and the law.

Erica Burman is Senior Lecturer in Developmental and Educational Psychology at the Manchester Metropolitan University.

Critical Psychology
Series editors

John Broughton
Columbia University, New York

David Ingleby
Vakgroep KPG, Utrecht

Valerie Walkerdine
Goldsmiths' College, London

Since the 1960s there has been widespread disaffection with traditional approaches in psychology, and talk of a 'crisis' has been endemic. At the same time, psychology has encountered influential contemporary movements such as feminism, neo-marxism, post-structuralism and post-modernism. In this climate, various forms of 'critical psychology' have developed vigorously.

Unfortunately, such work – drawing as it does on unfamiliar intellectual traditions – is often difficult to assimilate. The aim of the Critical Psychology series is to make this exciting new body of work readily accessible to students and teachers of psychology, as well as presenting the more psychological aspects of this work to a wider social scientific audience. Specially commissioned works from leading critical writers will demonstrate the relevance of their new approaches to a wide range of current social issues.

Titles in the series include:

The crisis in modern social psychology
And how to end it
Ian Parker

The psychology of the female body
Jane M. Ussher

Significant differences
Feminism in psychology
Corinne Squire

Lev Vygotsky
Revolutionary scientist
Fred Newman and Lois Holzman

The mastery of reason
Cognitive development and the production of rationality
Valerie Walkerdine

Child-care and the psychology of development
Elly Singer

Rewriting the self
History, memory, narrative
Mark Freeman

Deconstructing developmental psychology

Erica Burman

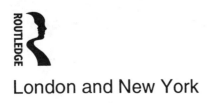

London and New York

First published 1994
by Routledge
11 New Fetter Lane, London EC4P 4EE

Simultaneously published in the USA and Canada
by Routledge
29 West 35th Street, New York, NY 10001

© 1994 Erica Burman

Typeset in Times by LaserScript, Mitcham, Surrey
Printed and bound in Great Britain by
Biddles Ltd, Guildford and King's Lynn

British Library Cataloguing in Publication Data
A catalogue record for this book is available from the British Library.

Library of Congress Cataloging in Publication Data
Burman, Erica.
 Deconstructing developmental psychology/Erica Burman.
 p. cm. – (Critical psychology)
 Includes bibliographical references and index.
 1. Developmental psychology. I. Title. II. Series.
 BF713.B87   1994
 155 – dc20   93-5880
                                                     CIP

ISBN 0–415–06437–6 (hbk)
ISBN 0–415–06438–4 (pbk)

Contents

Acknowledgements   vii
Introduction   1

1   Origins   9

Part I Constructing the subject

2   Researching infancy   23
3   Attributing sociality   35
4   Discourses of the child   48

Part II Social development and the structure of caring

5   Familiar assumptions   65
6   Bonds of love – dilemmas of attachment   77
7   The rise of 'fathering'   94

Part III Developing communication

8   Language talk   107
9   Discourses of caregiving talk   124
10   Language and power in developmental research   138

Part IV Cognitive development: the making of rationality

11   The production of Piagetian psychology   151
12   Piaget and child-centred education   163
13   Morality and the goals of development   177

References   190
Name index   207
Subject index   212

This book is dedicated to
my nieces and nephews,
Hannah, Rachel, David and Jonathan,
in the hope that its contents
will one day be irrelevant to them.

Acknowledgements

In addition to all the people whose work has been so useful, and influential, for me, I want to thank:

Kath Holland, Ian Parker and Sharon Witton for comments on the manuscript;

Julian Pine for supplying lots of papers;

Liz Bondi, Katrina Long, Ian Parker and Diane Samuels for their general support during the process of its preparation;

Heather Walton and Berenice Burman for proof reading;

Valerie Walkerdine for her enthusiastic response to my tentative proposal to write this;

David Ingleby for the faxes full of comments;

Elena Lieven, John Morss and Rex and Wendy Stainton Rogers who, in addition to their constructive commentaries on earlier drafts, have encouraged me to realise that there really is a network of critical developmental psychologists;

Sue Jameson for all those articles;

the library staff at Elizabeth Gaskell, the Manchester Metropolitan University, for discharging lots of books that have been so entertaining and useful;

the psychology technicians for the computer first aid;

successive cohorts of students taking developmental psychology on the BSc Psychology at the Manchester Metropolitan University who have been subjected to various forms of the material outlined in this book over the past six years, including the feminist students who, year after year, confirmed that it was important and worthwhile;

and the women I work with on the MA in Women's Studies at the Manchester Metropolitan University who display a healthy suspicion of psychology.

Erica Burman

Introduction

God forbid that any book should be banned. The practice is as indefensible as infanticide.

(Dame Rebecca West, 1928)

Sooner murder an infant in its cradle than nurse unacted desires.

(William Blake, *Proverbs of Hell*)

Deconstructing Developmental Psychology is a critical introduction to developmental psychology. Critical in the sense that it comments upon rather than replaces mainstream accounts of developmental psychology. Introductory in the sense that it aims to present in an accessible way a synthesis of various existing critiques and discussions that are often complex and seemingly very specific in their remit, but which have major and important consequences for the project of developmental psychology. This book focuses on the relation between academic research and social policies and practices, in particular to highlight and often question the desirability of the effects of developmental psychological research (and also the possibility of the division between theory and application).

As the title suggests, my aim is to deconstruct developmental psychology, that is to identify and evaluate the guiding themes or discourses that structure its current dominant forms. To identify suggests an active search for patterning, while evaluation implies a process of commentary. I use the term 'deconstruction' in the sense of laying bare, of bringing under scrutiny, the coherent moral-political themes that developmental psychology elaborates, and to look beyond current frameworks within which developmental psychological investigation has been formulated to take up the broader questions of where these themes fit into the social practices in which psychology functions. I am using deconstruction here not as a formal analytical framework but rather to indicate a process of critique. In this sense this arises from a critical movement within psychology (exemplified by Henriques *et al.* (1984) and Parker and Shotter (1990)) which takes as its topic the structure of psychological practice. In this book I will be addressing the discourses that developmental psychology both constructs and informs, using the term 'discourse' to refer to socially organised frameworks of meaning that define categories and specify domains of what can be said and done. I will be concerned with developmental psychological *accounts*, not simply in terms of the language within which these are cast, although this is important; rather this book explores how these accounts reflect and engage with the practices associated with them. In this sense my concern is with how, why and in what ways sets of ideas in developmental psychology have functioned outside as well as within its relatively restricted domain.

Developmental psychology, more than any other variety of psychology, has a powerful impact on our everyday lives and ways of thinking about ourselves. Its effects are so great that they are often almost imperceptible, taken-for-granted features about our expectations of ourselves, others, parents, children and families. Due to the divide in the West between the public world of work and the private, domestic sphere inscribed by industrialisation, the home and our actions within it carry so much emotional investment that evaluation of relationships and behaviours conducted within it (as mothers, fathers, children) is deeply felt, and often feared. Part of the imperceptibility lies in the ways developmental psychology has structured the standards and even the forms of modern state intervention that accompany welfare policies of protection and care. Acknowledging these issues means going beyond the representation of developmental psychological research as scientific and benign in its effects.

ORGANISATION

The structure of this book reflects the main topics and categorisations employed by many widely available developmental psychology texts. In following this structure I do not mean simply to reproduce those categorisations, but rather to facilitate the co-ordination of this account with the others. Hence the titles of chapters and headings aim to highlight the discursive construction of topic areas. In commenting on these, this book traces the accounts of development along the semi-biographical or chronological path of the notional 'child'. In Chapter 1, I start by exploring the historical background to the contemporary role that developmental psychology and developmental psychologists have played. This sets the focus for the first major section of the book, Part I, 'Constructing the subject', which is concerned with how developmental psychology arrived at and investigates its unit of development. Here, Chapter 2 addresses this in terms of infancy research, Chapter 3 through discussions about social development and Chapter 4 by analysing historical and cultural influences that inform our conceptions of childhood and the limits of these conceptions.

Part II, 'Social development and the structure of caring', focuses on the role accorded to, and particular representations of, families and parents. Chapter 5 examines the ways in which families are discussed in developmental psychological accounts. Chapter 6 analyses the literature on the formation and importance of relationships, and Chapter 7 evaluates the preconditions and consequences of the shift in cultural and academic focus from mothers to fathers.

Part III, 'Developing communication', is devoted to the research on how children learn to talk (Chapter 8), and how child language can best be promoted (Chapter 9). Chapter 10 draws on a rather different set of perspectives to argue for the importance of analysing the power relations that structure adult–child interaction, including that of psychologist and child.

Part IV, 'Cognitive development: the making of rationality', deals with the role accorded to Piagetian theory within developmental psychology. Chapter 11 explores historical and cultural factors relevant to interpreting Piaget's work and Piagetian debates, and how these have entered into the ways the ideas have been incorporated within social practices. Chapter 12 develops this further in relation to the impact of Piaget's work in educational contexts. Chapter 13 addresses the application of Piaget's 'cognitive' model in the arena of morality through the work of Kohlberg, as illustrative of some of the major difficulties the cognitive developmental approach involves. This question also brings us back to the moral status of developmental psychology and its collusion in the organised amorality of contemporary life.

KEY THEMES

A number of key issues have structured the forms and functions of developmental psychology. These stretch across the seemingly (within current formulations) disparate arenas of social, cognitive or language development. While treating each topic separately I have tried to indicate continuities, highlighting the specific forms the recurring structural themes take within particular domains. The repetition of these issues in itself is evidence not only of their pervasiveness, but also of the greater unity of preoccupations that developmental psychology has informed and reflected, as a vital contributor to modern state practices.

Put briefly, these themes are as follows. Firstly, that tools of measurement produce research objects and research subjects. Developmental psychology has been driven by the demand to produce technologies of measurement. These methodological parameters have reflected broader ideological assumptions in selecting and abstracting child and mother as its units of enquiry.

Secondly, in many respects mothers have replaced children as the primary focus for developmental psychological investigation, reflecting wider themes of regulation – in terms of a) active intervention in women's lives, b) indirect impact through women's subscription to developmental psychological accounts about how children develop and what is 'best' for them, and c) the broader impact of developmental psychology as it informs the cultural climate and structure of provision and services available for children (and working mothers). It is the adequacy of mothering that developmental psychology is called upon to regulate and legislate upon, and the continuity with which this issue crops up across the range of topics in developmental psychology is a manifestation of the widespread and routine subjection of women to the developmental psychological gaze.

The third recurring issue is that normative descriptions provided by developmental psychology slip into naturalised prescriptions. These are fuelled by the appeal to biology and evolution, which is called upon in areas as diverse as attachment theory, language development and education. Representations of children frequently function as a projective slate on to which fantasies of nature and its relation to society are inscribed. Developmental psychology makes claims to be scientific. Its use of evolutionary assumptions to link the social to the biological provides a key cultural arena in which evolutionary and biologistic ideas are replayed and legitimised. Closely associated with its technologies and its guiding preoccupations has been its use to classify and stratify individuals, groups and populations so as to maintain class, gender and racial oppression.

A fourth strand within this book concerns the relation between psychology and psychoanalysis. A psychoanalytic reading of developmental psychology offers glimpses into the repressed themes of fear that underlie the scientific demand for control and prediction. Psychoanalysis is increasingly being used as a resource to critique psychology (Parker, 1993; Walkerdine, 1990), including developmental psychology (see, e.g., Henriques *et al.*, 1984). This enables a questioning of what lies behind the privileging of objectivity and control over the ambiguity, flux and ambivalence of the issues raised by caring for children.

The fifth, and final, theme concerns how the selection of children as objects of developmental psychological enquiry leads to a failure to theorise the psychological context they inhabit. This contributes to individualistic interpretations of socially structured phenomena that can lapse into victim blaming, as where mothers are treated as responsible for the social ills of the world in which they are trying to rear their children. Where the focus moves beyond the individual to consider class and culture, these have frequently, explicitly or implicitly, been treated as responsible for failures of child development or education, while the motivations or resources drawn upon by those who make such evaluations all too often remain unexamined. This book attempts to open up these structural themes for scrutiny together with their underlying assumptions and the practices to which they give rise.

HOW TO READ THIS BOOK

Children and childhood are rhetorically invoked in multiple ways for sometimes (as in my introductory quotations) divergent or contradictory purposes. Similarly, there are various ways of approaching developmental psychology: from the point of view of the child, from that of parents and families, and from the position of professionals or agencies directly or indirectly involved with children. Accounts are usually cast in terms of the first approach, of what the child is, does and what it will do next. In this book, I adopt the second position and explore the consequences of focusing on the child. These consequences are pervasive both for adults who do (and do not) care for children and for professionals involved with services for children. In fact, I will be taking the child-centred focus of developmental psychology as itself a topic of enquiry and critique.

This book therefore concentrates less on 'facts' that developmental psychology has unearthed than on how particular topics arise as interesting areas of enquiry. The perspective I am adopting is to look at developmental psychological knowledge as constructed within social practices rather than as a distinct content area. This means that this book is not only concerned with what developmental psychology has 'found' and the claims that it makes, but also considers the significance of the types of research and research outcomes in three ways: the circumstances in which the research was carried out, the social and political influences that made the topic seem relevant, and the role and impact of that research. In other words, developmental psychology is treated as a topic of enquiry in its own right, with objects and subjects of study (children, families, mothers) constructed in relation to it.

My aim in this book, then, is to pose questions about what is all too often assumed to be given or obvious. For example: why is developmental psychology always presumed to be about 'the child'? What are the consequences of this for the theory and practice of developmental psychology? How would this be different from discussing 'children' or 'contexts in which people grow and change'? This book challenges the common-sense view of developmental psychology, treating this view as a resource through which to explore developmental psychology's project and practice.

In accordance with this perspective, I frequently refer to 'the child', the 'individual' or the 'subject' of developmental psychology using the feminine pronoun 'she'. This practice departs from the conventions used in many psychology textbooks. If it sounds strange, it is worth considering why this might be so. In more general terms, this should lead us to consider *whose* development we are talking about – that of an individual? An abstract 'knower'? Everyone's development? (Are there claims to universality here?) Does it reflect all cultures? Classes? Men's and women's experiences? What are the consequences for developmental psychology of its forgetting of gender as a structuring dimension of development?

Throughout the book, I will be drawing links between what may seem like rather conceptual debates within the discipline and their effects within the practices in which developmental psychology participates. Developmental psychological knowledge informs a number of professional practices, such as health, education and welfare, that touch everybody's lives. In particular, it forms part of the knowledge base for health visiting and social work, as well as education and law. For example, on what basis do law courts arrive at an understanding of what constitutes a child's 'best interest'? What underlies an education welfare officer's opinion that a child's 'social and emotional needs' will be better catered for outside mainstream school? What criteria do adoption agencies use in evaluating whether or not adoption is likely to be successful? These are some of the ways in which developmental psychology reverberates far beyond the theory or the experimental laboratory, as well as beyond the pages of child advice magazines and toyshops.

To facilitate the connection between the arguments elaborated within the book and the general implications for theory and practice that flow from them, each chapter has suggestions for further reading and some practical demonstrations or activities that exemplify its key points. These activities can be used to structure individual or group work. They are based on my experience of teaching students of psychology, nursing, healthcare and youth and community work, and involvement in training teachers and social workers. They are intended as a resource that can be adapted or extended to a variety of audiences and contexts.

CULTURAL CONSTRUCTIONS

As already mentioned, the approach here is not the 'child-centred' variety generally found. Rather the starting point is that children and childhood are *constructed*; we therefore have to study not only 'the child', but also the context (that is, the interpersonal, cultural, historical and political situation) that produces her. This book focuses on families, on the ways in which parents, and in particular mothers, are positioned in relation to children, and the effects that cultural prescriptions for 'good mothering' as relayed through developmental psychology have for women. As Piaget (1950) said: 'Child psychology is a branch equally of sociology and psychology, since the social environment is an integral component of development.' More recently, Goodnow and Collins (1990: 10) comment:

> For us an exclusively child-centered focus is limited. Child development is not the whole of developmental psychology. Moreover parents are interesting in their own right. Their experiences, satisfactions and development are topics to be explored without any necessity to justify the exploration on the grounds of effects on children.

The developmental psychology generally studied is usually conducted on, and written by researchers from, Western societies. Indeed it is typically Anglo-US, and the bulk of this work is North American – although it exerts its influence throughout the English-speaking world. In the main I will also be drawing on those sources, not because I wish to subscribe to the same assumptions, but rather because we need to analyse the structure of the dominant approach in order better to comment on its implications, especially in terms of its impact in post-colonial countries whose psychological services (and perhaps psychologies) are moulded by that colonial legacy. However, there is a longstanding (but until recently relatively separate and philosophically different) Soviet tradition (Valsiner, 1988), and of course a Western European one. I will be commenting on the selective importing of Piaget's work and its subsequent insertion into existing practices. This offers a prime example of the cultural and philosophical tensions between different strands of developmental psychology that are taken up later in this book.

This book focuses primarily on infancy and early childhood. Traditionally, developmental psychology has not only concerned itself with plotting the growth of individuals, but has also compartmentalised the human life span so that 'development' is usually portrayed as confined to early life, and psychological change during and after adulthood is limited to intellectual decline. Such views have recently been disputed, and 'development' has come to be seen as a 'life-span' affair. However, this tends to magnify rather than resolve the problems of naturalising the life span in the name of extending the trajectory of developmental progress. In this book, I will be problematising developmental psychology's study of the child as isolated individual, rather than solely criticising the focus on childhood as a life stage. Nevertheless, the arguments elaborated in relation to childhood throughout this book also apply to the assumptions guiding the models of adulthood and ageing. These wider applications have been addressed by Lichtman (1987).

Finally, this book highlights the nature of the normative assumptions guiding developmental theory and research, and assesses the impact of these on our understanding of 'the child' or 'the parent–child relationship' in relation to both the professional and non-professional social practices developmental psychology informs.

CLAIMS AND DISCLAIMERS

While it may be tempting to treat this book as just a commentary on, rather than a contribution to, developmental psychology, this book should also be considered as part of developmental psychology. A deconstruction of developmental psychology is no less a part of developmental psychology for that. These ideas should not be marginalised as 'outside'. Commentaries on the practice of psychology have for too long been seen as the province of sociologists and historians. There is now increasing recognition that behind the mask of detached, disinterested objective research lie interpretative and subjective features that, as is the way of repressed material, exert their influences in forms of which we are not aware. Rather than condemning developmental psychology to serving and reproducing this unconscious agenda (which is very much *man*-made), we should be moving towards some awareness of the historical and current reasons for the particular ways developmental research has been structured. This should enable a more informed re-evaluation of the possibilities and problems of developmental research.

The resources I have drawn upon in writing this book have been feminist and post-structuralist ideas (and in particular the feminist re-workings of post-structuralist ideas). In both dimly perceived and consciously developed ways, the history of my own (multiple and contradictory) subject positionings within developmental psychological discourses – as child, daughter, sister, aunt, child-free, child-less, daughter of single parent, feminist, child-centred, woman-centred and so on – has been instrumental in the elaboration of this account. I list these not, or not only, to engage in the confessional mode of expression conventionally adopted within an 'Introduction', but to emphasise that I, as author, am as subject to the power of the discourses developmental psychology produces and reproduces as the putative children and families I discuss in this book. I, like everyone else, cannot stand, or rather speak, outside them. But I can try to describe and analyse their consequences, and maybe by such interventions create new ways of doing developmental psychology.

Chapter 1

Origins

Many experimental psychologists continue to look upon the field of child psychology as a proper field of research for women and for men whose experimental masculinity is not of the maximum. This attitude of patronage is based almost entirely upon a blissful ignorance of what is going on in the tremendously virile field of child behavior.

(Murchison, 1933: x)

Nowadays the status of developmental psychology is not clear. Some say that it is a perspective or an approach to investigating general psychological problems, rather than a particular domain or sub-discipline. According to this view we can address all major areas of psychology, such as memory, cognition, etc., from this perspective. The unit of development under investigation is also variable. We could be concerned with the development of a process, or a mechanism, rather than an individual. This is in marked contrast with the popular representations of developmental psychology which equate it with the practicalities of child development or, more recently, human development (with the relatively recent recognition that development is a 'life-span' affair, Baltes *et al.*, 1980).

These paradoxical, mixed conceptions of developmental psychology testify to different aspects of its history. If we look at the origins of developmental psychology we begin to get a picture of 1) the social movements from which it arose, 2) the social movements in which it participated, and 3) how these have set the terms of developmental enquiry that reverberate even now. This chapter will elaborate how modern developmental psychology arose in the late nineteenth century to answer particular questions related to evolutionary theory and anthropology as well as philosophy. In so doing, developmental psychology participated in social movements explicitly concerned with the comparison, regulation and control of groups and societies, and is closely identified with the development of tools of mental measurement, classification of abilities and the establishment of norms. It is associated with the rise of science and modernity, subscribing to a specific, gendered model of scientific practice. All of these features are reflected in the terms of developmental research, including the reproduction of the division between rationality and emotion.

CHILD STUDY

The new psychology of the mid- to late nineteenth century placed itself within and between various disciplines: natural history, anthropology, physiology and medicine. Most accounts take Charles Darwin as the author of the first child study with his 'Biographical sketch of an infant', which, though published in 1877, was based on notes made in 1840 (Riley, 1983; Rose, 1985; Walkerdine and Lucey, 1989). Not surprisingly, Darwin's interest was in the relative contribution of genetic endowment and environmental experience; identifying the characteristics that differentiate humans and (human children) from animals, placing great weight on human ingenuity and creativity, especially as exhibited in language. This was one among many early observational, diary studies of young children, although, as Bradley (1989) points out, there had been many conducted earlier, especially by women, but these have been eclipsed from the history of developmental psychology. In retrospect, both this study and the importance it has been accorded can be taken as prototypical of the form developmental enquiry was to take.

Firstly, the infant is depicted as a biological organism abstracted from its familial and material environment. By virtue of being very young, and having had less opportunity to learn, the infant is seen as close to nature, devoid of the trappings of adult training and (Western) 'civilisation'. In contradictory ways, romantic and scientific models combine to locate within the child both *more* knowledge ('the child is father to the man') and (by virtue of the child's lesser and different understanding) the *route* to knowledge. In this, developmental psychology naturalises the romantic fiction of children as innocent bearers of wisdom by producing them as objects and subjects of study.

The perspective underlying this project partakes of the theory of 'cultural recapitulation', that is, that the individual in her or his lifetime reproduces the patterns and stages of development exhibited by the development of the species – 'ontogeny recapitulates phylogeny'. The study of infants in the mid-nineteenth century, along with that of 'primitives' and of natural history, was motivated by the quest to discover the origins and specificities of mind, that is, the human adult mind. This enterprise was related to similar ventures in anthropology and animal observation that were closely allied with European (and particularly British) imperialism, maintaining the hierarchy of racial superiority that justified colonial rule. The child of that time was equated with the 'savage' or 'undeveloped'; since both were seen as intellectually immature, 'primitives' and children were studied to illuminate necessary stages for subsequent development. As James Sully wrote in his 1881 article 'Babies and science':

the modern psychologist, sharing in the spirit of positive science, feels that he must, being at the beginning, study mind in its simplest forms. . . . [H]e carries his eye far afield to the phenomena of savage life, with its simple ideas, crude sentiments and naive habits. Again he devotes special attention to the mental life of lower animals, seeking in its phenomena the dim foreshadowing of our own perceptions, emotions etc. Finally he directs his attention to the mental life of infancy, as fitted to throw most light on the later developments of the human mind.

(Sully, 1881: quoted in Riley, 1983: 47)

In addition, the apparently bizarre beliefs and behaviours of both 'primitives' and children were seen as relevant to the understanding of neurotic and pathological behaviour. As well as recapitulationism, Lamarckism (the belief in the heritability of acquired characteristics) underlay the new developmental psychology. Here it was the experience, rather than innate predispositions, that was seen as reproduced in childhood and in dreams. A set of equivalences was elaborated whereby the conception of the child was related to the 'savage', who, in turn, was seen as akin to the neurotic. Comparison between child, prehistoric man (*sic*) and 'savage' presupposes a conception of development, of individual and of evolutionary progress, as unilinear, as directed steps up an ordered hierarchy. The specifically Darwinian notion of natural selection, however, emphasises variability rather than uniformity. While Darwin's subscription to recapitulationism and Lamarckism was equivocal and implicit (Morss, 1990: 14-16), these were the features that were taken up to structure the emergent developmental psychology. It should be noted that these views were widely held, and that, among others, both Freud and Piaget subscribed to them in their writings.

While Darwin's study can in many ways be taken as prototypical (in various senses) of several others conducted by researchers such as Taine, Preyer and G.S. Hall in the 1880s (Riley, 1983), John Morss (1990) argues that the effect of Darwin's work within the emerging developmental psychology was to reinforce *pre*-Darwinian versions of biology, focusing on heritability rather than variation. Child study 'societies' soon flourished, observing children, weighing and measuring them, documenting their interests, states, activities. This development reflected the increasing importance of science – and a particular model of science at that – not only as a set of procedures for conducting research, but as a set of practices associated with the modern secular State.

THE GENDERED DIVISION OF LABOUR AND THE SCIENTIFIC GAZE

The child study movement 'observed' children. Guidelines on how to go about this emphasised the importance of being objective. In doing this a split or opposition was created in the process of knowledge construction – a gendered division. Fathers were seen as having the necessary detachment and rationality to engage in scientific endeavour and mothers as too sentimental to participate. In his article (which was partly satirical – both of the practice of studying babies and of the current interest it was inspiring) Sully (1881) comments on the new phenomenon of the 'psychological papa':

> Men who previously never thought of meddling with the affairs of the nursery have been impelled to make periodic visits thither in the hope of eliciting important psychological facts. . . . [T]he tiny occupant of the cradle has had to bear the piercing glance of the scientific eye. The psychological papa has acquired a new proprietry right in his offspring; he has appropriated it as a biological specimen. This new zeal for scientific knowledge has taken possession of a number of my acquaintances.
>
> (Sully, 1881: quoted in Riley 1983: 48–9)

Women were excluded from the investigative enterprise because they were declared constitutionally incapable of regarding their children with the requisite objectivity. The mother's approach to infants

> unfits her from entering very cordially into the scientific vein. She rather dislikes their being made objects of cold intellectual scrutiny and unfeeling psychological analysis. . . . To suggest a series of experiments on the gustatory sensibility of a small creature aged from twelve to twenty four hours is likely to prove a shock, even to the more strong-minded of mothers.
>
> (ibid.)

Even if she does want to participate, her efforts are to be treated as suspect and as more of a handicap than anything else:

> if the mother gets herself in time infected with the scientific ardour of the father, she may prove rather more of an auxiliary than he desires. Her maternal instincts impel her to regard her particular child as phenomenal in an extra-scientific sense. She . . . is predisposed to ascribe to her child a preternatural degree of intelligence.
>
> (ibid.)

The Murchison quote at the beginning of this chapter indicates how little had changed fifty years later. The equation between science and masculinity was so strong, and research practice so 'virile', as to be able to counter the supposedly feminising tendencies that proximity to children produces.

There are five ways in which the child study movement of the late nineteenth century prefigured the terms of developmental enquiry. Firstly, it set out to investigate the mind. Secondly, the mind was seen as instantiated within the study of the development of the minds of children. Thirdly, it researched knowledge, viewed as a natural and biological capacity – that is, subscribing to an assumption that there is a normal core of development unfolding according to biological principles. Fourthly, it participated in the practices of education, welfare and medicine. Fifthly, it institutionalised the ancient split between emotion and rationality, played out in the gendered practice of scientific research.

However, while the early child studies clearly privileged biological and universal questions concerned with the development of species, race and mind, there was still room to look at children's emotional proclivities and personalities. But, by the 1930s, clear lines of demarcation were being drawn between the elaboration of developmental norms for diagnostic use (seen as the domain of general psychology and medicine) and psychoanalysis (seen as the arena of the particular personality traits and specific idiosyncratic processes). The contrary and complementary relation between psychology and psychoanalysis came to reflect the split between the rational, conscious, uniform, individual subject of psychology, and the emotional, unconscious, contradictory, fragmented mental states associated with psychoanalysis (Urwin, 1986).

THE RISE OF PSYCHOLOGY TO MEET THE DEMANDS OF PREVAILING SOCIAL ANXIETIES

The late nineteenth century was a time of social upheaval and unrest all over the world, and with revolutions brewing throughout Europe. In England, increasing urbanisation brought about by rapid industrialisation produced the appalling conditions of the Victorian slums, while the poor health of army recruits for colonial wars made the physical state of the general population a matter of widespread concern. Popular (that is upper-class) attention focused on the 'quality' of the population, in particular on those sectors of society considered unstable and unruly. The concern with the quality of the 'stock' and with the moulding, and ameliorating, effects of environmental conditions was reflected in the 'nature–nurture' couplet which was invented by Francis Galton in 1875, and which has since become the widely adopted formulation through which to pose questions about the origins of knowledge and learning in psychology. This early focus on change is somewhat ironic when it is recalled that 'nature–nurture' originates as a way of describing the *immutability* of human behaviour.

It has been widely documented (Hendrick, 1990; Meyer, 1983; Rose, 1990; Walkerdine, 1984) that the establishment of compulsory elementary schooling in the 1880s in England (and around the same time in France) reflected popular anxieties about 'pauperism' (seen as a trait rather than a set of circumstances) and crime, which popular education was seen as rectifying by inculcating good habits, or at least keeping potentially disorderly groups busy and under scrutiny. Reading of the Bible was considered especially important, as well as learning skills suited to one's gender and station in life (Hunt, 1985).

The notion of 'degeneracy' elided mental and moral qualities to the extent that the object of political anxiety and scientific intervention became the 'feeble-minded', who came to signify physical, moral, mental and political dis-integration. In terms of the increasing currency of social Darwinist ideas (applying notions of 'survival of the fittest' to human societies), the fact that poorer sections of the population were reproducing at a faster rate than the educated middle classes provoked fears of contamination and upheaval. A state-of-the-art

Handbook of Child Development of 1933 still devoted a chapter to 'The feeble-minded child' in which there is a discussion of relation between feeble-mindedness and delinquency. It ends with the following:

> Since feeblemindedness is not a disease that we can hope to cure, what methods are to be adopted to lessen the enormous burden that feeble-mindedness places on the community? The only procedures seem to be training, segregation and sterilization. Training all the feebleminded as much as possible to reduce their liability to the community. The segregation of as many of them as possible is wise in order to diminish the chances of feeble-minded offspring. The segregation of feebleminded women of child-bearing age is particularly necessary. . . . Perhaps the percentage is increasing in view of the very noticeable modern trend among the more intelligent families to limit the number of offspring, with little corresponding limitation among the less intelligent families.
>
> (Pintner, 1933: 837)

Controlling and regulating those social elements considered potentially unruly presupposed the means to monitor them. Nikolas Rose (1985) discusses how 'individual psychology' emerged to fulfil this role of classification and sur-veillance. The psychological individual was a highly specified and studied entity whose mental qualities and development were understood by virtue of com-parison with the general population. So knowledge of the individual and the general went hand in hand: each required the other, and each was defined in terms of the other. The division of the mad from the sane, the criminal from the lawful and educable from the ineducable, shifted from moral-political criteria to the equally judgemental, but scientific, evaluation of mental testing.

CATCHING THEM YOUNG: MENTAL TESTING AND THE PRODUCTION OF THE NORMAL CHILD

The psychology of the individual, then, was the forerunner of the arenas now known as personality and developmental psychology, and depended heavily on testing for both its knowledge base and functioning – though psychology did not achieve its monopoly on testing without a struggle (Rose, 1985). Individual psychology in late nineteenth- and early twentieth-century Western Europe reflected and translated the social preoccupations with population quality and mental abilities into policy recommendations, prescriptions on infant and child management, and education. As Donna Haraway notes:

> Comparative psychologists have been extraordinarily creative in devising testing situations and technology: the testing industry is central to the pro-duction of social order in liberal societies, where the prescriptions of scientific management must be reconciled with ideologies of democracy.
>
> (Haraway, 1989: 236–7)

But the technology of testing both requires and relies on the very institutions that permit its administration. Hence 'individual psychology' became central to the existence of the mental hospital, the prison – and the school and child guidance clinic. The emergence of both the individual and the child as objects of social and scientific gaze was therefore simultaneous.

> Developmental psychology was made possible by the clinic and the nursery school. Such institutions had a vital role, for they enabled the observation of numbers of children of the same age, and of children of a number of different ages, by skilled psychological experts under controlled experimental, almost laboratory, conditions. They thus simultaneously allowed for standardization and normalization – the collection of comparable information on a large number of subjects and its analysis in such a way as to construct norms. A developmental norm was a standard based upon the average abilities or performances of children of a certain age in a particular task or a specified activity. It thus not only presented a picture of what was *normal* for children of such an age, but also enabled the normality of any child to be assessed by comparison with this norm.
>
> (Rose, 1990: 142)

By virtue of producing the unit of enquiry, the standardisation process set up a reciprocal dependence between the normal and abnormal: it is the normalisation of development that makes abnormality possible; and vice versa – in the sense that the special education system has always deeply structured, rather than merely supplemented, the mainstream schooling system (Ford, 1982). So, despite the current image of special schools as some extra or distant facility drawn upon in exceptional circumstances, they are what make mainstream schools 'mainstream': that is, the latter function as 'normal' schools precisely because they are bounded by institutions for those designated as 'abnormal'. In 1956 a book by an erstwhile President of the British Psychological Society, C.W. Valentine, appeared, entitled *The Normal Child and Some of his Abnormalities*, which went through eleven reprints up to 1974. As the editorial foreword by Professor C.A. Mace puts it, the book sets out

> to answer a question of great concern to parents and teachers today: *Is this child 'normal' or shall I take him to the clinic?*
>
> (Mace in Valentine 1956: 9)

Hence 'the clinic' becomes the arbiter of 'normal' development through its position as the domain of its converse, 'the abnormal'.

Moreover, this process of normalisation prompted a naturalisation of development, overdetermined by two related factors. The new psychology's claims to be a science of the mental sought to emulate medicine's status as a science of the body. This emulation was expressed within the confounding of the notions of medical with mental through the hybrid notion of mental hygiene. This endowed a scientific legitimation upon practices of social regulation and reform.

KINDERGARTEN COPS: THE NATURALISATION AND REGULATION OF DEVELOPMENT

There were two ways in which development was naturalised. Firstly, the notion of mental age underlying IQ tests, considered as analogous to chronological age, assumed that ability could be distributed (at quantifiable and equal intervals) on a quasi-physical scale. The work of North American psychologist Arnold Gesell was highly influential in drawing up the norms and 'milestones' that underlie developmental health checks, and in promoting a maturational view of development as a process of natural unfolding whereby development is equated with growth. The blurb to the fourth (1971) edition of *The First Five Years of Life* (Gesell, 1950) claims that it contributes 'more than any other book to the foundations of systematic developmental psychology'. While (in contrast to more behaviourally oriented positivist researchers) he favoured 'naturalistic', clinical interviews over psychometric tests, Gesell presented descriptions (or what he called 'characterisations') of development as absolutely age-graded. Years and months dictated capacities and achievements. The following example, while meant to ring a lighter note, highlights more general themes. The abstraction of developmental time is associated with that of exchange, such that developmental maturation is linked to the return on a financial investment. Child development parallels capitalism:

> Three is a delightful age. Infancy superannuates at Two and gives way to a higher estate.
>
> (Gesell, 1950: 40)

Secondly, the production of the individual mirrors the incorporation of the mental within the medical: the natural has to be closely scrutinised to prevent it lapsing into the pathological. The presumed equivalences between mental and physical development systematise the scrutiny of children, extending beyond the measurement of apparent to hypothetical qualities, and beyond the child to the family in ways that are now central to welfare policies. Note how the emphasis on care subsumes the mental within the physical and reinforces the role of the expert as empowered to make family interventions in this recent extract from *The Handbook of Child Surveillance*:

> Child health surveillance is a programme of care initiated and provided by professionals, with the aim of preventing illness and promoting good health and development. . . . [A]lthough we have described some of the methods of early detection in detail, we have also stressed the importance of primary prevention and of working with parents as the most effective means of helping children.
>
> (Hall *et al.*, 1990: x)

The normal child, the ideal type, distilled from the comparative scores of age-graded populations, is therefore a fiction or myth. No individual or real child lies at its basis. It is an abstraction, a fantasy, a fiction, a production of the testing apparatus that incorporates, that constructs the child, by virtue of its gaze. This production, rather than description, of the child arose from the technologies of photography by which hundreds of children doing the same tasks could be juxtaposed, compared and synthesised into a single scale of measurement, from one-way mirrors through which children could be observed, and of psychometric tests. The production and regulation of children extended beyond testing environments to the settings by which children were cared for and instructed. Gesell (1950) provides plans of the prototypical nursery school, the complex design of which is structured around a hidden child observation room. All child behaviour is available to be documented, becomes normalised into child development, and child development comes to inform the mundane minutiae of childcare. As Urwin and Sharland (1992) argue, the organisation and arrangement of the body is taken as the route to the regulation of the mind. And this is not dead history. In August 1991 media reports of John McCarthy's release after five years of being held hostage in Lebanon focused on his mental state (and his subsequent consumption of that signifier of homecoming, a full English breakfast). The commentators included 'a psychologist' who stated that he will have lost the use of his 'freedom muscle'. The mental is assimilated to the physical.

JAGGED EDGE? CONFLICTS AND CONTINUITIES

In drawing out these connections, no causal determination can be attributed to the psychological study of children, but rather this is simultaneously both a reflection of the wider preoccupations and an instance of strategies developed to further them. As Valerie Walkerdine puts it, political motivations cannot be said to have

> caused in any simple sense certain developments in the science of the individual. Rather each should be taken as mutually implicated, making and re-making the other possible, intertwining to produce a discursive and political nexus. The rational, the savage, the animal, the human, the degenerate, the normal, all become features of the modern scientific normalization and regulation of children.
>
> (Walkerdine, 1984: 173)

Moreover, highlighting the continuities between past and present forms of developmental psychology should not lead us to underestimate shifts and conflicts between them. The child study movement, based on the accumulated observations of individual children and inspired by evolutionary ideas, focused initially on questions of heredity. But soon afterwards its attention was devoted to the role of education in alleviating or compensating for the deficiencies of heredity (Riley, 1983). Cyril Burt is now infamous for the falsification of his twin studies (Hearnshaw, 1980), but was responsible in large part for creating the profession of educational psychology in Britain. (Now the British Psychological Society, which condemned Burt, is being pressurised, against the background of a revival of streaming and testing in British schools, to rehabilitate him.) While adhering to a notion of a fixed, quantifiable and heritable cognitive capacity, he also subscribed to a staunch environmentalism by which hereditary dispositions could be mitigated. Philanthropic and innatist perspectives can coincide with as well as contradict each other.

With the impact of behaviourist ideas from the 1910s onwards, environmental – meaning school as well as family – influences became the main focus of developmental psychological accounts. Child training accompanied improvements in sanitation and social reform. Education (of the child and the parents) gradually superseded segregation as a strategy of demographic management – though, as the above examples indicate, it was none the less regulatory. If anything, a strategy of education rather than segregation required a commitment to greater intervention and control. It should nevertheless be recalled that many of the founding fathers of statistics, and of individual psychology, such as Galton and Pearson, were in the forefront of the eugenic movement in Britain. Rose (1985) discusses in detail why and how the more 'enlightened' ideas of the reformers prevailed over those of the eugenicists even before those ideas were further discredited by their application in Nazi Germany, and Ulfried Geuter (1987) documents the flourishing of psychology in Nazi Germany. The point is that modern psychology came of age with the political utility of mental testing. As Lewis Terman, himself reponsible for the development and popularisation of one of the foremost standardised tests, asserted in 1920:

> It is the method of tests that has brought psychology down from the clouds . . . that has transformed the 'science of trivialities' into the science of human engineering. The psychologist in the pre-test era was, to the average layman, just a harmless crank, but now that psychology has tested and classified nearly two million soldiers, has been appealed to in the grading of nearly two million children, is used everywhere in our institutions for the feebleminded, delinquent, criminal and insane, has become the beacon light of the eugenics movement, is appealed to by congressmen in the shaping of national policy on immigration . . . no psychologist of today can complain that his science is not taken seriously enough.
>
> (Terman, quoted in Olsson, 1991: 191)

While hailed by some as the forum in which to resolve age-old philosophical questions about what knowledge is innate and what acquired, the emergence of modern developmental psychology was also prompted by other more pragmatic concerns to classify, measure and regulate, in particular, those populations deemed a social threat to the prevailing order. Hence the division between theory and its application becomes unimportant, since the social need for the technology and data provided by individual psychology constituted the condition and rationale for its existence (Ingleby, 1985). This infusion of scientific enterprise with social-political agendas is not, of course, specific to psychology nor to the development of testing. Science, as the tool of reason and progress fostered and harnessed by the modern State, put into practice enlightenment philosophies of protection and care of citizens, the realisation of which presupposed greater monitoring and control. Even the authors of the early child studies were quick to move from observation to advice, from empirical 'fact' to social application.

What is perhaps different about standardised testing is that the moral evalua- tion that underlies the description is rendered invisible and incontrovertible through the apparent impartiality of statistical norms and administration through the power of the institutions that can enforce statistical description as moral- political *pre*scription. There is a central ambivalence here about the relation beween the natural and the nurtured that mirrors the tension between scientific objectivity and social application structuring psychological research: it seems that the natural course of development has to be carefully monitored, supported and even corrected in order to emerge appropriately. That which is designated as natural or spontaneously arising is in fact constructed or even forced.

As Adrienne Harris (1987) suggests, the drive towards rationality in models of development may be a reflection of the rationalisation of the modern State, taking place at the level of individual psychic, rather than industrial, processes. The norms and milestones that structure developmental psychology present a picture of orderly, progressive graduation through stages to ever greater competence and maturity. In addition to being the modern economic strategy for efficient pro- duction, rationalisation is also, in psychoanalytic terms, a psychic *defence* against anxiety, that is 'the process by which a course of action is given *ex post facto* reasons which not only justify it, but also conceal its true motivations' (Rycroft, 1974: 136). In psychoanalysis we can infer from defences the structure of what it is that is repressed. What is wilfully left out or repressed from developmental psychology is the chaos and complexity (including the emotional chaos) of the research process. The investment in portraying development as progress works to deny our histories of the personal costs in 'growing up'. More than this, turning the complex disorder of individual development into orderly steps to maturity reflects explicit social interests in maintaining social control within and between social groups and nations. The technologies of description, comparison and measurement of children that underlie the descriptive knowledge base of developmental psychology have their roots in demographic control, comparative anthropology and animal observation that set 'man' over animals, European man over non-European, man over woman, as well as politician over pauper. So the history of developmental psychology offers glimpses of its structural and structuring influence in its coming of age as the authoriser and arbiter of child, family and professional relations within the modern Welfare State. The next step is to look more closely at how these origins are sustained or transcended in contemporary developmental psychology.

FURTHER READING

On the preoccupations that prompted and maintained the emergence of developmental and individual psychology, see:

Cooter, R. (ed.) (1992) *In the Name of the Child: health and welfare 1880–1940*, London: Routledge (a useful collection addressing historical and cultural perspectives).

Rose, N. (1985) *The Psychological Complex: psychology, politics and society 1869–1939*, London: Routledge & Kegan Paul.

Rose, N. (1990) *Governing the Soul: the shaping of the private self*, London: Routledge (see especially Chapter 11).

On the selective interpretation of Darwinian biology and its implications for developmental psychology, see:

Morss, J. (1990) *The Biologising of Childhood*, Hillsdale, NJ: Erlbaum (especially Chapters 2 and 11).

On the child study movement, see:

Riley, D. (1983) *War in the Nursery: theories of child and mother*, London: Virago (especially Chapter 3).

Urwin, C. (1986) 'Developmental psychology and psychoanalysis: splitting the difference', in M. Richards and P. Light (eds) *Children of Social Worlds*, Oxford: Polity.

SUGGESTED ACTIVITIES

1   Drawing on Rose (1985), Rose (1990) and Cooter (1992), comment on extracts illustrating psychology's preoccupation with population regulation and control.

2   Drawing on extracts from Van der Eyken's (1973) *Education, the Child and Society: a documentary history 1900-1973*, such as Cyril Burt on 'mental deficients', comment on the underlying assumptions and discourses that structure these accounts.

3   Discuss the changing lexicon of 'special education', highlighting the relations between terminology and social practices (e.g. 'imbecile', 'feebleminded', etc., to the more recent formulations of 'children/people with learning disabilities'). Note that this does not involve claims that the language is being used somehow to refer to what is essentially 'the same' entity – this would run counter to the ideas elaborated in this chapter about the constitutive effects of psychological discourses. The issue is not to trace continuities or homologies, but to explore the positions set out within the different practices.

Part I

Constructing the subject

This part addresses the theoretical and practical consequences of developmental psychology's identification of the individual child as its unit of study, exploring the implications of this in relation to the study of infancy (Chapter 2) and of social development (Chapter 3). Chapter 4 highlights how developmental psychology both draws on and feeds into dominant images of childhood.

Chapter 2

Researching infancy

But trailing clouds of glory do we come
From God, who is our home:
Heaven lies about us in our infancy!
(Wordsworth, *Ode, Intimations of Immortality*, 1807)

'I was born yesterday but . . .' Babies know a lot more, a lot younger than we used
to think.
(*Independent on Sunday*, 10 March 1991)

Most contemporary accounts of infancy start with the derivation of the Latin
word 'infans' meaning literally 'without speech', the period which used to be
taken to refer approximately to the first eighteen months of life. But since
developmental psychology is discovering so much about babies' abilities, the age
at which particular achievements occur is ever earlier, so that there is a continual
danger that infancy research will collapse back into neonatal (first two weeks)
examination. I will be suggesting that this dynamic follows from the earlier
practices and assumptions I identified in Chapter 1. This chapter draws on that
historical framework to trace briefly the phases and fashions of infancy research.
After this broad survey, key pieces of research are discussed, as paradigmatically
illustrating more general features of infancy work. Continuities are identified in
the topics the research addresses, which in turn raise further questions about the
significance of its sustained preoccupations and its absences.

TRENDS IN INFANCY RESEARCH: ABSOLUTE BEGINNERS?

Psychology, and in particular developmental psychology, is heir to a longstanding set
of philosophical, epistemological questions about the nature and growth of knowledge, and indeed was from the start hailed as the forum in which to test out

competing theories (much as computer modelling is claimed to do now). By this account, biology and epistemology meet in the study of developmental psychology. Taking a broad look at twentieth-century Anglo-US and European psychology, general social preoccupations and moral orientations are reproduced within the history of infancy research. The child study movement of the late nineteenth century and early twentieth century was motivated by questions drawn from evolutionary theory, that is, comparing animals and humans, and different groups of humans, to evaluate the role of heredity. But, from the 1920s until approximately the 1960s, behaviourist ideas shifted attention away from genetic endowment to environmental history, with a corresponding preoccupation with child training. The model of the child was as passive recipient of experience, with emphasis placed on quality of environment such that parents were seen as responsible for moulding and producing an appropriate moral character. The philosophical framework for this model of the child was empiricism, where the mind is conceived of as a blank slate (Locke) or, in pragmatic varieties, as 'blooming, buzzing confusion' (James). Since the behaviourists were reluctant to attribute any internal structure or organisation to the 'organism' – consistent with their denial of unobservable mental activity or events (which was in part their 'response' to introspectionist approaches) – the acquisition of knowledge was held to occur through conditioning, that is, through selective reinforcement based on environmental contingencies or learning from experience.

While it would be simplistic to treat these as sequential shifts, broadly speaking the 1960s saw a change of model from an incompetent infant assumed to know nothing, to a competent infant depicted as arriving already equipped with, or at least predisposed to acquire, sophisticated skills. This change arises in part from technological developments which could attest to the complex capacities of even newborns, but it also reflects the eclipse of behaviourism and the rise of cognitive psychology. The reversal of perspective (from blank slate to pre-programmed) is evident in the moral tone of righteous indignation with which books like Stone *et al.*'s (1973) *The Competent Infant* are presented. The very term 'competent' is used 'to stress that, from his [*sic*] earliest days, every infant is an active, perceiving, learning and information-organising individual' (Stone *et al.*, 1973: 4). Accounts of this period celebrate the achievements of modern science as miraculously transforming the understanding of infant development:

> all at once it seemed possible to obtain empirical answers where previously there had been largely theoretical speculation and inference . . . in what had previously seemed to be chaotic variability of response and responsiveness took on new meaning and order.
>
> (Stone *et al.*, 1973: 6)

Science promises order in measuring the individual via infant research, and the metaphor of comprehension becomes almost literally a process of grasping the mystery of infancy by means of new techniques. Technology is accorded a key role in revising the image of the newborn:

Still another handle was fashioned by the electronic transformation of auto-
nomic (particularly cardiac) measures and instrumentation . . . . aided by
measures of brain electrophysiology it became possible to determine what
infants, even neonates, could see or hear, or otherwise take in . . . . new
approaches and methodologies in learning have transformed our understanding of the young infant's capabilities.

(ibid.)

While new technologies undoubtedly played an important role in generating new
research, the driving force behind the 'discovery' of neonatal qualities was not
only to do with the accumulation of more facts from the accelerating pace of
infancy studies but was also due to the replacement of behaviourism by biologism and cognitivism.

The rhetoric of wonder and (self-)congratulation of the 1970s technical reports
is continuously replayed in current popular accounts: 'Born brilliant. It's amaz-
ing what your newborn can do' reads the November 1989 cover of *Practical
Parenting*, with the inside story starting:

Just arrived – isn't he clever! A newborn baby is much more interesting than
anyone could imagine. . . . Take time to study your baby, get to know him and
discover the many different ways that make him unique.

Another account reads:

Baby brilliance – the secrets revealed. Exciting new research suggests that
babies know more and learn much faster than we think?
(*Under Five*, November/December 1990)

The modern commitment to science as progress, with developmental psychology
accumulating facts on the way to complete knowledge, is thus reinscribed within
the process of documenting the individual infant's increasing maturity.

From the 1970s, as a corollary of the representation of the ever-more-able
child, a new research ethos emphasised how the infant takes an active role in
moulding the environment in which she participates. The 'child effects' work
(Bell and Harper, 1977) investigated what the child elicits from her caregivers,
rather than solely her adaptation to them, and began to piece together a picture of
reciprocal learning histories of both caregivers and their charges; how each
responded to and learned from the responses of the others. Subsequently, infancy
research from the mid-1970s onwards became the forum to test out and develop
Piagetian theory, since the sensorimotor period was seen as the arena where
Piagetian claims are at their most specific (e.g Butterworth, 1980).

The late 1970s to 1980s saw a diversification of research. One strand continued with an unabated cognitivism, now combining the test and application of
Piagetian theory with cognitive science (Leiser and Gilliéron, 1990). A second
strand, influenced by hermeneutics (e.g. Newson and Shotter, 1974), tried to
achieve a reprieve-by-synthesis of (cognitive) innatism and (behaviourist)

environmentalism, that is, to move beyond the positions which either denied any structure in the child's head (behaviourism) or put it all in her head (1960s–70s cognitivism). After all, if all the attributes and capacities are already there, what is it that could be said to *develop*? The reaction to behaviourism thereby threatened to fall back into innatism, and most developmental psychologists wanted to avoid this. Most current work is now wavering somewhere in the space between child and environment, which is also the space between child and adult caregiver. The fact that this is represented as a *space*, and that child and adult are treated as prior categories is itself part of the problem because these categories reproduce the divisions they strive to repair. As we will see in subsequent chapters, the current emphasis following from this is on communication, and on the processes by which infant behaviour is interpreted. The focus is currently on adult expectations, attributions and framing of child activity which are taken up in Chapter 3. But before we look at this, we need to explore how infancy research continues to reproduce the theoretical frameworks that initially gave rise to it.

HANGOVERS: CONTINUITY OF QUESTIONS ADDRESSED BY INFANCY RESEARCH

Throughout the study of infancy, research has been organised around a recurring set of preoccupations which include: firstly, depicting infancy as the evolutionary baseline; secondly, treating infancy as providing insight into adult development; and thereby, thirdly, demonstrating the association between research and its application.

Infancy as evolutionary baseline

The study of infancy was explicitly undertaken to illuminate the old philo-sophical debates about the nature and development of knowledge: What is innate? What is acquired? What is the role of experience in the construction of knowledge? These were transformed into specific questions, such as the extent of early plasticity of the nervous system, and age limits on learning capacities. Developmental psychology positioned itself as the testing ground for these age-old epistemological preoccupations, and in so doing it took on board the nineteenth-century framework of comparative psychology, comparing rates of development or states of knowledge between different (age and cultural) groups and species. More recently, different approaches have emerged to investigate these questions. Some researchers engaged in the experimental study of sensory deprivation in animals, from which it was claimed relevant extrapolations could be made. Examples of this work include Colin Blakemore's report that cats raised in visual environments consisting only of vertical and horizontal stripes behave as though they are blind to diagonals (Blakemore and Cooper, 1970) or Harry Harlow's (1959) maternal deprivation studies with rhesus monkeys (discussed in Chapter 6).

A second, supposedly less interventionist, approach was the ethological study of animals (Blurton Jones, 1972), especially those designated as the primate evolutionary ancestors to humans. This comparative framework can also extend (by a worrying set of associations) to the study of human societies still living in the 'ecological niche' within which *homo sapiens* is said to have evolved, that is, hunter-gatherer societies. Note the implied relation suggested between these two groups – with resonances of the nineteenth-century hierarchisation of societies (Gould, 1984). Ethological work has also been applied to the analysis of infant and child behaviour as a set of observational techniques that claim to provide neutral descriptions of clusters of actions, rather than preconceived interpretative categories (Hinde, 1983).

Within contemporary neonatal research, there are claims for a move away from evolutionary explanations in accounting for early infant behaviours such as the neonatal stepping and rooting responses previously designated as 'reflexive' (Bremner, 1988). These are now being interpreted as having specific individual functions, so that, for example, the stepping is said to help the foetus turn in the intrauterine environment, which, it is hypothesised, may, in the early stages of prenatal development, prevent adhesion to the wall of the womb and later facilitate engagement of the head in the cervix in preparation for labour. The tone of this interpretation is that we have outpaced evolution in ontogenetic development, that spontaneous foetal activity arises as adaptation to the womb and that there are continuities between prenatal and neonatal behaviour. However, despite the explicit distancing from evolutionary accounts and their assumptions, including the appeals to the 'primitive', the emphasis on the *function* of behaviour in specific contexts still harks back to evolutionist assumptions about adaptation and survival value which structure the agenda of infancy research in particular directions.

Overall, the commitment to an evolutionary framework prioritises 'the biological' and accounts for the heavy emphasis on physical, and especially perceptual, abilities in the early infancy literature. This also assumes that perception is more 'basic', and therefore simpler to investigate. This trend continues within the arena of artificial intelligence – although here the emphasis on vision and sensory research can also be related to other, military interests (Bowers, 1990).

Blooming babies and adult aids

The contemporary version of the nineteenth-century notion that 'the child is father to the man' takes the form that babies can tell us how we come to know what we know, how they are more receptive to learning and how we might learn from them for later remediation. Claims are made for the study of infancy as providing insight into the development and functioning of adult capacities which may be so skilled as to be automatic. To take some widely cited examples, Tom Bower's studies with infants just a few weeks, sometimes days, old led him to suggest that they use almost the same repertoire of visual cues as adults do to interpret depth (though not to the same extent), in the form of interpreting virtual images of cubes of varying sizes and distances away, and show the same susceptibility to visual illusions. The measure used as the index of this knowledge was (operantly) learnt by association with a friendly (female) experimenter playing 'peekaboo' (Bower, 1966: 40). Moreover, close study of infants has been used to challenge some of the dominant assumptions of psychological models. For example, it was assumed that sensory knowledge (touching, seeing, hearing, etc.) is acquired in separate modalities which are only later combined (matching what you hear with what a particular object looks like; knowing how to make your facial expression correspond to that of your conversational partner). Research in the 1980s, by contrast, suggested that the starting point was one of an initial intersensory co-ordination which only subsequently separated into specific modalities. Meltzoff (1981), working on cross-modal matching, controversially claimed that infants less than one month old could imitate the facial gesture of an adult on their own face, which of course they could not see. Since they cannot see their own faces, they cannot know what expression they are producing. This early imitation would therefore involve the infant possessing an abstract representation of something she has not seen. But, theoretically important though these issues may be, they are nevertheless cast within an evolutionary perspective by which the study of infancy is seen as the route to understand the adult course of development.

In addition, work on how infants conceptualise and discriminate 'the world' has been directed towards the early identification of delay and handicap, the development of remedial devices and therapeutic interventions. A celebrated example of the practical application, as well as test, of intersensory co-ordination reported by Bower (1977) involved babies being fitted with devices emitting ultrasonic waves which bounced off objects and were reflected back to the wearer's head. The device then picked up the waves and translated them into sounds which conveyed auditory information about the layout of the environment. Bower (1977) used the device with blind babies and young children of ages varying from a few months to a few years old and reported that all those fitted could translate this auditory information back into information about the visual world, sometimes within minutes of being fitted. The applications for children who have visual impairments are manifest (though, after the equipment's promise had been demonstrated, its expense has meant that the applications are still potential rather than actual). But, at the level of theory, Bower claimed that infants a few months old can respond to abstract properties of sounds and translate them into visual information, reporting that adults fitted with the device took weeks of training before they could accomplish this, and thus arguing for the greater sensory plasticity of infants. The theoretical implications of this were taken to present a direct challenge to the dominant model of the construction of knowledge and perception, although, after the initial enthusiasm, it seems that both theoretical claims and results may have been overstated (see Bremner, 1988: 92–9).

The relevance of this work for our purposes here lies as illustrative of the ways different questions – some theoretical about the course of development and others 'applied' for remediation purposes – are fused together. As the research literature suggests, it is important to see that what are at stake in interpreting an infant gesture (as, for example, defensive or indicative of awareness of an impending collision) are key theoretical issues about the origins and nature of knowledge. But, and this is a big but, perhaps this is not the only way to ask these questions. These are not the only ways to interpret the infant's actions.

CLIFFHANGERS: FEAR OF FALLING?

At this point I want to develop this argument by looking in some detail at an early classic infancy experiment, Gibson and Walk's visual cliff (1960) which set out to address the question of how we see in three dimensions, that is, how we perceive depth. This experiment is classical in the sense that it continues to be described in current developmental psychology textbooks (e.g. Dworetsky, 1990: 137; Kaplan, 1991: 186; Mitchell, 1992: 59; Seifert and Hoffnung, 1987: 215) complete with diagrams and details of the apparatus. It therefore takes on a pedagogic role as a memorable experiment combining those vital ingredients for success in infancy research: ingenuity and technology. Its underlying assumptions are correspondingly maintained and reproduced within successive cohorts of students who read and learn about it.

Gibson and Walk couched their question, which they trace back to the Greek philosophers, as a nature–nurture issue: Is the ability to process and interpret visual cues about depth innate or learned? It was also posed as a comparative question within an evolutionary context: What is the species variation in this ability, and how is this related to differences in species habits and habitats? They developed an apparatus to investigate this: a simulated 'visual cliff', which permitted control of optical auditory and tactile stimuli, while also protecting experimental subjects from harm (by suspending the checked board indicating depth on the underside of a heavy glass sheet). Later versions permitted adjustment of the depth so that this too could become an experimental variable. The researchers observed the behaviour of infants on this visual cliff, placing each child on the centre of the board (a 'safe' area), asking the baby's mother to call the child to her, firstly from the 'cliff' side and then from the 'shallow' side of the board. Out of the thirty-six infants tested, the authors reported that all of the twenty-seven who moved off the board crawled out on the shallow side at least once; only three crept over the cliff side; many crawled away from their mother when she called from the cliff side; others cried because they couldn't come to her without crossing an apparent chasm (Gibson and Walk, 1973: 19).

The researchers claimed this demonstrates that most infants can discriminate depth by the time they can crawl. This, in turn, indicates dependence on vision for depth discrimination: although the infants could touch a solid surface, they refused to cross because of the visual depth cues. They also argued that awareness of depth precedes the locomotor abilities to act on that knowledge, in that many of the infants might have had a nasty accident while they were deciding which way to go had it not been for the protection of the glass. They did not, however, claim to have proven that depth discrimination and cliff avoidance is innate, since they acknowledged that by the time infants can crawl they will have had a substantial visual and locomotor experience.

Gibson and Walk continued with many permutations on the same theme, investigating the role of specific pattern cues, the effect on animals reared in the dark (so depriving them of visual experience on which to apply any visually based predispositions) and so on. But it is worth reflecting for a moment to see what this work indicates about the styles and preoccupations of infancy research.

Evolutionary or communicative test?

Firstly, there is clearly an explicit continuity of interest in comparative work and evolutionary considerations. The entire study was cast within the framework of nature and nurture, of relating response to species and species lifestyle. Age of onset was related to that of autonomous locomotion, interpreting reactions in terms of the necessity to each species tested. Kittens, chicks, turtles, rats and goats were all compared to see the extent to which onset of responsivity varied. For example, Gibson and Walk suggested that night foragers, like rats, might rely primarily on tactile information from their whiskers, while predators like cats which depend on vision may be more susceptible to the illusion. Apparently, turtles were unperturbed by the 'cliff', which the authors interpreted as arising either from the fact that they had no need to fear a fall or because the glass reflections gave the impression of water.

Secondly, there are problems with casting this investigation as a global nature–nurture question. Identifying the different prerequisite abilities presumed for the target behaviour (in this case discriminating between 'shallow' and 'deep' sides of the cliff) raises difficulties of what in experimental terms would be interpreted as either spurious or artefactual indicators of 'knowledge' (false positives) or failure to respond appropriately for reasons other than the variable under manipulation (false negatives). Gibson and Walk used infants who could already crawl and therefore cannot be said to have investigated whether appreciation of depth is innate (nor did they claim to have done so). Turning to animals to investigate neonatal responses leaves them open to the criticism of making unwarranted extrapolations from animals to humans. They relied on a fear response, but it is possible that infants could register and even use the depth information and that they merely might not yet have learned to associate this information with danger. A subsequent study, using younger infants who were placed on different sides of the visual cliff, reported a change in heart rate according to the side on which they were placed. However, the direction of the heart rate change – deceleration – is conventionally interpreted as an interest rather than a fear response (Wolman, 1982).

Criticisms so far have been of the classical scientific variety. But as important for present purposes is a third problem, that this framework suppresses the analysis of the task as a *social* situation. The emphasis on the problem of perceptual discrimination leads to a failure to consider the construction of the laboratory test as a social situation. A more recent study applying some of the research on face recognition to the 'visual cliff' experiment suggested that the infants' reaction (whether or not they are willing to cross the deep side of the cliff) depended on the (standardised) facial expression the mother (and it is still only done with mothers!) had been trained to assume (Sorce *et al.*, 1985). When the infants' mothers assumed an expression considered to indicate fear none of the infants crossed the cliff, whereas nearly all of them (fourteen out of the nineteen in that condition) crossed when she smiled; most of them crossed when she looked interested, but rarely when she looked angry (understandably since anger might serve as a restraint, prohibiting approach towards the mother); where the mother looked sad six of the eighteen infants in this condition crossed towards her, but they looked at their mothers more frequently than any other group, suggesting that they were puzzled or uncertain. Whatever the limits of such facial recognition tasks, what this study intimates is that presenting the task as an epistemological enquiry ignores motivating factors, and reduces what is clearly a complex communicative encounter, dependent on particular aspects of a relationship, to a question about individual perceptual competence. It is most revealing that research should first have concentrated on the issue of babies' depth discrimination and only much later begun to appreciate the children's sophisticated abilities to interpret the mother's facial expression – which seems at least as impressive. Moreover, this experiment illustrates how misleading it is to regard the infant alone as the appropriate unit of analysis. Rather we must look at the whole material and communicative system within which the infant acts.

PROBLEMS OF INFANCY: TECHNICAL OR CONCEPTUAL?

A typical account of infancy research starts at precisely this point in the narrative, discussing the difficulties of researching a subject population where there is a very limited behavioural repertoire to use as measures (hence earlier underestimations of infant abilities) of what infants 'know'. Much literature deals with the problem of interpreting infant behaviour, highlighting also the complex relationship between different response measures, a relationship which is confounded both by differences in relative maturation of response systems and because the same reaction can have different meanings at different ages. Heartrate change is taken as indicating that the infant has registered a difference, but the basis on which she has discriminated a difference may be less easy to determine. Overall, debates in the literature have been preoccupied with the problem of determining between competing interpretations for the same experimental result: whether, for example, a reaction of head retraction is defensive, indicating awareness of impending collision with a virtual object moving towards them (also eye widening, hands in front of face) in Bower *et al.*'s (1970) looming object procedure, or simply arises from infants' visual preference for the edges of objects, so that they draw their heads back to watch the edges recede as the object moves away. By one account the response indicates 'fear' and by the other the 'same' response indicates 'interest' (the latter arising from features irrelevant to the investigation of infants' depth-perceiving abilities).

But, more than anything else, what these debates illustrate is the pre-occupation of the infancy literature with methodological issues, with major sections of research reports devoted to descriptions of apparatus and techniques. While this is undoubtedly important, the focus on method and technology distracts attention from reflection on the rationale for the experimental question – which is largely taken to be self-evident. Either it is assumed that the earlier a behaviour can be documented the closer it is to being innate, or research on infancy is presumed to have implications for later intervention, with early detection contributing to later remediation, irrespective of whether it is clear that the behaviour under investigation is necessarily and solely indicated as the antecedent of the later difficulty.

While there is no doubt infancy is a challenging and difficult area of human development to investigate, it could be argued that it simply represents in a particularly graphic form what are general problems for psychological investigation. Problems cited include those of variable and conflicting results, whereby slight differences in a baby's age, state of arousal, birth factors, posture, stimulus materials, techniques and so on all produce ambiguous and conflicting measures. But rather than being seen as technical difficulties to be overcome, what these difficulties demonstrate is that we cannot make a clear distinction between what a baby somehow 'knows' and how that knowledge is obscured by so-called 'performance variables', since the two are much more deeply interrelated than the split between these two terms would suggest.

If we take as a further illustration of this DiPietro *et al.*'s (1987) study of behavioural and heart-rate differences between breast-fed and bottle-fed infants, we see the relationship between environmental issues of method of feeding and seemingly internal issues such as temperament as inextricably involved. In this study the authors reported that birth factors, such as the type of delivery or the drugs taken by the mother during or after childbirth, were reflected in the state of the breast-fed baby. Method of feeding was related to how fussy, active or placid a baby rated. Hence, factors associated with the circumstances of the birth become interpreted as a property of the child in the classification of neonatal temperament. Generalising this further, it seems that casting discussions in terms of traits and behaviour, inside and outside, and even organism and environment sets up oppositions which treat as separate those entities that may be far less clearly differentiated.

Discussions about the indeterminacy of early responses, then, highlight that there is no such thing as 'raw potential': the behaviour we see exhibited by an infant can occur only within a social situation that, firstly, elicits it and, secondly, interprets it, thereby constructing it. It is now well established that environmental events can modify infant behaviour from the earliest moments of life – seen in the DiPietro *et al.* (1987) bottle- vs. breast-feeding study and also, for example, in the Sandler *et al.* (1970) study where newborns were found to exhibit different rates of crying in relation to different caregivers. One theoretical consequence of this is that there is no easy separation between internal and external, and that the exhibition of infant behaviour must be regarded as both reactive and interactive. Attending to Ben Bradley's (1989) claim of the irreducibly rhetorical character of models of infancy, we should pause to reflect both on what the emerging representation of infancy achieves and the implications this has for the knowledge claims concerning the rest of 'development'.

Adrienne Harris (1987) argues that the dominant conception of infancy portrays it as the atomistic acquisition of skills, built up in steps that link to later, more complex skills. She suggests that the research preoccupation with tracing skilled performance mirrors the societal value placed on productive aspects of labour, while the negative, maladaptive features of infant action are screened out of the picture. The cognitive model of the infant as problem solver mirrors that of the assembly worker, with research privileging those activities and products which will enhance performance. The result is that the indeterminate, ambiguous and non-instrumental features of infant behaviours are suppressed. The effect of this, she suggests, is that it encourages parents to see the technological capacities of their offspring at ever earlier ages, contributing to the compression of developmental time in the rush to competence and 'mastery' (with its masculine connotations). Inscribed within models of the infant, then, are a cluster of problems. The dynamic of changing models is towards a reflection of rational, modern capitalism, with, as we shall see in Chapter 3, the psychological subject portrayed as separate and endowed with a rational and adaptive agency. Perhaps even more significantly, as demonstrated in the interpretation of the Gibson and Walk study, it renders the context in which the infant acts invisible, thereby both nullifying and naturalising the work of 'parenting' – which is, within current social arrangements, usually mothering.

FURTHER READING

On the rhetorical and ideological status of babies, see:
Bradley, B. (1989) *Visions of Infancy*, Oxford: Polity.
Harris, A. (1987) 'The rationalisation of infancy', in J. Broughton (ed.) *Critical Theories of Psychological Development*, New York: Plenum.
Morss, J. (1990) *The Biologising of Childhood*, Hillsdale, NJ: Erlbaum (especially Chapter 6).

SUGGESTED ACTIVITIES

Taking accounts such as those reproduced in T. Greenough (ed.) (1973) *The Nature and Nurture of Behavior: developmental psychobiology* (San Fransisco: Freeman), or Stone,

L., Smith, H. and Murphy, L. (eds) (1974) *The Competent Infant* (New York: Basic Books), explore the relevance of the arguments outlined in this chapter in relation to the following questions:

- what claims is infancy research used to warrant?
- what models of the relation between infant and adult capacities are being invoked?
- what other interpretations can be put forward for the phenomena described (with particular reference to features of the experimenter/caregiver/child relation)?
- what issues and features are absent within a) the topics of, and b) the relationships set up within, infancy research?

Chapter 3

Attributing sociality

So runs my dream: but what am I?
An infant crying in the night
An infant crying for the light:
And with no language but a cry.

(Alfred, Lord Tennyson, 1860)

A baby's smile is a language everyone understands.

(Salada tea bag tag, 1991)

Two main aspects of the legacy of nineteenth-century developmental psychological research form the focus for this chapter. One is the division between social and 'non-social'. The second is the priority accorded to biology in accounts of infant and early child development. I will explore the forms these take in varieties of recent developmental psychological research, and then evaluate some efforts made to escape the terms in which these questions were posed.

The developmental psychology of the early 1970s assumed the human infant started as a biological organism which had to be incorporated into an already existing social system. Drawing on work on attachment theory which harks back to evolutionary and animal work, researchers in this paradigm emphasised how the human infant is born equipped with a reflexive repertoire of behaviours that function to elicit care, nurturance and attention. This is interpreted in an evolutionary framework as being of 'survival value' to the species as well as to the individual (since the child is portrayed as the species' future). For example, there is research which documents distinctively different crying patterns exhibited by neonates that adult caregivers rapidly learn to differentiate and so attend more effectively to the infant's needs (Wolff, 1969). By this kind of account, then, there is an attempt to overcome the split between the biological and the social by referring to the adaptedness of the neonate for human social interaction, with this seen as functioning as a social signal to caregivers. The infant is viewed as making a gradual transition from a biological to a social being. The efforts researchers made to overcome this divide between the biological and the social are reflected in the titles of books of this period. To take as indices the titles of two well-known and influential works of this period, Rudolph Schaffer's (1971) *The Growth of Sociability* suggests a development from lesser to greater involvement with and awareness of the social world, while Martin Richards' (1974) edited collection *The Integration of the Child into a Social World* conjures up the image of a transition from isolation into sociality, with the epithet 'social' qualifying 'world' functioning retrospectively to designate the world the child had previously inhabited as pre- or non-social.

The problem with this genre of research is that it was surprisingly unspecific in its analysis of what it was that made the social world social or what demarcated it from any other variety of world. The 'social' here staggers under a heavy theoretical load, coming to mean communication, enculturation, participation and (bearing in mind the political preoccupations discussed earlier in this book) adaptation. In Chapter 1, I discussed how, with the advent of cognitivism, 1970s developmental psychology superseded earlier behaviourist accounts of infancy, claiming that they provided an impoverished picture of children's abilities. This trend was also reflected in the investigation of children's social development. I will outline some of this work now to illustrate its variety and the corresponding fluctuations of the image of the child on offer.

INNATE PREDISPOSITION TO BEING SOCIAL: BORN TO PARTY?

Corresponding with the 'discovery' of infants' competencies, a narrative of neonatal and infant development emerged which traced the adaptedness of the young child for social interaction, an adaptedness that in some sense was regarded as genetically 'prewired', but that formed the basis for involvement and then interaction with others. Infants were shown to distinguish between and orient towards human voices. Claims were made about infants selectively attending to faces (Fantz, 1961), and exhibiting different patterns of behaviour towards 'social' and 'nonsocial' objects, where these terms mapped on to animate (persons) vs. inanimate (things) (Brazelton *et al.*, 1974). A rather different line of work, but one that also sprang from the technological revolution of infancy research brought about by film and video, was the 'micro-analysis' of infant–adult behaviour. Continuing Gesell's paradigm of photographic records, this was based on close scrutiny of film played at slow speeds (or even frame by frame). Researchers made startling claims about regularities they could pick out in mother–infant interaction.

Two strands of micro-analytic work can be distinguished. Condon and Sander (e.g. Condon, 1977) applied the work on interactional synchrony of body movements with talk to the caregiver–infant context. Social psychological research had already suggested that as adults we move our bodies in subtle but characteristic ways when we are speaking, and listeners move in similar ways as if in sympathy with the speaker (that is, in relation to changes of tone, etc.). Condon and Sander claimed to be able to see similar patterns at work in the movements of infants whose mothers were talking to them (see Condon, 1977). They argued that this synchronous matching of movement with speech constitutes a basic form of social response which is fully functional at birth. Within these claims, then, what is social is accorded so pre-existent a role that it is threatening to lapse back into biology.

In a similar vein, Colwyn Trevarthen's work (e.g. 1977) argued for the existence of an innate predisposition for co-operative turn-taking exchanges, which were regarded as paving the way for linguistic dialogue. This was interpreted in terms of the development of mutual intentionality, that is the sharing of mental states and purposes, whereby (consistent with the 'child as agent and contributor to her own development' reaction to behaviourism) the infant is depicted as interpreting the actions of the caregiver as well as vice versa. The emphasis in Trevarthen's analysis was on the active involvement of the infant in communicative interaction – with partners negotiating together to achieve 'joint action', that of constructing and elaborating joint purposes.

Ben Bradley (1989) provides a more extensive review and commentary on the presuppositions and adequacy of this work. For present purposes a few points should suffice. Firstly, unlike Condon and Sander, Trevarthen described several different stages in the development and achievement of intersubjectivity (sharing of mental states) rather than postulating that all was present and ready from birth. However, in different ways these accounts present an impoverished and insufficiently analysed understanding of what it means to be social and, in their efforts to connect early infant reaction patterns to later interaction, they fail to specify what it is (if anything) that by their account distinguishes sociality from biology. Perhaps another way of reading this is as an illustration of some of the difficulties with maintaining the opposition between a social and a biological realm; dissolving one into the other, as these accounts threaten to do, will not solve the problem. Further, while the more recent focus on communicative development may seem to depart from the biological and evolutionary concerns of the early work, it nevertheless retains some of the same starting assumptions, albeit now cast in more neutral terms.

PROBLEMS: QUALIFICATIONS AND MODIFICATIONS

The claims of infant predisposition to sociality have been subject to a number of other criticisms. Firstly, there has been a failure to replicate some of the key studies which inform the theoretical account. So, there are disputes about the specificity of response to animate and inanimate objects (Sylvester Bradley, 1985), and about the interpretation of infant movements from the micro-analytic studies. Bradley (1989) argues that the process of selection of material for analysis both reflects and contributes to a sanitised and romanticised representation of infant lives (and of the lives of those who look after them).

Related to this, a second point is that determining what an infant response 'means' is not a 'biological given' or inevitability, so it is not sufficient to invoke some kind of innate pre-adaptedness. For example, the meaning of a particular action may be culture-bound and State-dependent. In many cultures babies are in constant physical contact with their mothers who carry or strap them on their bodies (Konner, 1977; Whiten and Milner, 1986). Despite the 'culture-free' and universalist terms of their formulations, then, crying need not necessarily serve as a signal to bring the parent to the baby, as the evolutionary theorists suggest, nor to signal hunger. What crying means will be defined by the particular circumstances of its exhibition and cannot be entirely pre-ordained by some genetic programme. This has implications for how we research and interpret parental behaviour, in particular for more recent discussions of 'maternal sensitivity', a 'quality' that, it is claimed, can be tested and measured and related to child social awareness (Light, 1979; Yarrow et al., 1975). If we take the notion of the social construction of meaning seriously, a mother who does not immediately respond to her child is not necessarily 'pathological' or 'insensitive', since signalling systems are a matter of cultural definition and individual elaboration by mother and child. This perspective on the research on 'sensitivity' is a theme we shall be returning to in subsequent chapters.

All this highlights the difficulty of identifying a specifically *social* response. Fantz's pioneering work on the visual preferences of infants for face-like patterns was soon revised on the grounds that it seemed that the crucial factor was the complexity of the experimental stimuli rather than specific response for face-shaped configurations (Cohen et al., 1979). Perhaps the clearest illustration of this comes from the literature on smiles.

Smiling, the development of smiles and their interpretation have occupied many pages of social developmental psychological texts. A 1970s study noted that mothers' voices were the most effective at eliciting smiles from infants of 5 weeks old (Sroufe and Waters, 1976). Smiling in infants has been seen as an index of recognition which has been used as an illustrative measure of infant capacity to discriminate specific individuals (Lamb, 1988). While smiling is a very rewarding response for caregivers, since we interpret it as communicative, it is not only communicative. It may not even *be* communicative. Infants have been observed to smile in so-called 'non-social' contexts at the point at which they seem to have solved a problem or (in behavioural language) detected a contingency relation. These so-called 'smiles of successful cognition' are reported as exhibited in circumstances where infants learnt that they could control the sound or movement of a mobile above them by operating a microswitch at the turn of their heads (Hunt and Uzgiris, 1964). The key factor in eliciting the smile seemed to be control, and in other studies of developmentally delayed or visually impaired babies, their first smiles were elicited in those contexts of discovery in which an action on their part produced a particular (and presumably pleasurable) result (Watson, 1973). Now, rather than engaging in the elusive quest for the quintessentially social smile, the variety of contexts in which this index of sociality is exhibited must lead to a questioning of the viability of the social vs. non-social distinction, or at the very least a closer inspection of the criteria by which such demarcations are made.

Some of this theoretical work has been carried out in debates as to the status of ascriptions of intentionality to infants. When can an infant be said to be purposive or intentional in its behaviour? There is a danger of going overboard in reacting to the outside-in approaches of the behaviourists in returning to an already constituted, socially mature model of the child. This would simply be a backdoor way of returning to the biological determinism of an inside-out approach, since all the qualities defined as constituting sociality are portrayed as already built-in (as in the Condon and Sander study). By depicting the child as already social, the category social is being collapsed back into the biological and thus rendered meaningless. But, at an intuitive level, there is a clear difference between interpreting the howls of a 3-week-old baby as meaning 'I want to be fed', and interpreting an 8-month-old baby's actions as intentional when she crawls to the door, looks back at you, looks at the door again and starts to cry. In the second case we would perhaps feel much more confident about attributing purposes, goals and communicative intent. We must be clear, though, that *we* are doing the attributing and have our own investments in reading actions in this way.

Research in the 1980s recognised and tried to address these problems by emphasising the *as if* quality of early parent–child interaction: how we treat infants *as if* they were fully initiated social partners, *as if* they were able to participate in a social system. This work claimed that it is by treating the infant as socially competent that she becomes so.

FRUITFUL ILLUSIONS: ADULT ATTRIBUTIONS AND SELF-FULFILLING PROPHECIES

I am going to take Kenneth Kaye's (1982) book *The Mental and Social Life of Babies* as indicative of a genre of research which emphasises how infant behaviour is framed within a context of adult attribution and interpretation. This is a good example of a constructionist approach which I analyse here to identify residual tensions and challenges for this project. By this account, initially the caregiver does all or most of the interactive work in maintaining the communication or activity, but gradually the infant assumes more responsibility for this. Such ideas are now widespread in developmental psychology, as extensions of Jerome Bruner's notion of 'scaffolding' in the precursors to language development (see Chapters 7 and 8 for more detail), and Kaye presents an influential account which attempts to elaborate precursors within prelinguistic activity for the emergence of communication (including language) and sense of self. Kaye sets out to elaborate what he calls a 'holism without romanticism', to provide an account of how infants are initiated and come to participate within the social world. He attempts to do this without either postulating the infant as a pre-given separate (asocial) unit or resorting to the claim that the newborn baby arrives equipped with all human social characteristics and skills. In other words, he explicitly rejects some of the earlier (what he calls 'romantic') claims of primary intersubjectivity and interactional synchrony. The account blends evolutionary concerns about species adaptation with information-processing models to present a 'holistic' approach whereby the primary unit is the social system rather than individual interactants, out of which the 'personhood' of the infant gradually emerges. Hence, by treating the baby as social it becomes so.

> The human infant is born social in the sense that his [sic] development will depend from the beginning upon patterns of interaction with elders . . . . interaction does begin at birth but . . . infants only become individual partners gradually, as a direct result of those interactions.
>
> (Kaye, 1982: 29)

This seems a promising start, particularly because Kaye presents a clear analysis of what he considers a social system is, and elaborates criteria for different levels of participation within it. For Kaye, the two key features of properly social systems are sharing a history and common ends. He discusses examples which fall within each section of a four-by-four matrix of separate/shared purposes vs. shared/independent development, which I summarise as follows. Enemy armies share a history in the sense of participating in the same battle, with rather different goals but with their fates intertwined; a wolf and caribou (a variety of Alaskan deer) share neither the same history nor the same goals, even if they share the same habitat – the wolf that preys on the lame and straggling deer relies on an understanding based on species knowledge rather than a specific relationship with each deer; strangers in an elevator share a goal in the sense of wanting to go to the fifth floor, but the history of that journey is (usually) independent in the sense of not requiring the other for it to take place. Bees are excluded from being social on the grounds that their mutual functioning and adaptation arises from the evolution of roles (drone and worker) within the species rather than from relationships between individual members. In summary, members of the system are portrayed as requiring some knowledge of it and their place in it before it is truly social – hence the *gradual* emergence of the mother–infant interaction as a social system:

> Members of a system know when other members are or are not performing their roles. And it is not enough for only one member to be responsible for that awareness: A mother and infant do not begin to be a social system until the infant, too, has expectations of how the mother will behave. These must be expectations based on experience together, not genetically programmed information like the expectations spiders have about the behaviour of flies.
>
> (Kaye, 1982: 35)

(The example of a social system that receives the most elaboration is about softball. It is fortunate that Kaye's discussion is concerned with accounting for the emergence of culturally specific knowledge as well as developmental regularities that are continuously produced and reproduced across cultures!)

Kaye applies this perspective to an arena for which claims of the earliest pre-adaptation between adult and child have been made – namely breast-feeding. He claims that the infant's pattern of sucking in bursts and pauses, combined with the mother's tendency to jiggle the nipple of her breast (or the teat of the bottle) during the pauses, constitutes the earliest form of mutual adaptation and turn-taking. Apparently all mothers tend to jiggle and all babies tend to pause after jiggles, but within the first few weeks of the infant's life mothers learn to adapt their jiggles to maintain feeding because pauses after jiggles tend to precipitate a resumption of feeding. Hence the infant reinforces the cessation of the jiggle. Kaye goes on to claim that this pattern has evolved specifically to set up feeding as a primitive turn-taking interaction, since there seems to be no physiological reason for the burst-pause alternation (babies breathe while they suck). Rather, the pauses function to 'prompt mothers to fit into infants' patterns' (Kaye, 1982: 40), that is, 'to bring the mother into the feeding as an active taker of turns with the baby' (ibid: 89). The mother *adjusts* her jiggles to contingencies she learns about the infant's sucking patterns, and hence comes to *share and organise* the infant's world by structuring and participating in the feeding rhythm. What was initially a neurologically organised patterning provides, by virtue of the mother's anticipation and engagement (that is, the adaptation of the rhythms of her jiggles), the rudiments of a socially structured patterning. By treating her infant as a turn taker, the narrative goes, she starts to give the infant turns to take, setting up patterns so that eventually, in terms of other behaviours, the infant will start to take her own turn and assume her place in the social world.

The account goes on to highlight how adults supply, frame and place stimulation to entice infants into social participation as a self-fulfilling prophecy, extending in the rest of the book from the establishment of the earliest feeding patterns to face-to-face interaction, game playing, language development and even the development of 'selfhood' and clinical implications. Here we will leave it to take stock for a minute.

PAUSING TO JIGGLE AND THINK

While Kaye's account offers considerable improvement over earlier ones in terms of clarity both of definition of sociality and of the evolution–learning relation, it is still caught within the framework of the very biological–social opposition it tries to transcend. Firstly, the preoccupation with biological and evolutionary issues remains with the concern to sort out how neurological responses by babies come to function as social, through mothers' adaptation of their 'instinctive' action (jiggling) to the infants' reactions (sucking and pausing).

Secondly, although developmental psychology is hailed as providing the way out of the teleology of philosophy (by attending to the how rather than the why of development), the focus is still on the route by which the finished adult mind emerges – which still preserves a privileged status for the 'finished product' in guiding the investigation. Moreover, there is a lapse back into biologism since the existence of the current final product is held to arise from its adaptive value for our evolutionary ancestors, presumably because it must have been adaptive to have endured (Kaye, 1982: 15). Despite Kaye's efforts to avoid this, then, there is a short step from what is to what has been, and therefore from what is to what is best. A thoroughly normative account of development is thereby produced. Ultimately, the goal seems to be about demarcating humans from other kinds of animals and confirming the specialness of 'man' which is seen to reside in 'his' adaptability, particularly in relation to communicative and symbolic capacities.

Further, the conception of evolution here has extended from the 'baggage' a child brings with her on her developmental journey to construct the environment in which she travels and arrives. Kaye discusses this in terms of intrinsic and extrinsic functions which he claims are not the same as nature vs. nurture. The reason for this, as it turns out, is that *both* are regarded as innate. Paradoxically, in formulating what initially looks like a thoroughly social approach to development it collapses back into being even more biologically determined. The explanation for the fit between parent and infant is one of mutual evolution; the mother's reaction (jiggling) to the neurological response by the baby (sucking) is also 'instinctive':

> certain social mechanisms – interaction mechanisms for feeding, play and instruction – are the products of evolution every bit as much as those features we think of as innate to the individual organism. In fact it can be argued that such jointly evolved social mechanisms are likely to be more stable, once evolved, than particular traits intrinsic to either infant or the adult alone.
>
> (Kaye, 1982: 24)

While Kaye is careful to disclaim the developmental fallacy that earlier behaviours must be causally related to subsequent developmental achievements, nevertheless this research falls into the classical model of identifying the earliest exhibition of a basic unit of interaction (turn taking) which becomes the building block for everything else. In the very analysis of what makes the system social, we return to the project of partialling out the biological and the social. While in this account, unlike many previous ones, the individual is seen as produced by rather than pre-existing the social, nevertheless the biological and evolutionary perspective reduces culture to biology. Although 'the human infant is born social in the sense that his [sic] development will depend from the beginning on patterns of interaction' from which 'infants only become individual partners gradually as a direct result of those interactions' (Kaye, 1982: 29), the impetus towards sociality is analysed only in evolutionary terms.

The tensions and contradictions within this, otherwise very interesting, account, point to a more general trend towards biological reductionism. The problems elaborated above indicate the conceptual and theoretical difficulties that lie within efforts to connect the biological and the social, and it is ironic that Kaye frames his project of 'holism without romanticism' as one of rescuing empirical scientists (who treat the child as an isolated unit) from the romantic (read unscientific) humanists.

In terms of connections with broader themes taken up throughout this book, this evolutionary perspective should also be noted as both fragmenting cultural variation into individual differences and moving the focus of the analysis once again away from difference in favour of cultural universals. These are seen to owe their status not to their cultural reproduction, but to a biological ordination: 'the universal aspects of infants' culturally transmitted nurturing environments turn out to be also a matter of nature' (Kaye, 1982: 29).

COSY COUPLES: SOCIAL AS INTERPERSONAL

The confusion between the social and cultural (with its attendant corresponding homogenisation of difference) arises from the impoverished representation of the social on offer. In the first place, the social is reduced to, or seen as quint-essentially represented by, the dyadic. Further, the social is equated with com-munication, which is seen only as the 'interpersonal'. The dyad of 'social' developmental research is almost always the mother–infant. This suppression of other relationships that surround and involve infants and young children is an overwhelming illustration of the permeation into research of particular ideo-logical assumptions about the structure of families, about which relationship is the most important for a child, and how the social world is categorised into the domestic and the public (see Chapter 5).

Despite the proclamations of wonder and congratulation at maternal skills and responsivity (a double-edged commendation – for woe betide you if you lack them), mothers are continually depicted in the literature as almost appendages, pieces of furniture constituting children's environments. For example, in the Sorce et al. (1985) variation on the visual cliff experiment discussed in Chapter 2, the narrative slips in its reference, moving from designating the infants as the 'subjects' to designating the mothers, who thus become research subjects (and so objects) of the experiment – as if the mothers had no existence independent from the babies.

Subjects were middle class volunteers . . . whose infants were normal at birth. In response to postcard inquiries, they had expressed an interest in partici-pating in studies of normal psychological development. Subjects coming to our laboratory were included if (a) they did not become too distressed at any time *prior* to noticing the drop-off, (b) they spontaneously referenced the mother's face after observing the drop-off.

(Sorce et al., 1985: 196)

Moreover, the knowledge produced by developmental psychological accounts itself contributes to the ways a mother complements and completes her infant's actions, since she is exhorted to orient her child rearing around it:

Since it is usually the child's mother who is his [sic] guide during the early years, it becomes extremely important for her to have a knowledge of the general route along which he is travelling . . . . If she has in mind a preview of the genetic sequence through which a behavior is likely to develop, she is in a position to foresee and interpret the developing behavior in all its variations.

(Gesell, 1950: 240)

In addition, accounts analyse dyadic relationships as if they take place in a social vacuum, ignoring how they are structured by culture. Within Kaye's (1982) matrix the examples of a social system provided are all of the dyadic variety. To return to his examples, are we dealing with one social system or many? In what senses do husbands and wives necessarily share the same goals or the same history? Do pupils and teachers always mesh together so congruently? In the effort to account for a shared social reality, developmental psychological accounts occlude variability of perspective and position. The conception of the social as the extrapolation of the (already sanitised) interpersonal promotes an over-harmonious view of relationships – eliminating all traces of conflict and disharmony in psychology's representation of relationships (a point taken up in Parts II and III). The focus on the interpersonal dyad leaves out of the picture the wider social structural relations, relations of power (in Kaye's examples gender, age and professional relations), and thus correspondingly works to obscure the ways those wider structural relations enter into and are (re)produced within micro-social relations. Lacking that broader perspective, interpersonal relations and interactions become rendered simply as the exchanges of separate equals. A very *particular* social system (the biological mother in the home) is thereby depicted here as *generic* (as if no other caregiving systems are possible). A liberal model of society as consisting of separate, autonomous agents engaged in joint activities for mutual benefit is reproduced within a developmental model seeking to describe processes of engagement and enculturation. There is a failure to treat the representation of the 'social system' as itself historically and culturally constructed. This omission, combined with the social role model that underlies both this analysis of social systems and its liberal model of social exchange, works to naturalise patriarchy and capitalism, and to flatten out social relations within it as equal and harmonious.

Even in Kaye's model, which in many respects presents a much more sophisticated and elaborated constructionist account of the creation and emergence of the autonomous child, the project still boils down to apportioning responsibility to the partners in the interaction. Like other developmental models it tends towards being drawn back into the framework of preconstituted individual agents, rather than focusing on what it is that is achieved. In some respects, this impetus towards individualisation and atomism is itself a product of the social role theory that underlies Kaye's model in his exemplary social system. The mechanism for learning is socialisation, and the norms for behavioural performance are roles (albeit now reconceptualised as a mutual process). Since the account cannot provide a socially structured explanation of the emergence of the roles (owing to the absence of a wider conception of the social), to postulate that the capacity of the system functions as if the infant were playing the role, as well as flowing from the infant's own readiness, does nothing to help ward off the divisions and dualisms of individual and society, and of biology and society. It is this failure to treat the typical categories of psychological research – of parenthood, personhood, gender, class, etc. – as discourses that are reflected in, and in part produced by, developmental psychological practices that facilitates the incorporation of this constructionist model into the dominant atomistic and individualistic approach.

It is now beginning to be recognised that people other than 'the mother' interact with and provide the environment for an infant. When the category of the social is extended beyond the dyadic to consider the relationships between father and children and between siblings, we begin to see how highly selective and impoverished are the topics that have been the preoccupations of developmental psychology. In particular, we see the consequences of the emphasis on the physical, its separation from the emotional, and the suppression of the emotional in developmental psychological investigation. Judy Dunn and Carol Kendrick's (1982) and Dunn et al.'s (1991) analyses of sibling relationships, for example, provide a picture of children's social awareness, capacity to interpret another's emotional state and to empathise with one another at ages when such skills of understanding of 'social cognition' had previously been considered impossible. While still harking back to an evolutionary framework, their work also strongly suggests that we need to restore the study of emotions to the developmental agenda, and to reconsider our conceptualisation of the emotion–cognition relation. They report that traumatic events such as the birth of a sibling can herald rapid developmental advances rather than the regressions that are typically expected or noted. As was argued in Chapters 1 and 2, the question of what is considered 'progress' or 'regress', and why, restates rather than resolves problems about the construction and categorisation of development. But at the very least we are beginning to see research that explores the differences in early experiences as a result of different positions, instead of trying to suppress that difference.

THE GENERAL AND THE PARTICULAR IN DEVELOPMENTAL PSYCHOLOGY

The tension between the biological and the social is inscribed within psychology in general, and in developmental psychology in particular. This tension is reflected in the general psychological project to explain both the general and the particular in the human condition. Psychology has tended to deal with this tension by suppressing the particular, the emotional. Despite its name, the 'psychology of individual differences' (of which developmental psychology is a key component) addresses similarity rather than differences, with difference explored only in relation to technologies of scores on attitude tests, personality tests or ability scales. Emotions become stable, generalisable variables conceived of as analogues to relatively fixed cognitive processes. This contributes to a psychology which has abstracted its unit of analysis such that its notions of 'interaction' and 'the social' are highly impoverished. So far in this book I have tried to point out how these considerations have been both reflected in the historical origins of developmental psychology and reproduced within its recent history. We can see the culmination of this failure to theorise the social, and the abstraction of the 'individual' as the unit of analysis, in the way computer programs are regarded as being capable of modelling thought processes. Here we have a dramatic illustration of psychology's models of the individual and all they fail to address: the computer metaphor provides a representation of the human mind as individual, rational, isolated and disembodied. Moreover, the individualistic assumptions that permeate developmental psychology both feed into and are reflected by the rhetoric of child rights. Judith Ennew and Brian Milne (1989: 48) provide a dramatic illustration of the direct consequences of these theoretical issues, where what they call the 'individualism' of the international human rights policies on children facilitates the abstraction and dislocation of children from their nationality or culture, which have made practices of trans-racial and/or trans-national adoption a matter of only recent debate.

Any adequate developmental psychology has to address the question of the relationship between the biological and the social, but the failure of so much developmental psychological research so far lies in how it has regarded these as polarised factors of development that somehow combine in an additive way. In this chapter we have seen how impoverished developmental models are when they attempt to graft the biological onto the social – the language of 'socialisation' falls into this, with the social portrayed as a layer or coating over the biological (like a choc-ice). What we have to get away from is a conception of biology as somehow prior to or underlying the psychology, to rather, as Denise Riley (1983) argues, how it is lived out in particular times, places and conditions.

The seemingly abstract concerns of developmental psychological research have their reflections in the wider cultural arena. In terms of more popular representations, the social world of children, especially infants, is almost always one where 'parent' signifies mother, where mother and child are used to convey meanings of purity and naturalness. Developmental psychology both partakes of and informs cultural representations of the origins and nature of social organisation that are recycled within models of social development. But just as it is by no means clear that we can determine if a baby's cry or smile has meaning, and, even if it has, that this is not fixed or shared except by historical and cultural convention, so significations of children, what childhood is and what meaning this holds, are by no means as stable and homogeneous as has been assumed – as we will see in Chapter 4.

FURTHER READING

Bradley, B. (1989) *Visions of Infancy*, Oxford: Polity.
Kaye, K. (1982) *The Mental and Social Life of Babies*, London: Methuen.

Morss, J. (1990) *The Biologising of Childhood*, Hillsdale, NJ: Erlbaum, Chapters 6 and 9.

Riley, D. (1983) *War in the Nursery: theories of child and mother*, London: Virago (see especially Chapter 2).

SUGGESTED ACTIVITIES

Examine a range of developmental psychological textbooks, both current and from the 1960s onwards, exploring definitions of what it means to 'become social' and the positions set out for the 'socialising agent'. What conception of society is on offer? Contrast this with the kind of account provided within a Vygotskyan-informed perspective (see, e.g., Harré (1986) 'Steps towards social construction', in M. Richards and P. Light (eds) *Children of Social Worlds*, Oxford: Polity; and F. Newman and L. Holzman (1993) *Lev Vygotsky: revolutionary scientist*, London and New York: Routledge).

Chapter 4

Discourses of the child

Once upon a time we all lived in the land of childhood.
(Adolescence, Channel 4, 26 April 1992)

Childhood is the kingdom where nobody dies
Nobody that matters, that is.

(Edna St Vincent Millay, 1892–1950)

Discourses of childhood are central to the ways we structure our own and others' sense of place and position. They are part of the cultural narratives that define who we are, why we are the way we are and where we are going. This chapter addresses the range of ways childhood is depicted, the extent to which developmental psychological accounts reflect these representations, and the consequences of this for the adequacy of current forms and functions of developmental psychology.

The definition and demarcation of childhood are replete with social and political meanings. Whether cast in terms of nostalgia or repugnance, the category of childhood is a repository of social representations that functions only by virtue of the relationship with other age and status categories: the child exists in relation to the category 'adult'. While most developmental accounts treat movement within, and transition beyond, childhood as largely maturationally determined (as reflected in the chronological organisation of textbooks), a moment's reflection reveals that the membership prerequisites and privileges associated with the entry to adulthood are only tenuously linked with some criterial common point. As Jo Boyden and Andy Hudson (1985) note:

The distinction between children and adults is given as a basis on the one hand for granting additional rights (for instance, the first to receive relief in times of distress), and on the other, for restricting both the enjoyment of certain rights and the exercise of certain obligations.

(Boyden and Hudson, 1985: 4)

To take just a few contemporary and immediate examples, in Britain today there are a number of competing definitions of adult maturity simultaneously applied to different spheres of activity which vary in the age of maturity employed: political majority, legal responsibility and sex. In the last case it should be noted that different criteria for maturity are employed depending on whether your sexual partner is of the same or opposite sex. The entry limits on these three arenas of adult activity vary within Western Europe as well as across wider cultural spheres. There is variation within systems as well, with different criteria employed on the basis of gender. In Judaism, for example, boys are considered adult at age 13 while girls attain this status at 12. At a more general level, to take perhaps the most telling example, in many countries, the UK included, young men of 16 are treated as too young to vote or marry without permission, but old enough to kill or be killed for their country. But even before we look to 'other' cultures or to history, a diversity of definitions of maturity is apparent. To what extent is this diversity reflected in developmental psychological accounts? The question of whether 'we all lived in the land of childhood' (as the documentary claimed) turns out to be indissociable from that of who 'we' are, and whose land it is.

DEVELOPMENTAL PSYCHOLOGY AND THE CULTURAL CATEGORISATION OF THE LIFE SPAN

Do children grow or are they made? This variant of the nature–nurture question is what structures both the popular and the academic imagery of child development. The cover of one current textbook (Dworetzky, 1990) shows a budding flower emerging from the soil beneath the beneficent glow of a sun (with bud and sun of the same colour) – all this in a naive child-like style. Another (Kaplan, 1991), entitled A Child's Odyssey, conveys a picture of development as a journey, beset with difficulties and dangers, which are, moreover, negotiated sequentially and separately. Reproductions of Impressionist rural and garden scenes are interspersed throughout this text. The corresponding nuances of nostalgic romanticism this conveys perhaps underscore how as readers we learn about developmental psychology through the lens of our own recollected childhood as retrospectively reconstituted within dominant models of the child. Small wonder perhaps at the alternation between a rhetoric of mystery or wonder and business-like calculation of how much further there is yet to go.

The important point here is that both varieties of account portray development as natural and inevitable. The trajectory of development is seen as basically uniform, with 'cross-cultural perspectives' appearing as optional extras within 'Applications' sections, in which it is largely child-rearing strategies or differences in moral codes that are presented for consideration. That is, cultural issues are treated as informing the 'content' of development rather than entering into its structure in any more fundamental way. Further, the distinctions most textbooks make between the main account and 'applications' or 'issues' maintains an implicit assumption that developmental psychological knowledge is not otherwise informed by 'applied' interests or values – an assumption that I questioned in Chapter 1.

One reason why culture can be portrayed as a kind of optional or exchangeable extra in this way lies in the structure of the texts. Firstly, most textbooks follow a chronological format from birth (or even conception) to adolescence or, with the recognition that development is 'life span', to death. Some accounts specify age limits on the periods they distinguish, as in Dworetzsky and Davis (1989) who distinguish 'Beginnings: 0–1 years; Early Childhood: 1–6 years; Middle Childhood: 6–12 years; Adolescence: 12–18 years; Early Adulthood: 18–40 years; Middle Adulthood: 40–65 years; Late Adulthood: 65+ years of age' (vii–x). It is impossible to read this without noting at the very least the remarkable lack of sensitivity to cultural and class variation in life expectancy. Most accounts distinguish between early and middle childhood, with 'toddlerhood' emerging as a new category between infancy and early childhood (in Kaplan, 1991). At a more detailed level, Fogel's (1991) account of infancy breaks this period down into seven sections, each of which is accorded not only age limits but also a specific subjective orientation (in some instances even assuming the 'voice' of the infant), with 'The psychology of the newborn (the first two months)'; 'Attention and anticipation (two to five months)'; 'The origins of initiative (six to nine months)'; 'Becoming a cause and becoming vulnerable (ten to twelve months)'; 'Expression, exploration and experimentation (twelve to eighteen months)'; 'Conflict, doubt and power (eighteen to twenty four months)' and 'I'm not a baby anymore (twenty four to thirty six months)' (Fogel, 1991: ix–xiv).

In one sense this kind of 'developmental tasks' approach simply represents the application within an age category of what is frequently portrayed as the preoccupations that separate and govern age categories. But how much do these actually have to do with age? Dworetzky and Davis (1989) treat 'Loving and working' as the subtitle for 'Early adulthood' (p. xx) with the 'Applications' section devoted to 'Finding your one and only'. In 'Late adulthood' (subtitled 'Relationships and retirement'), the 'Applications' is about 'Stopping elder abuse'. Are these inevitable, or even prevalent, features of the human life span? Surely 'elder abuse' can occur only in societies where older people are infantilised and treated as dispensable, rather than integrated and revered. Important questions arise from these reflections. What we have here are features of white middle-class US society mapped onto models of development which are then treated as universal. What are the effects of condensing the intervals between stages from multiples of years to mere months, as in the infancy example? The earlier in the life span, the more crucial it seems the developmental achievements must be within an ever-contracting period of time. Are these achievements as culture-free as they are represented? What kinds of injunctions do they make to parents?

Secondly, the categorisation into age-graded intervals brings with it a further segmentation of developmental description. Many of these comprehensive texts subdivide each period into 'physical', 'cognitive' and 'psychosocial' (or 'social and personality'), in some cases with a chapter on each (e.g. Seifert and Hoffnung, 1987), but more often combining the treatment of 'physical and cognitive development' and 'social and personality development' (e.g. Dworetzky, 1990; Dworetzky and Davis, 1989; Kaplan, 1991; Santrock, 1989). There are two features to note here: firstly, the connection between the cognitive and the physical works to privilege the realm of the cognitive as the primary arena for psychological development (and incorporates the physical within this), and places it in linear succession to the emphasis on biology in development; and, secondly, it reinstates the now familiar division between the rational and the irrational, that is, the cognitive and the emotional (see Chapter 2) with the first seen as essential and the second as contingent.

BRINGING UP BABY: VARIABILITY IN CHILDCARE ADVICE

A rather different picture emerges from the history and sociology of childhood. Here, debates focus on the extent and variability of conceptions of childhood, conceived of as a modern, Western notion (Ariès, 1962). While it is not possible to make a simple translation from representations (whether pictorial or literary) of children to child-rearing practices, or from newspaper accounts to what parents actually did to, and felt for, their children (Pollock, 1983), nevertheless childcare advice does constitute an important resource from which to speculate about the cultural content of, and importance accorded to, childhood and parenting practices. It can therefore provide an alternative vantage point from which to look at contemporary developmental psychological accounts.

Various models have been put forward to categorise historical fluctuations in childcare advice discernible even within England and the US. Newson and Newson (1974) and Hardyment (1983) write in terms of prevailing moralities which have governed approaches to childcare. From the mid-eighteenth century to mid-nineteenth century they identify a 'religious' morality, with a focus on preparing children for death since, with the high infant mortality rates of the time, a parents' duties were seen as best fulfilled in striving to ensure their child's life in the hereafter. With the prospect of little time to prove a child's goodness in life, a battle ensued to save the child's soul. For some this means there was little scope for indulgent, permissive parenting. As Susanna Wesley wrote to her son John (founder of the Methodist movement) 'Break his will now and his soul will live' (in Newson and Newson, 1974: 56). Child activists Ennew and Milne relate the powerlessness of children to their status as legal minors in every society, pointing out that in eighteenth-century Europe, child theft was not theft unless the child was wearing clothes. Otherwise child theft was like the theft of a corpse. The body was not inhabited by a legal person in either case.

(Ennew and Milne, 1989: 12)

After World War I medicine succeeded religion as the dominant moral authority governing childcare. This is sometimes attributed to a decline in infant and child mortality rates due to sanitation reforms in the mid- to late nineteenth century (combined with a general crisis of faith from the War), but it should be recalled that the highest recorded infant mortality rates in Britain were reported in the first part of the twentieth century (Rose, 1985). The narrative of modern progress that sometimes informs these accounts of childcare advice must therefore be problematised.

With the shift from medical to mental hygiene, the emerging psychology partook of medicine's authority to promise earthly survival in return for adherence to 'scientific mothercraft'. The earlier preoccupation with hereditary inclinations and predispositions was superseded by the application of behaviourist principles to childcare. The work of Watson and the New Zealand stockbreeder Truby King, who applied principles he developed rearing cattle to the upbringing of children, both advocated 'regularity of habits', and gave rise to what Daniel Beekman (1979) has called the 'mechanical' child.

> The establishment of perfect regularity of habits, initiated by feeding and cleaning by the clock is the ultimate foundation of all round obedience. Granted good organic foundations, truth and honour can be built into the edifice as it grows.
>
> (Truby King, 1937, cited in Newson and Newson, 1974: 61)

The authoritarian religious expert on child development was succeeded by the equally authoritarian medical expert. But the 1930s to the 1950s saw the rise of a different moral orientation towards children, emphasising children's 'needs' and 'natural development'. This was the period when psychoanalytic ideas were beginning to make their impact in early child education and with this came the importance accorded to play, to emotional as well as physical needs, and to continuity of care (Urwin and Sharland, 1992). As Newson and Newson put it 'At last the dirty, happy, noisy child could be accepted as a good child' (1974: 63). A less punitive approach was advised in dealings with children, particularly in relation to those enduring preoccupations of childcare advice: toilet training, thumb sucking and masturbation. But this was uttered in no less coercive pronouncements to parents.

The final period Newson and Newson (1974) distinguish is what they call 'Individualism and the fun morality' which they identify with the period after World War II. In part they attribute this change to the inward turn towards personal, domestic matters as an escape from recalling the atrocities of Hiroshima and Nazi death camps, and otherwise as part of a new confidence and assertiveness that marked this more affluent (for some) period. These developments (in 'choice' and consumption) were reflected in the childcare advice, firstly, in the less authoritarian tone of address and, secondly, by an emphasis on flexibility rather than prescription. The problem here is that enjoying parenting has become mandatory. In terms of the contemporary situation, this aspect still seems predominant, although there are rumblings of a backlash to permissive parenting in favour of more punitive parent-centred approaches within moral panics about childhood crime and failure at school. Contrariwise, in publicity about child abuse, moralities of 'natural needs and development' are still very much in evidence (Kitzinger, 1990; Stainton Rogers and Stainton Rogers, 1992).

It seems, then, that even within a relatively homogeneous cultural group, different historical periods have represented the process of rearing children very differently. While only one of these periods employs an explicit rhetoric of needs, it is important to recognise that all types of advice laid claim to the moral authority to define the requirements not only for good parenting, but also for what made an appropriate child, albeit often concerned with what the children would become rather than how they fared at the time. In this sense, the rhetoric of children's needs, while attractive, has been invoked over the years in quite diverse and often conflicting terms. There is a corresponding danger that children's 'needs' become some kind of inviolable category that is treated as self-evident rather than as informed by and reflecting the socio-political pre-occupations of particular cultures and times (Woodhead, 1990).

CHILDHOOD AS DEPENDENCY

Changing images of the child can be related to broader social tensions within emerging modern industrialising states. There are three points to note here. Firstly, the contrasting models frequently coexist and compete, rather than succeed each other in a harmonious fashion. Secondly, and following from this, there are continuities between images at different times – many conceptions reverberate on in powerful ways today. Thirdly, debates about the nature of the child have been central to the ways the State has interacted with, and regulated, its citizens. The eighteenth-century French philosopher Rousseau is credited with inventing the modern notion of childhood as a distinct period of human life with particular needs for stimulation and education. In contrast to evangelical doctrines of 'original sin', this model upheld the innocence of the child, the proximity of children to nature, and their freedom from contamination with the ugly lessons of civilisation. But this was not all it achieved:

> The new child was a figure of the 'Cult of Sensibility' associated with Rousseau. . . . At the basic level, therefore, this construction related to the contest for a particular kind of society – for a particular kind of beliefs – which was to stand between eighteenth century rationalism and nineteenth century industrialisation.
>
> (Hendrick, 1990: 38–9)

Industrialisation in the late eighteenth century ushered in the formalisation of child labour in factories. Outrage over the conditions of child labourers had less to do with exploitation than with fears of unruly and potentially undesirable activities made possible by an independent income. Martin Hoyles (1989) relates the invention of childhood innocence to the cult of the 'infant Jesus' which worked to eclipse children's active political resistance. Harry Hendrick (1990) argues that a debased version of the eighteenth-century philosophy of child nature was invoked to justify making children dependent through schooling, imposing a middle-class ideal of childhood as a period of helplessness. This was then treated as a cultural universal to block the reproduction of working-class resistance through controlling the activities of young people.

> They [eighteenth-century notions of child nature] were thoughtful expressions of a developing social and political philosophy (extending well beyond a concern with children) which was finding an audience among a class anxious about what it deemed to be the rebellious and aggressive attitudes and behaviours of young people (and of their parents). Thus juvenile lawlessness was seen as one of the heralds of political insurrection.
>
> (Hendrick, 1990: 44–5)

This was achieved through the introduction of compulsory mass schooling, linked to a theory of child nature which presented the initial state of the child as ignorant (thereby disenfranchising their community and 'street' knowledge) and positioning the working-class child as in need of education and socialisation. A standard curriculum produced a segregated and surveyed population with an emphasis on Bible study, along with gender-appropriate training suited to working-class boys and girls' allotted station in life (Hunt, 1985). A national childhood was constructed through schooling, which, although it was officially classless, rendered the child (and therefore the family) always available for reformation of their working-class morals. The process of schooling demanded a state of ignorance in return for advancement of opportunities for limited few. In terms of the impact on children at the time, Hendrick (1990) suggests that the main effect of the introduction of compulsory schooling was to diminish children's sense of their own value and take them out of the sphere of 'socially significant activity':

> [T]here was nothing coincidental in mid-century penologists and social investigators seeking to return children to their 'true position' (to their nature), as it also involved making them more amenable to the classroom. . . . The reconstruction of the factory child through the prism of dependency and ignorance was a necessary precursor of mass education in that it helped prepare public opinion for shifts in the child's identity (from wage-labourer to school pupil), for a reduction in income of working class families (as a result of the loss of children's earnings), and for the introduction of the state into childrearing practices.
>
> (Hendrick, 1990: 46)

CHILDHOOD AS UNIVERSAL

From this specific historical picture based in mid-nineteenth century Europe, we can see a move away from a diversity of class and cultural conceptualisations of childhood to the imposition of a standardised model that drew together a set of concerns with child education, management and control as well as philanthropy. This standard childhood, as administered in part through schooling, achieved uniformity and coherence among urban and rural populations; it reflected the Victorian domestic ideal of the family – based on order, respect and love – with corresponding organisation around age and gender asymmetries; and it made possible the twentieth-century construction of the compulsory relation between family, State and public welfare. Childhood, conceived of as a period of dependency, meant that education and socialisation were required to lead and train the child in the 'appropriate' direction. Hence representations of childhood were central to social policies.

It is worth reflecting on the links between notions of childhood, schooling and child labour when considering contemporary debates on the welfare of children in Third World countries. The mass media encourage us to think about 'all our children' (the BBC leaflet to the series of this name is subtitled 'A guide for those who care'), and charitable aid to Third World countries is focused on the welfare of children (as in sponsoring a child: 'Experience the joy of sponsorship says Michael Aspel', advertisement in the *Guardian*, 13 February 1992). We are exhorted by Plan International UK to 'change the world . . . one child at a time', to consider ourselves 'A World Family'. Cosy and caring as this 'world family' sounds, it ignores cultural and economic differences and treats economic inequalities outside the history of colonialism and imperialism which produced the impoverishment of the Third World in the first place. It positions those countries as responsible for their own 'underdevelopment' instead of recognising the vested interests that maintain Third World countries as dependent markets and sources of cheap labour – primarily that of women and children. In evaluating the significance of the suppression of the impact of imperialism within these texts, we should recall that children are directly involved in the sex tourism industry which was made possible by imperialist (often specifically US) wars in South East Asia (Boyden and Hudson, 1985), as was international trafficking in children (Ramirez, 1992). Moreover, additional consequences follow from this focus on the child. Social change is rendered gradual, discretionary and individual through working at the level of 'one child at a time'.

In these ways the child *as child* functions as an index, a signifier of 'civilisation' and modernity. The 'right' to childhood is adopted as a transcultural universal that links First and Third Worlds in a relationship of patronage and cultural imperialism. The adoption of this notion (which is structured in the 1959 UN Declaration of the Rights of the Child and the 1989 Convention on the Rights of the Child) bears witness to interests which, while seeking to enable and protect children, are also in danger of rendering them passive, dependent and malleable.

This is useful in evaluating current discussions of child labour in Third World countries, involving around 150 million children (Boyden with Holden, 1991). The issue here is to proscribe exploitative and dangerous work practices rather than pathologise Third World cultures and families for failing to uphold modern Western notions of dependent and playing children. What Boyden (1990) calls the 'globalization of childhood' functions as a medium for perpetuating ethnocentric and racist assumptions and prevents us from attending to the specific conditions and meanings of children's participation within local economies, without which little real aid and action is possible (see Chapter 13 for more on these issues).

From this historical perspective on legal and social policy, therefore, a certain ambivalence about the State's role in relation to children can be detected. While the model of the vulnerable, ignorant child positioned them as requiring protection, children were also portrayed as a source of disruption requiring control and discipline. In their analysis of policy and welfare practices relating to children that have given rise to legislation in Britain, Dingwall *et al.* (1984) argue that childhood has generally been treated as a 'social problem' whereby the dominant focus of social policy and practice has been on the perceived capacities of young people to threaten public order. Children's problems of abuse and neglect have tended to be collapsed together with the treatment of child *as* problem, as reflected even now within the types of care and provision available.

Returning to the developmental psychology textbooks, a similar elision is distinguishable. Dworetzky and Davis (1989) move from discussing children's needs in early life to taking as their 'Application' for their 'Adolescent social and personality development' chapter the question of 'Preventing teenage pregnancy'. It is worth pointing out here that the majority of the world's children are born to women under 20 (Phoenix, 1991), and that this is the time considered by most cultures as appropriate for childbearing. So whose development is being depicted here? 'Sexual precocity' is, however, a threat to the dominant, sanctified, passive model of childhood. New arrivals within US child development texts are coverage of 'teenage suicide' (Dworetzky, 1990; Seifert and Hoffnung, 1987) and 'childhood obesity' (Kaplan, 1991), both of which are problems within the US (but while most of the world is starving and struggling to survive). In Bukatko and Daehler (1992) the chapter on 'Social cognition' treats this as equivalent to 'self regulation'. Issues of social inequalities, disaffection and unemployment are alluded to in the last of the new (to the second edition) sections on 'The child and the year 2000' in Kaplan (1991). These, however, are presented as choices or almost life careers for young people, with the headings 'The non-college bound student'; 'Gender and achievement; minorities in high school; dropping out of school'; and 'Delinquency'. The focus on individual development leads to an acknowledgement of structural disadvantage only insofar as it is treated as a property of the individual: yet another reminder of the problems with opting for a model of change 'one child at a time'.

SIGNIFICANCE OF ADVICE LITERATURE

The identification of these problems is often coupled with advice. Firstly, there is the significance of its presence (and volume). Newson and Newson (1974) comment on the paucity of this literature prior to the mid-twentieth century. They provide a useful reminder that the preconditions for a psychology of child development, with its concerns about psychological adjustment and abilities, are a low rate of infant mortality and an adequate standard of living. Consider then what they term the 'cult of child psychology', the explosion of popular as well as academic literature that assaults us in supermarket queues and newsagents, and that finds its way among the recipes and quizzes in general newspapers as well as in those magazines specifically directed to women. Developmental psychology participates within the everyday popular understanding of parental roles, family relations and indeed personal identities of mothers, fathers, children and all who are involved in teaching or caring for them in contemporary Western culture. In Britain, the Royal College of General Practitioners has recently approved a publication, *Emma's Diary* (Lifecycle Marketing, 1991), to be distributed free in doctors' surgeries and clinics. This contains adverts not specifically associated with childcare as well as a week-by-week description of the progress of pregnancy and childcare. The demand for information about childcare and development is presented in newspaper coverage as aiming 'to satisfy pregnant women's craving for facts about parenthood', with pregnant women described as 'information guzzling' (*Independent on Sunday*, 16 February 1992: 24). The popular notion of pregnancy as producing compulsive appetites is here extended to include women's desires to know. So essential is the role currently accorded to knowledge about child development that it can even be represented as part of a pregnant woman's bodily needs. Nested within these ideas is a form of biological reductionism which collapses the biological fact of pregnancy into a period of receptivity to information about children (shades here of Winnicott's 'primary maternal preoccupation', and of the attachment and 'bonding' research discussed in Chapter 6). And following from the biologistic analogy, the notion of critical periods, or deadlines by which this knowledge must be demonstrated, is maintained.

But, secondly, what functions does this advice play? Do we find it helpful, reassuring? How can we understand the development of this eager market? It has been suggested that one reason why mothers (and fathers) turn to books arises from the erosion of extended family ties within which cultural understandings of child rearing would otherwise be communicated. Indeed, distinct class differences have been noted between those mothers who rely on their mothers' advice and those who seek out professional sources of information (Jones, 1987; Vukelich and Kumar, 1985). Again this is a useful prompt to recall the social divisions that make spurious simple descriptions of 'society' as homogeneous even within one geographical area. While the readership of the early child manuals was primarily middle class, one clear reason for the increasing dependence on professional advice lies in the ways this explicitly devalues oral sources as uninformed and old-fashioned, cautioning women not to rely on their mothers' or older women's advice. In this sense the advice is self-maintaining.

It is clearly difficult to assess the impact or 'effects' of this literature. Harriette Marshall's (1991) analysis of the content of some influential contemporary British sources highlights their dominant themes. Motherhood is presented as a woman's 'ultimate fulfilment', with mother love as 'natural' (and, correspondingly, failure to love as requiring psychiatric treatment). There is an emphasis on 'modern' mother-hood, with a dependence on professional experts for advice, and the desirable forum for the bringing up of a child is defined as a happy, heterosexual, nuclear family. This was presented as both inevitable and enduringly stable, wherein the expressed commitment to flexibility and 'sharing the caring' in the accounts gave way to positioning the mother as primarily and ultimately responsible for the 'normal development' of her child through actively stimulating, as well as caring for, her child. Rather as indicated by the slip in the Sorce *et al.* (1985) study discussed in Chapter 3, her identity as a woman is absorbed into that of mother, she is treated as responsible for her child's subsequent deeds and misdeeds through the emphasis on the importance of early experience and she is drawn into the discourse of develop-mental psychology through this positioning, as both originator and monitor of her child's development.

Marshall speculates how, given this load, it is possible for a woman to feel confident that she is fulfilling her maternal duty. While the women in Cathy Urwin's (1985a) survey report consulting manuals for reassurance, these are also the source of considerable anxiety. Developmental milestones structure mothers' observations of their offspring, such that they worry about the rate of progress, and induce competition between parents by inviting comparisons between children, reflecting the structuring of 'normal development' as measurable through the ranking of individuals. Development thus becomes an obstacle race, a set of hoops to jump through, with cultural kudos accorded to the most advanced, and the real or imagined penalties of professional intervention or stigmatisation if progress is delayed. Small wonder then at the marginalised position of 'learning disabled' children and their families. As well as the ten-dency to load responsibility for the next generation's moral performance on women, and to locate social problems within 'faulty mothering', this account also fails to accord any role to societal and structural influences.

THE CULTURAL ORGANISATION OF DEVELOPMENT

The popular and 'academic' literature on how children develop reflects dominant cultural assumptions about children's natures and treatment. It also informs these to the extent that they become the resource for the circulation of everyday under-standings about what children (and through them mothers, fathers and others) around them are like. The variability of advice gives rise to variability of practice. Newson and Newson (1974) take as their example the case of breast-feeding, which has been subject to fluctuation according to class and generation. While in the 1920s and 1930s bottle-feeding was a means for the British middle classes to display their status as able to afford the technology to feed and manage babies, by the 1980s breast-feeding had come to be associated with a middle-class commitment to the notion that 'Breast is best' (Stanway and Stanway, 1983), a principled desire to give your baby the best start to life, backed up by studies correlating breast-feeding with subsequent cognitive performance. The point here is not to advocate one form of feeding over another, but to indicate how the fluctuating demands on women made by medicine and psychology neglect the social factors that constrain women's choices, and thus often function simply to stigmatise further those who fail to measure up to this moral imperative.

A major consequence of this variability is that women are segmented and separated from each other's experiences and solidarity, both by generation and by class. Firstly, women who adhered to the expert advice of their day, by, for example, staying home with their child rather than engaging in paid work, are now portrayed as over-involved and clinging. Before them, their mothers who had not indulged their children and had fed them by the clock had gone on only to be later positioned as cruel and heartless. Meanwhile, within the current rhetoric of 'flexibility', women are presented with the 'choice' about feeding method. But the decks are heavily loaded in favour of breast-feeding: what mother can resist the injunction to foster the development of her child or, worse, impede it by failing to provide 'baby's birthright'? What of the mothers who do not have 'the choice' not to work, or who cannot for other reasons breast-feed their baby? This is not to condone the cynical peddling of baby milk substitutes to poor women in the Third World. Rather, in both contexts, the rhetoric of freedom of choice functions as a more subtle form of oppression by failing to recognise the inequality of access to the conditions it presupposes.

CONSEQUENCES

This chapter has focused on the forms and variations of discourses of childhood, and the significance of these variations. Three main issues emerge. Firstly, definitions of childhood are relational, they exist in relation to definitions of adults, of mothers and fathers, of families, of the State. These relational terms of child, adult and State have come to function in mutually dependent, mutually constitutive ways. While this may be an easy point to accept at an intellectual level, its ramifications are far-reaching. Discussions of children's natures necessarily reflect, and invoke, models of political organisation. Just as the needy, dependent child requires the attentive, indulging mother, so the child on whom environment inscribes its learning schedules requires the regulating, training mother.

Secondly, as feminists have recognised (Thorne, 1987), changes in gender relations will bring about changes in our conceptualisation of children. Developmental psychology's commitment to a view of children and child development as fixed, unilinear and timeless is not only ethnocentric and culture-blind in its unwitting reflection of parochial preoccupations and consequent devaluation of differing patternings, but is also in danger of failing to recognise changes in the organisation of childhood subjectivity and agency. Ann Solberg (1990) documents the increased power gained by the greater participation in household labour of Norwegian children of dual earner parents, as indicated both by their own and their family's perceptions. This study involves analysis of the subjective meanings invested (by children as well as adults) in being older or younger, or more or less big or grown up. The participation of women in paid work outside the home in this example has created the conditions for new forms and variations of childhood to emerge. If childhood is seen as static, universal and timeless then this can only be viewed as an aberration to be deplored. But to do this would be to proscribe any change from existing social arrangements and to refuse to recognise opportunities for the development of new subjectivities. Further, the fact that this study seems so novel in testifying to a relation between children's productive labour and enhanced social position itself speaks volumes about the ignorance or repression of the fact that most of the world's children work. That is, we fail to recognise the cultural specificity of our developmental models, which are not only partial and unaware of this, but also oppressive in prescribing what are Western norms for Third World countries.

Thirdly, and finally, there is the question of the positioning of children and knowledge. Children are defined as lacking knowledge, hence requiring protection and education. To challenge this conception may seem to render children responsible for the difficulties that befall them, as is evident in discussions of child abuse (Kitzinger, 1990). In their textbook, Seifert and Hoffnung (1987), alongside a section on 'The concept of childhood in history', present an account of the modern construction and institutionalisation of children as benign, noting that:

> In the twentieth century, society became increasingly concerned about protecting children from the harsh world outside the family. Children were thought to need the special protection of parents and institutions dedicated to serving children, such as schools.
>
> (Seifert and Hoffnung, 1987: text to figures pp. 12–13)

Attribution of knowledge to children is bound up with images of the child and what we imagine them and ourselves to be. Discourses of childhood function as regulatory both overtly and internally. They produce a sense of adulthood and childhood not only for us but also for children. Accounts such as that quoted above fail to distinguish between a variety of social relations, both within and between cultures, that constitute a 'society'. They portray as unproblematic both the position of the family as haven in a heartless world, and the State as involved in protecting and educating children. These are the issues to which we turn next.

FURTHER READING

James, A. and Prout, A. (eds) (1990) *Constructing and Reconstructing Childhood*, Basingstoke: Falmer Press (a fascinating and wide-ranging collection, all of which is useful in the elaboration of issues raised in this and other chapters in this part).

Stainton Rogers, R. and Stainton Rogers, W. (1992) *Stories of Childhood: shifting agendas of child concern*, Brighton: Harvester (a very entertaining and readable account that explores current issues and dilemmas).

For accounts that specifically address childcare advice, see:

Marshall, H. (1991) 'The social construction of motherhood: an analysis of childcare and parenting manuals', in A. Phoenix, A. Woollett and E. Lloyd (eds) *Motherhood: meanings, practices and ideologies*, London: Sage.

Newson, J. and Newson, E. (1974) 'Cultural aspects of childrearing in the English-speaking world', in M. Richards (ed.) *The Integration of the Child into a Social World*, London: Cambridge University Press.

Urwin, C. (1985) 'Constructing motherhood: the persuasion of normal development', in C. Steedman, C. Urwin and V. Walkerdine (eds) *Language, Gender and Childhood*, London: Routledge & Kegan Paul.

Also the chapters by

Urwin, C. and Sharland, E. (1992) 'From bodies to minds in childcare literature: advice to parents in inter-war Britain' and Thom, D. (1992) 'Wishes, anxieties, play and gestures: child guidance in inter-war England', both in R. Cooter (ed.) *In the Name of the Child*, London: Routledge.

SUGGESTED ACTIVITIES

Gather together a selection of childcare advice literature, from the key books – ranging from current (such as those by Hugh Jolly and Penelope Leach) to the 'experts' of the 1950s and 1960s such as Benjamin Spock. Many public, and college, libraries have endless amounts of such material. Students may also have access to such materials as well. It is also useful to include literature that is provided free of charge at health centres, doctors' surgeries or family planning clinics, or is distributed by health visitors, and to analyse material in childcare magazines, of which there are currently many. Having allocated this material to individuals or pairs, address the following questions:

- what is the gender of the child depicted (and how do you know)?
- what is the gender of the primary caregiver?
- what is the gender of professionals (if they are depicted)?
- what is the tone of the advice offered?
- what models of family relations are represented?

Simple questions such as these can generate interesting commentary and debate, particularly if the material under scrutiny spans a significant period of time, or is clearly addressed to different audiences (as in those who buy vs. those who are statutory recipients of services). Tensions or contradictions can also be fruitful, as in variation between articles and advertising copy within a single text such as a magazine, or between narrative and image. An exercise like this can bring to life questions about variety and variability of childcare literature over time and within and between cultures that make the discursive construction of childhood and the correlative positions elaborated for mothers, fathers and others very concrete.

Part II

Social development and the structure of caring

Along with 'the child', developmental psychology constitutes homes and families as its object of enquiry. This part correspondingly explores the impact of developmental psychological research on families in Chapter 5, highlighting in Chapter 6 what this has meant in terms of its conceptions of mothers and mother–child relations and, in Chapter 7, of its depiction of the role of fathers. Particular connections are made with issues of policy and practice.

Chapter 5

Familiar assumptions

Parents . . . remain the most cost-effective social service for children's well-being.
(Whitfield, 1980: 108)

Representations of children function in relation to representations of those who look after and live with them. Indeed, a family is often defined in terms of caregiving roles for dependent children, to the extent that couples living together without children are rarely classed as a 'family' (Van Every, 1992). We saw in Part I how the individual-centred focus of developmental psychology sets up an opposition between 'child' and 'environment' such that the separation between 'child' and 'context' seems taken as pre-given. This 'context' has come in for much scrutiny and evaluation, not least in terms of its purported child-rearing qualities. While the 'environment' for children's development has often been treated as synonymous with the mother (e.g. Yarrow *et al.*, 1975), the family as the context for child rearing is central to social policy and welfare and is also the site for heated debate about social relations and social change. The significance of these social policy debates and the ways they enter into developmental research is the topic of this chapter.

THE STATE OF THE FAMILY

While the Right claims a special allegiance to it, social commentators of all political persuasions see the family as the basic unit of social life, and political parties compete to be the party of 'the family' (Egerton, 1991). Yet discourses of 'the family' function in contradictory ways, positioning it sometimes as a refuge from the stresses and strains of the outside world, and sometimes as threat to its orderly functioning. Alongside the celebration of security, commitment and romantic love in which the home is depicted as a conflict-free haven, there are anxieties about the 'break-up' of the family through rising divorce rates and rising numbers of young, 'teenage' mothers. Domestic violence and child abuse are increasingly being taken seriously as widespread phenomena. Before entering the debate about whether families are *really* disintegrating, we need to consider the extent to which families have changed and are variable.

Discussions about families often treat the family as a universal, common and unchanging structure without reference to cultural or historical specificity. Yet patterns of mortality and fertility dramatically affect the composition of families. In the 'developing' world today (as in the northern hemisphere in pre-industrial days) where infant and child mortality rates are high, parents are more likely to have more children in the hope that some will survive. Indeed anthropologist Nancy Scheper-Hughes (1989a: 10) suggests that a high birth rate may well be a *response* to a high death rate. Changes in life expectancy alter the age and composition of families. While the key demographic issue currently pre-occupying the rich, industrialised northern hemisphere is an ageing population, with people living longer, its preoccupation with the impoverished south is with reducing the birth rate. As Diana Gittins (1985) points out, 'till death do us part' has a different meaning in modern technological societies where, with increased life expectancy, a marriage can last sixty or seventy years. It is in this context that moral panics about divorce rates and 'broken' homes need to be evaluated.

Economic factors enter into the structure and composition of families. Historical accounts of the family generally point to the role of industrialisation not only in bringing about the transition from village to urban life for most people, but also as creating the division between the 'public' sphere of work and the 'private' realm of home – coinciding with the greater separation of and segregation between women and men's labour. In pre-industrial Europe productive activity was carried out in or near the home, and all family members worked, although tasks varied according to age and skill (Gittins, 1985). Families were often distributed by sending children into service (for girls) or apprenticeship (for boys), and might be extended by the inclusion of servants who were treated as family members. Hence household size would vary according to the number of dependants and servants it could suppport. Variation in land ownership and inheritance patterns affected who was able to marry and when. For example, women have only recently been able to own and inherit property in their own right (from 1870 in England), and a woman with no dowry might have been unable to marry. Marriage therefore has played an important role for women as a source of material security, and as almost their sole route for social mobility. The different histories and political role of both aristocracy and bourgeoisie in Britain and France owe much to variation in inheritance laws (with land passing to eldest sons in Britain and divided equally between all sons in France for example). Finally, it must be remembered that a large proportion of the population (up to 20 per cent) remained single in pre-industrial Europe: celibacy (irrespective of how celibate people actually were) was seen as a chosen and valued way of life, often but not always linked to religious devotion.

While it is unlikely that there was ever an idyllic 'golden age' of happy and supportive extended families (Abbott, 1989) as some critics of modern life suggest, it is clear that families have taken and do take on different forms according to culture and historical period. Moreover, attending to this history indicates that the nuclear family, composed of man and woman and children, with the man as breadwinner working outside the home and the woman responsible for housework and childcare, is itself a family form which came to prominence in the late nineteenth century. It is not possible to make absolute distinctions between varieties of family forms at different historical periods, since these forms are both more continuous and less uniform over time (according to economic factors among others) than has usually been assumed. Nevertheless, there is no doubt that the nuclear family emerged as the privileged form. Gittins (1985) comments that, while the industrial revolution was spurred on by the low waged labour of women and children, the call for a 'family wage' was a central demand of the developing trade union movement. Echoing the middle-class norm of women and children as dependants of their husband/father, this demand called for men to be treated as primary wage-earners. Since most families could not afford to live on one income alone, an ideal of family life was being promoted that few could attain. In addition to naturalising women's roles as mothers and home-makers, the model of the nuclear family therefore reinforces the low-waged status of women workers. It should be noted that the so-called 'third industrial revolution' of the computer age relies on the low-paid labour of southern hemisphere women and children (Mitter, 1986).

FAMILIAR ASSUMPTIONS

Perhaps the most pervasive assumption about families is that they are necessary. The idea that we could not do without such important and worthwhile social institutions is based primarily on the mere fact of the continuing existence of families, although, as we have seen, they are not fixed in structure and composition. 'Functionalist' approaches to the family within sociology (such as those of Parsons and Murdock) assume that the family is a universal and basic social unit as the site for co-operation and exchange of resources and services. The allocation of resources is taken to include money, food, skills and space, while services range from the division of labour between production and reproduction (i.e. childcare, household labour vs. paid work) to sexual relations. These assumptions clearly legitimise the maintenance of traditional gender and age roles. They present a sanitised image of the home as a conflict-free arena, thus ignoring power relations between family members, and presume that all members share the same interests (Brannen and Wilson, 1987). The very assumption of co-residence as a criterion for constituting a family both includes those who would not consider themselves a family (such as prisoners) and excludes those who would (where one parent works away from home). Further, the emphasis on the family as a site of 'co-operation' ignores other sources of co-operation and support and suggests that it functions autonomously, thus failing to recognise both the interrelationships between families, and State incentives which bolster and maintain this particular form of social organisation. For example, the legal system is so structured that cohabiting women can be advised to marry their male partners for material security (Fieldman, 1991).

The model of the nuclear family, consisting of heterosexual couples with their genetic, 'naturally' conceived children, with the man bringing home the wage and the woman keeping the home, is increasingly recognised to be a fiction. Over a third of children in Britain are born to single mothers, over a third of marriages end in divorce (more in the US) and 70 per cent of women are economically active (part-time or full-time) (Equal Opportunities Commission, 1991). As Robert Dingwall (1989) points out, over a quarter of a million children in Britain live in residential institutions (especially if we include young people in boarding schools). Yet the nuclear family continues to lie at the centre of social policy in terms of defining relationships and responsibilities (with women rendered economically dependent on men, and men emotionally and physically serviced by women), and children treated as the property of their parents.

Jayne Van Every (1992) points out that the power of this model of the family makes itself felt more on those who fail to conform to it than those who do. Clause 28 of the British Local Government Act of 1987 defines lesbian and gay relationships as 'pretended families' and paragraph 16 of the 1989 England and Wales Children Act precludes lesbians and gay men from fostering or adopting children. The furore over 'virgin births' which hit the British press in March 1991 highlighted widespread outcry at the possibility of women having babies without sexual contact with a man, while justification for DI (Donor Insemination) and infertility treatments being selectively available to women in heterosexual relationships is made on the grounds that such a relationship will satisfy the child's 'need' for a father.

The definition of a normal mother as married and in her mid-twenties positions young mothers, most of whom are single, as 'social problems', particularly in terms of their likelihood of being inadequate parents and of dependence on state benefits. While both of these assumptions are questionable (Phoenix, 1991), single mothers are thereby either rendered invisible within normative definitions of mothering or recognised only in order to be treated as deviant – what Ann Phoenix and Anne Woollett (1991) call a 'normalized absence/pathologized presence'.

Familial organisation is of course culturally as well as historically variable, as are age of marriage, structure of living arrangements, styles of management of behaviour and definitions of family responsibilities. This is clearly relevant to policies and practices around childcare and families within modern 'multicultural' societies. It is dangerously simplistic to generalise within and between cultural groups, especially since migration changes the availability of extended family networks and physical organisation of characteristic childcare and rearing practices (Phoenix, 1988; Stainton Rogers, 1989). Nevertheless it should be noted that women-headed households are a predominant family form for many people of West Indian background, and this renders black women subject to further stigmatisation and pathologisation within contemporary familial ideology (Phoenix, 1987).

In contrast, research into children's own ideas about families indicates that children are aware of normative definitions of families, but that their definitions reflect their own experiences. Margaret O'Brian and Pam Alldred (1991) report that children's drawings of their families were not always confined simply to the people they lived with, that in group discussion they employed variable definitions at different times and expressed awareness about the complexity and diversity of family relationships.

DEVELOPMENTAL PSYCHOLOGICAL RESEARCH AND THE FAMILY

There is now some acknowledgement within developmental psychology that families are both changing demographically and constitute differing environments for the different individuals within them that also vary over time (Cohen, 1987; Daniels and Plomin, 1985). Despite this, most developmental psychological research conforms to dominant familial assumptions of the nuclear family containing a male breadwinner and female childcarer. This connects with dominant definitions of femininity which characterise motherhood as women's ultimate fulfilment, a characterisation to which all women, mothers or not, are subjected (Phoenix et al., 1991).

Practical as well as ideological motivations inform the mother-focused orientation of most research. It is mothers rather than fathers who tend to be at home during the working day, and who therefore make the most convenient research 'subjects', and limiting the study to mother and child reduces the complexity of data collection and analysis (White and Woollett, 1992). As Penny Munn (1991) points out, the overwhelming emphasis of developmental psychological research on the early years of child rearing produces an impoverished conception of the family unit as 'mother and child', ignoring the fact that most women have more than one child, and that therefore the familial context in which most children develop – even within exclusive childcare by mothers – is far from dyadic (see Chapters 8 and 9 for a discussion of the consequences of this on child language research). A consequence of the 'normalized absence/pathologized presence' of black, single and working-class mothers within developmental psychological research is a homogenisation as well as normalisation of accounts of mothering and children's development:

> we have less information about normal interaction patterns in unconventional families and problems in normal families, so we do not have a good basis for assessing the relative advantages and disadvantages of different family forms.
> (White and Woollett, 1992: 11)

The terminology used within developmental psychology texts reflects familiar assumptions, with 'normal' family meaning 'nuclear' family, and variations correspondingly defined in relation to that norm. An 'intact' family is a nuclear family, which can be 'broken', 'reconstituted' or 'extended' (see, e.g., White and

Woollett, 1992). 'Non-traditional' families, even when they are studied (e.g. Lamb, 1982) rarely 'vary' beyond cohabiting couples, and lesbian and gay parents are absent from all current developmental psychological texts (cf. Pollack and Vaughn, 1987). Women have been so absorbed into definitions of mothering that research investigating their specific identities as women who are mothers is important, rather than homogenising all mothers as the same (e.g. Phoenix *et al.*, 1991). However, acknowledgement of the recent 'expansion' of women's economic and political roles can turn into a position which treats attention to the conflicting interests of family members, particularly of women and children, as unhelpful (Dornbush and Strober, 1988). The changing conceptions of the relation between the interests of women and children are taken up by Singer (1992).

THE FAMILY AND THE STATE

The definition and boundaries of families connect with wider institutions and practices. While the general shift to the Right in Britain is not yet sufficiently organised, successful or monolithic to constitute (as in the US) a 'moral majority' (Durham, 1991), policy and legislative changes already reflect ideological assumptions about appropriate and desirable citizens. The nuclear family reflects heterosexist and ethnocentric assumptions. The recent proposal in Britain to chase up fathers who default on alimony, while presented as a measure to support mothers, for example, may force some women into unwanted negotiations with their ex-partners, and clearly works to move financial responsibility for provision from the State to individuals.

Setting up the division between public and private serves many functions. While the relationship between these is complex historically, ideologies of femininity and family can be seen as central to doctrines of racial supremacy. The invariably white imagery of the cultural icon of mother and child functions as the conjoined index of both 'nature' and 'civilisation'. These twin (and contradictory) notions tie patriarchal ideologies of femininity and family to the specifically racialised configurations set up by colonialism. Not only is white defined as the norm, but the white couple of mother and child signify vulnerability and the need for protection from unnamed dangers outside. Vron Ware's (1992) analysis of varieties of British and US femininities within the context of eighteenth- and nineteenth-century imperialism demonstrates the central role this iconography played within the terrorism of colonial rule, so that the subjugation of black people (as, for example, through the threat or actuality of lynching) was defended on the grounds of claiming to protect white women:

> One of the recurring themes in the history of colonial repression is the way in which the real or imagined violence towards white women became a symbol of the most dangerous form of insubordination. In any colony, the degree to which white women were protected from fear of sexual assault was a good indication of the level of security felt by the colonial authorities. . . .

Protecting the virtue of white women was the pretext for instituting draconian measures against indigenous populations in several parts of the Empire. . . . White women provided a symbol of the most valuable property known to white man and it was to be protected from the ever-encroaching and disrespectful black man at all costs.

(Ware, 1992: 38)

More recently, families are positioned as the primary site for the socialisation of children to such an extent that there are recurrent calls for parents to be legally responsible for children's bad behaviour. Moreover, in a climate of increasing privatisation and reduction of welfare services and benefits, the rhetoric of celebration of family support clearly works to exonerate the State from its responsibilities. While kinship has functioned and continues to function as the basis on which to organise financial and caring support, this is by no means automatic or unchanging (Finch, 1989). Not only do recent welfare policies position women as responsible for childcare (Moss, 1990), but it has become increasingly clear that 'care in the community' for people who are physically and mentally disabled rests on unpaid care by women (Dalley, 1988; Finch and Groves, 1983).

While the sanctity and privacy of the family is contrasted with the public arena (to the extent that wife battering is frequently condoned and rape in marriage is only in the early stages of a process of becoming illegal in Britain), those who infract the dominant norms of child rearing and parenting are subject to intervention by a variety of professional and welfare agencies. State provision of childcare is primarily directed at those families deemed to have 'special needs'. These women are correspondingly accorded less 'privacy' than those who can afford nannies or *au pairs*:

So while provision of council day nurseries seems benevolent, and is indeed essential to some women who live in poverty, they also allow easy surveillance of the children being placed in them. . . . What is being suggested is that the privatization of 'the family' together with social constructions of 'good parents' which omit many mothers, particularly those who are black, working class and single, makes some mothers liable to state intervention based on their structural position rather than because they are inadequate.

(Phoenix and Woollett, 1991: 20)

Since families, and within existing childcare arrangements particularly mothers, are seen as reproducers of culture (Yuval-Davis and Anthias, 1989), professionals have regarded educating parents as preventive social work. Bowlby was active in developing the profession of social work for this purpose (see Chapter 6). As the extract at the beginning of this chapter indicates, 'Education for Parenthood' programmes aim to create responsible and autonomous families, in which developmental psychology (in the form of knowledge about child development and maturation), along with nutrition, domestic technology, economics and health care, is seen as a vital resource to foster appropriate moral reasoning within the child.

The boundary between public and private perhaps becomes most controversial in cases of (suspected) child abuse. Handelman's (1989) analysis of the management of a case of suspected child abuse highlights how 'caring' professions such as child protection workers, health visitors or social workers are embedded within a bureaucracy of 'helping' services that are structured around the bipolar dimensions of punishment and rehabilitation. The tension between care and coercion is epitomised by the use of the term 'co-operation' as a description of the recipient of the service's response to the intervention. This can mean either partnership or submission to authority under threat of losing the child. The fact that these two rather different reactions are treated as equivalent highlights the elision between punishment and support within the services. Handelman traces how the bureaucratic procedures for the management of a 'case' and the corresponding structures of professional accountability can construct, rather than prevent and aid, the situation (in this case of child neglect) they are designed to ameliorate. Her analysis is based on the example of a mother whose resistance to professional involvement is pathologised to such an extent that she is eventually compulsorily admitted to a mental hospital. The structures for prevention of child neglect and maternal deprivation had created the very phenomena they supposedly set out to prevent.

In terms of recent developments, the England and Wales Children Act (1989), introduced within a market-oriented context, extending economic relations of exchange to social theory, tried to balance up 'rights' of parents with those of children. Despite the overt separation between economic and social spheres (with the market regulating the public sphere and the family the social), the Act has worked to bolster the authority of the State in the name of protecting individual rights and liberties (Parton, 1991). Here the regulation of families becomes particularly overt within policies which have abandoned thoroughgoing policies of childcare provision to focus simply on child protection:

> the more voluntaristic indirect and universal childcare services have been remodelled and refashioned to meet the needs of the child protection system which emphasises much more of the targeting of provisions and concentrates on the direct observation and regulation of behaviour. Nowhere is this more evident than in the replacement of day nurseries with family centres.
>
> (Parton, 1991: 207)

Central to the boundary between family privacy and state intervention is conformity to normative definitions of acceptable family organisation and relations which, although conducted by social workers, draw upon developmental psychology as an academic resource which then gets recycled into common-sense norms about what proper parenting and families are like.

> What the recent very public debates about sexual abuse and parental rights have provided is not simply a vehicle for constructing and re-thinking the nature of child protection practices and social work, but the form and nature

of the family itself. If governing the family is to be successful, it means that most of us must know what good childcare and good parenthood is and what constitutes normal family relationships without ever having contact with a social worker.

(Parton, 1991: 214)

RIGHTS AND WRONGS: DOES PRACTICE MAKE PERFECT?

Developmental psychology therefore both contributes to and reflects dominant assumptions and debates about families, both in structuring research agendas and in informing practice. As already noted in Chapter 3, discourses of 'rights' and 'liberties', reflecting the world-wide move towards so-called 'free'-market economies, figure prominently in the political arena, in which the struggle to determine children's rights constitutes a key area for the definition and legislation of familial ideology. While the normative role of developmental psychology in this is usually tacit, it becomes much more explicit where it informs legal discussions about children's rights, needs and 'best interests'. Parents and children may not share the professionals' view of the nature of the problem. The influence of individual psychology and family therapy in social work training can

lead to a social worker being preoccupied with relationships and family malfunctioning, whilst in stark contrast the preoccupation of many of their clients is lack of money and balancing of budgets.

(Fletcher, 1982: 2)

Historically within the British legal system (like many others), children, like women, were seen as the legal property of men, except where the child was conceived outside marriage (Freeman, 1989; Lowe, 1982). The move towards according children rights, as in the British Children Act (1989), redefines parents as having *responsibilities* towards children, which they forfeit in circumstances where they fail to meet their parental duties. However, Nigel Parton (1991) argues that in practice this is undermined by a consumer model of partnership borrowed from discussions of parental involvement in services for disabled children. The result is that the rights of parents are privileged over those of children. Further, the shift towards defining child abuse as a socio-legal rather than a socio-medical issue extends the power of the 'psychological complex' (Rose, 1985), in which, as we have seen, developmental psychology is a vital ingredient. This is because, paradoxically, in spite of the widespread criticism heaped upon social workers, they now play an even greater legal role in determining state intervention within families through the importance accorded to 'social assessments' which report on children's and families' welfare and development (Parton, 1991).

Objective and indisputably right as affirming 'children's rights' sounds, the call contains an irreducibly moral-political component which can be enlisted in different agendas. This can be illustrated in definitions of parental and child rights within criteria used for awarding the custody of children. Contrary to received wisdom, it is only comparatively recently that women have tended to get custody of their children. Within English law until the mid-nineteenth century the family was considered the father's 'empire', and fathers' legal rights over children and women were upheld irrespective of child welfare considerations. The Infant Custody Act of 1839 first allowed courts to award custody of children under 7 to women, but this was subject to the proviso that they had not committed adultery. Legislation in 1886 permitted courts to award custody of all children under 21 to their mothers. As Nigel Lowe (1982) points out, while this legislation extended the courts' powers to grant custody orders in favour of mothers, this was only at the courts' discretion and did not amount to any affirmation of mothers' custodial rights. In fact the equalisation of parental rights was achieved within English law only in 1973. Rather it has been the emergence of the 'child welfare principle' formulated in the 1925 Guardianship of Infants Act that has changed women's custodial positions.

In their analysis of key cases in English courts from the mid-nineteenth to the mid-twentieth century, Dingwall and Eekelaar (1986) document how normative and contradictory assumptions about what constitutes a proper family have entered into custody settlements. Consequently, varying definitions of children's best interests have been deployed, with factors such as financial provision (usually advantaging men) or living in a nuclear family (where the father has remarried) prevailing over continuity of relationship and the child's 'need' for her biological mother. Women's success in custody disputes over the last thirty years derives from 'the primary caretaker' rule, by which the child is awarded to the parent who has played the major role in day to day care, which within current arrangements is usually the mother (Smart, 1989). While some fathers' rights groups are arguing that this constitutes discrimination against men, Holtrust *et al.* (1989), Graycar (1989) and Boyd (1989) all argue that so-called egalitarian moves towards joint custody arrangements prevalent in Europe, Canada, North America, Australia and now emerging in Britain (Lyon, 1989) advantage men (who had previously lost out according to the 'primary caretaker' rule) and increase the likelihood of the harassment of women and manipulation of children. Maureen O'Hara (1991) takes this further to argue that the rhetoric of children's rights can work as a cover to assert the power and control of men, and renders even more vulnerable the custodial rights of lesbian mothers.

The problems with determining children's 'best interests' become most evident where the children, for reasons of age or disability, are unable to make their own opinions clear. One strategy for dealing with this is to appoint child advocates. However, as Martha Fineman (1989) argues from the North American experience, what this does is to create a further layer of professionals through which the same set of ideas about children and families is circulated. For what resources can a 'child advocate' draw upon except those already popularised by the childcare and welfare 'experts', then recycled as the child's putative wishes? While it may have the potential to do other things, child advocacy therefore threatens simply to strengthen the legitimacy of, and to naturalise, psychology in social policy.

The discourse of rights presumes that individual interests can be treated as isolated and separable from others. This is a particularly difficult model to maintain when dealing with children, whose material and psychological existence is constituted through relating to others (Roche, 1989). We have seen how developmental psychology tends to reproduce this model by researching the child as separate and abstracted from social relations. This has implications for the production as well as the topic of psychological research. Abramovitch *et al.* (1991) report that children who consent to participate in developmental psychological studies rarely understand the consequences of this and do not feel they have a genuine choice, especially if their parents or teachers have agreed. Waving the banner of freedoms, rights and choices simply cannot remove the issue of power relations between the parties whose rights conflict.

FAMILY RESEMBLANCES?

Developmental psychology has enlarged its focus of enquiry from the abstracted child to the 'context' only to halt at his or her immediate social surroundings of family, rather than examining the social-historical influences that construct the family unit. This has led to a failure to see the variety of forms of family organisation as connected with cultural and economic issues. In turn this leads to an idealised model of the family which perpetuates age and gender asymmetrical relations, ignores conflicts and stigmatises and pathologises those who fail to conform to this model.

The real effects of this are evident within the provision of educational psychological services dealing with children identified as 'having problems'. These either treat the child *with problems* as *being* the problem or else position the child's family as responsible for creating the problems (Marks, 1993). It is now increasingly recognised that the identification of children's needs is a matter of resources rather than flowing from anything intrinsic to the child or family so that professional assessments are constrained by the knowledge of the limited forms of provision available (Wolfe, 1981). A consequence, then, of developmental psychology's inability to theorise the relation between the individual child and the wider social and political context is an academic and welfare discipline which blames difficulties on either child or family, or both, and which fails to implicate the wider social forces which construct and maintain the child's relations within his or her family. The rhetorical use of the term 'family' functions to tie individuals together into small units, to deny their relation with broader social action and reaction, and to act as a buffer zone to mask wider social responsibility. Hence 'community care' means care by families (i.e. women). So by this account we do not need social services (except where families are not doing their job properly) and we do not need social change.

Clearly the ties that hold women and children at home together are not only self-imposed. The mother is glued to the family through discourses of family structure, and within that structure the child is glued to the mother through discourses of attachment. This is addressed in the next chapter.

FURTHER READING

Phoenix, A., Woollett, A. and Lloyd, E. (eds) (1991) *Motherhood: meanings, practices and ideologies*, London: Sage (contains many useful chapters).
Smart, C. and Sevenhuijsen, S. (eds) (1989) *Child Custody and the Politics of Gender*, London: Routledge (reviews developments in custody legislation across Europe, the US, Canada and Australia).
Van Every, J. (1992) 'Who is "the family"? The assumptions of British social policy', *Critical Social Policy, 33*: 62–75 (a useful recent account).
White, D. and Woollett, A. (1992) *Families: a context for development*, Basingstoke: Falmer Press (an up-to-date review of psychological research with some links to its practical effects).

SUGGESTED ACTIVITIES

Using the cases discussed by Dingwall and Eekelaar (1986) (and more recent cases initiated by children themselves under new legislation), construct vignettes and ask individuals or small groups to consider what factors they would consider relevant to the decision making, and, if possible, what decision they would favour. If, as is likely, they feel they need more information on which to base their decision, then ask them to specify what further information they require and how it would inform their judgement – this then becomes an extra resource for discussion later. Then discuss the actual outcomes, and the factors that were considered relevant at the time. This exercise draws attention to the variation in cultural-political preoccupations over time which throws into question often unanalysed assumptions about mothers' or fathers' rights, and economic over affectional considerations (and the role played by developmental psychology within this; see Chapter 6).

Chapter 6

Bonds of love – dilemmas of attachment

It has been the fate of mothers throughout history to appear in strange and distorted forms. They may appear as larger than life or as invisible; as all-powerful and destructive; or as helpless and angelic. Myths of the maternal instinct compete, historically, with myths of a universal infanticidal impulse. Some of these contradictions and psychological projections can be found in the scholarly literature as well.

(Scheper-Hughes, 1989a: 3)

Harlow's imaginative research on the attachment behavior of infant monkeys brought the emotional and social development of the infant out of the field of clinical inference and speculation and made love an acceptable variable in the experimental laboratory.

(Stone *et al.*, 1973: 6)

Misogyny is deeply implicated in the dream structure of the laboratory.

(Haraway, 1989: 238)

Within the tripartite structure of 'physical', 'cognitive' and 'emotional' development set up by developmental psychological accounts, relationships between parents and children necessarily figure strongly in descriptions of children's social selectivity and responsivity. Mothers, positioned as the objects and sources of children's affections, feature in terms of their success or failure in promoting the child's development. While the claim that children need warm, continuous and stable relationships seems indisputable, the precise arrangements that fulfil these conditions continue to be a matter of fierce dispute, and many children grow up without them. The debates around childcare constitute a key arena for the interplay between developmental psychological research, social movements and social policy, with controversy focusing on how competing interpretations carry dramatically different implications for women's employment. But, central as this issue is, it is also a symptom of a more general and familiar agenda. The first part of this chapter reviews the themes characterising the research on attachment, while the second evaluates the assumptions guiding the research and the procedures which generate it.

JOBS FOR THE BOYS?

Free and available childcare has long been a demand of the feminist movement as a necessary prerequisite for women's liberation. At the same time, feminists have challenged the assumption that women are responsible for childcare (New and David, 1985). It is therefore not surprising that psychological theories that appear to confirm women's place in the home, that claim children suffer if they are not in the full-time care of their mothers and that suggest children who have personal or behavioural problems in their later lives have been inadequately mothered have attracted particular criticism. The popularity of John Bowlby's theory of maternal deprivation in the 1950s, at a time when men were returning from fighting in the Second World War, appeared to provide justification for excluding women from the (often heavy industrial) jobs they had taken over 'for the war effort'. While there is no doubt that most nurseries set up during the war to enable women to work were closed shortly afterwards, and that the 1950s was a period which glorified motherhood (as both the bearing of and caring for babies), to regard developmental psychology as responsible for this would be to overstate its influence and to underestimate other important influences, such as the institutionalisation of the psychoanalytically informed 'family fables' (Rose, 1985). Narratives of love going wrong employed by such services as child guidance clinics (Thom, 1992; Urwin and Sharland, 1992), all acted to perpetuate the assumption that women's futures lay in motherhood. Nevertheless, psychology played its part in the post-war celebration of home and hearth which defined and regulated women's fitness as mothers.

Clearly, as Denise Riley (1983) argues, the process by which a set of ideas gets inscribed within policy is not a simple translation process. Nor can it be reduced to the efforts or the creativity of a single author. Rather what has to be addressed is the question of what social-historical conditions made possible the emergence and reception of those ideas (Urwin, 1985b). What this perspective means is that we cannot postulate an absolute separation between theory and its application. In this case, the primary theorists of attachment and maternal deprivation, John Bowlby and Donald Winnicott, were very active in the promotion and popularisation of their ideas, writing newspaper columns and doing radio broadcasts. They were aware of the implications of their pronouncements for women's economic and social roles. But there is also a more complicated story of the interlinking of individual ideas, theoretical frameworks and social policy arrangements which needs to be told.

HOME ALONE

Bowlby's work on the effects of maternal separation was a major influence in reforming residential and hospital practices for the care of children. His con- clusions in his 1951 *Maternal Care and Mental Health* report commissioned by the World Health Organisation were based on studies of children evacuated from the cities away from their parents (demonstrating yet again psychologists and psychoanalysts benefiting from war as providing 'natural experiments', Wexler, 1983) and an investigation into the backgrounds of children who had histories of stealing and involvement in petty crime. From these, he argued that separation from mothers was an inherently traumatic experience for children, that children who failed to establish a firm attachment by the age of 3 would be unable to do so subsequently, and would suffer severe psychological problems (in his terms would become 'affectionless psychopaths'), and he urged early treatment and prevention programmes on the basis of early identification (he claimed by age 3). He reflected current norms about family organisation, arguing that a bad home was better than a good institution (the wisdom of which has increasingly been challenged). In some circumstances, however, blood ties were not enough. In accordance with dominant moral codes, he urged that unmarried mothers should submit children for adoption in the interests of securing a stable family life for their child. In this sense, Bowlby followed and confirmed developmental theory in assuming the presence of mothers at home, an assumption that was addressed or problematised only when a woman's full-time availability or devotion to motherhood was put in question.

While formulated to draw attention to the plight of children in residential care, Bowlby's ideas about care imposed impossible demands on the conscientious mother. With a familiar elision of mental and physical development, maternal care was likened to vitamins for the healthy growth of the young child, and the criteria for continuity of care were vague. Brief, regular and absolute separation were all lumped together so that day care, brief separation and death or divorce were treated as having equivalent effect and significance. As a result, any absence, brief or prolonged, was invested with the possibility of producing far-reaching effects and was inadvisable. The good mother must therefore be always available and always attentive. This rendering of the cosy world of innocent and dependent childhood both reproduces and produces the division between public and private realms. Women were portrayed as devoted to, attend- ing to and attuning to their children; they bask in her presence while she orients to their unspoken needs:

> She is his whole world, and the little excursions he makes beyond her are rooted
> in confidence that she is nearby to give him full protection. He has been weaned
> from the breast, but is still unweaned from complete dependence on the protection
> and love of this one person . . . . He is not far from her skirts all day, and in this
> close relationship she acts intuitively to meet his physical and emotional needs.
>
> (Robertson, 1958: 4)

For Gesell, the intermeshing of minds and reading of needs takes on an almost physical quality:

> It is almost as if the child's nervous system were completed by his mother, her part being that she must think ahead for the child.
>
> (Gesell, 1950: 240)

Significantly, it is knowledge of child development that is held to provide the resource for mothers to know what lies ahead. The dutiful, indulgent mother provides a secure environment in which the child learns the control and regulation of emotions. But separation, lack of bonding or emotional disturbance on the part of the mother would give rise to criminality and pathology. It followed that the roles of devoted mother and working woman were divergent and incompatible. The upshot of such a model was that any later moral or psychological aberrations exhibited by the child were attributable to the mother. This positions women as responsible for the ills of a world their maternal duties proscribed them from participating in:

> Through the child, the mother was made responsible for violence and social chaos in the world outside the family, a world from which she was more or less excluded.
>
> (Singer, 1992: 99)

As indicated in Chapter 3, the reduction of the social to the interpersonal, with the partner of the child in his (*sic*) environment defined as the mother (or else the environment is assumed to comprise the mother) adds up to a seemingly coherent theoretical whole, with the well-being of society identified with women at home (Walkerdine and Lucey, 1989). As we shall see, the definition and regulation of what constitutes good, sensitive mothering structured, and continues to structure, both discourses of child development and, through these, discourses of childcare provision and femininity. Maternal presence therefore functions as the essential feature in the maintenance of the social-political order. Mothers were, and still are, positioned as the relay point in the production of 'democratic citizens', that is, adults who will accept the social-political order by imagining that their concurrence is through independent choice rather than coercion. Once again, we see how definitions of child and mother on offer within developmental psychology work to maintain the existing social relations and forms of organisation.

WATCH WITH MOTHER

Subsequent studies modified the original gloomy picture, arguing that Bowlby's work should be regarded as an indictment of institutional rather than maternal deprivation (Clarke and Clarke, 1976), that separation need not be damaging (Rutter, 1982) and that secure relationships can be formed in later childhood (Tizard, 1991). Nevertheless, contemporary research on childcare continues to be dominated by a restricted range of questions that betray a theoretical legacy which positions women as responsible not only for the care of their children, but also for their current and future development. Day care is researched within a damage-limitation model, as a risk factor (Belsky and Rovine, 1988), or else is investigated in terms of the way it affects children's attachment to their mothers, rather than exploring the more useful questions concerning what different organisations of attachment relationships and caring contexts offer (Hennessy *et al.*, 1992).

Despite women's increasing participation in paid work, there has been little corresponding development of pre-school childcare provision. While there are significant variations in policy and provision across Europe, Britain has the worst level of provision (Penn, 1990). A commitment to pre-school education has given rise to the proliferation of play groups, but while these provide more childcare than any other pre-school service, they function for only an average of six hours per week. Provision is structured around the assumption that children are primarily to be cared for by their mothers, with care outside the family provided as an extra resource for children's development, not for mothers' convenience (Singer, 1992). Not only are mothers disenfranchised from participating in the productive sphere of paid work by employers' expectations of their engagement in full-time childcare, but those who out of financial necessity do work are correspondingly positioned as morally *reprehensible*. Even where these assumptions are starting to be eroded, with childcare provision so minimal, those for whom it is provided are thereby designated as inadequate. How much more pathological a mother must be if she needs to be taught what is supposed to 'come naturally'!

As Barbara Tizard (1991) notes, the attribution of the origin of adult problems to inadequate mothering in early life works to 'champion children at the expense of imposing guilt on mothers' (Tizard, 1991: 183). It also treats social problems as originating in the individual. There is every indication that 'mother blaming' is a pervasive and enduring explanandum in a wide range of clinical literature (Caplan, 1985). More recently, with the research trend towards communicative development, and the tendency to collapse development into ever earlier stages, the domain of early care is increasingly taken to include education, such that nursery and pre-school provision are now regarded as indistinguishable (Hennessy *et al.*, 1992). Research sets out to link early childcare with later social and cognitive development, enlarging the arena for which mothers can be held responsible. Jerome Bruner, known for his commitment to environmental 'compensation', illustrates how the onus for species-appropriate development lies in the mother's hands.

> the child's transition from his primate background into the use of the powerful cultural tool of language depends upon the development, indeed, the exploitation of the mother–infant bond.
>
> (Bruner, 1978: 63)

SHE'S GOTTA HAVE IT

Mothers are portrayed as so central to, and absorbed within, their children's development that any assertion of power or independence on their part appears to be at the expense of damaging children's self-confidence. Mothers' needs must be assimilated to those of their children for them to avoid censure as 'bad mothers'. As many critics point out, children separated from their mothers in residential care are also separated from their fathers and other friendship and family ties (e.g. Tizard, 1991). However, the focus on the uniqueness and exclusivity of the mother–child relationship has excluded men from having a role in childcare, while also sealing the separation between the worlds of work and home and the division of roles between breadwinner and childcarer. The beneficent gaze of the mother (aided and regulated by professional experts) relegated fathers' contributions to childcare to financial provision and emotional support to mothers. On a number of counts then, the term 'maternal deprivation' is something of a misnomer. Mothers (and fathers) could be said to be more deprived by their caregiving role than depriving. Yet women continue to be regarded as responsible for both children's upbringing and childcare provision. Despite the crucial role accorded to childcare, and its supposedly fulfilling qualities, its lack of value is reflected in the low pay of professional childcare workers (usually also women).

Even when recently challenged to address methodological and political criticisms of his work, Bowlby remained unrepentant about the irreconcilability of combining motherhood with career. From this it is clear that he regarded women who use other sources of childcare as not only surrendering their proper childcare responsibilities but as also demonstrating their lack of care and commitment to their children's development. Any woman who asserts her right to have an existence independent from her child is dismissed as abandoning her, with a clear dichotomy set up between women who put childcare first and those who will not, as:

> extreme feminists who take the line 'I can have children, I needn't look after them, I'm going to go ahead with my career and I'm damned if I'm going to be handicapped by looking after them.'
>
> (Bowlby et al., 1986: 51)

WEIRD SCIENCE

According to the theory, the securely attached child is endowed with the confidence to be able to leave her mother and explore his or her surroundings, whereas the insecurely attached child is 'clingy'. While babies and young children usually protest at being separated from familiar caregivers, from around 2½ years old children are expected to be able to adapt to the absence of their mothers. The paradigm by which attachment is investigated was developed by Ainsworth as a test of Bowlby's theory (e.g. Ainsworth et al., 1974). Typically, the reactions of children are observed, firstly, when they are brought into an unfamiliar setting with their mothers, secondly, when a strange adult enters the room, and, thirdly, when the mother leaves the child alone with the adult. If the child will not settle to play at some distance from her mother while she is there, the attachment is considered insecure. Conversely, this conclusion is also drawn if the child fails to protest at his or her mother's departure.

Clearly the ethics of treating children's distress as the variable under both investigation and manipulation should be questioned. Moreover, using this procedure to compare the strength of attachment relationships between children of employed and non-employed mothers is also methodologically suspect. Children of employed mothers may not experience separation as stressful since it is a regular part of their daily life. It seems paradoxical that children's success at adapting and gaining greater independence from their mothers should then be treated as a measure of disturbance. Furthermore, not only does the 'strange situation' test not take account of individual separation histories, it also fails to reflect real-life caregiving contexts when children are generally left with care-givers with whom they have some familiarity and in contexts to which they have become accustomed. As Alison Clarke-Stewart (1988) argues, this throws some doubt on studies claiming that children of employed mothers are less securely attached to their mothers. Similarly, White and Woollett (1992) note that the cultural value placed on maturity and autonomy within the US (as compared with other European as well as non-Western cultures) has produced a research bias in which variations in childrearing practices (of exposure to unfamiliar adults or amount of time spent interacting with children) suggest that US children have more secure attachment relationships than, for example, Japanese or German children. David Ingleby makes a similar set of points about the inappropriateness of using the Ainsworth Strange Situation Test to investigate the psychological states of Brazilian street children (Ingleby, 1989). Procedures such as these continue not only to be used, but are also applied to evaluate mothers as well as children (see, e.g., Fonagy *et al.*, 1991; Izard *et al.*, 1991).

INSENSITIVE MEASURES

Attachment research draws on a number of theoretical resources: ethology, systems theory and psychoanalysis. But the process of rendering psychoanalysis into terms that could be empirically investigated has produced an entirely different model. While for psychoanalysis the relation between psychical and external reality is complex, its investigation within developmental psychology collapses this subtle distinction into a single focal object, the mother. What we see played out in the history of 'attachment' is not only the uneasy coupling of developmental psychology and psychoanalysis. It is also, firstly, the productivity of a 'translation' process from theory to practice. (This is not to suggest that psycho-analysis did not already have its own 'practical' outlets, but that its introduction into developmental psychology called forth additional practices.) Secondly, the result of this (mis)rendering of psychoanalytic ideas within developmental psychology illustrates how the technology of research instruments not only produces the demand for measurement, but also thereby produces the object that is measured. 'Sensitive' and 'insensitive' mothers are produced by theories of maternal 'sensitivity', both through the incorporation of the theories within professional and policy structures and through women's consumption of those ideas. On both counts, then, the elision of phantasy and reality and the technologisation of empirical practice mean that the insertion of psychoanalysis within developmental psychological discourse as 'attachment' reinscribes the regulation of women as mothers.

Within conventional accounts, attachment is said to arise from mothers' rapid and appropriate responsiveness to children's demands of hunger, discomfort and boredom. Attractive as the concept is, it both fails to engage with the specificity and variability of caregiving, and (as we have already seen) in its attempts to identify optimal conditions for development it homogenises (treats as the same) normality and pathologises (treats as deviant) difference.

In the first instance, the myopic focus on mothers as the total environment for the child leads to a reification and abstraction of 'maternal sensitivity', and a corresponding failure to register how sensitivity varies according to situations and circumstances. Anne Woollett (1986) reports that mothers devote less attention to a younger child when other adults and older children are present and so in this context are correspondingly recorded as less 'sensitive'. Moreover, sensitivity exhibited by mothers and fathers seems to be differentially evaluated. Sensitivity 'is THE influential dimension of mothering in infancy: it not only fosters healthy psychological functioning during this developmental epoch, but it also lays the foundation on which future experience will be built' (Belsky, 1981: 8). In contrast, as White and Woollett (1992) point out, fathers' lack of contingency and sensitivity is interpreted as fostering independence and problem solving by making greater communicative and cognitive demands on children (cf. Parke *et al.*, 1989).

While what counts as sensitive and responsive mothering is graduated according to the age and development (Wachs and Gruen, 1982), what remains constant is the onus on the mother. This measure of the quality of mothering is then linked to a wide range of later social, behavioural and intellectual qualities within the child (e.g. Light, 1979). Moreover, class issues enter into the ascription of sensitivity. Many studies suggest that the patterns of interaction associated with 'sensitive mothering' are less likely to be exhibited by working-class than middle-class mothers (Boulton, 1983; Newson and Newson, 1968; Tizard and Hughes, 1984). Valerie Walkerdine and Helen Lucey (1989) argue that the class-coded discourses of developmental psychology function to regulate both middle-class and working-class women, who from their different positions are either enjoined to produce active, autonomous children or stigmatised for failing to exhibit interactional patterns deemed to promote this. They identify these evaluations of mothering with the post-World War II preoccupation with creating self-governing citizens. The scrutiny and regulation of mothers became a matter central to the maintenance of a democratic society (see Chapter 12).

BASIC INSTINCT

The apparatus of attachment theory thus naturalises class and cultural privilege. In addition, as we have seen, it is also based on a biological model of mothering. Since Bowlby's project was to replace psychoanalysis by an approach more in line with dominant notions of 'science', he turned to ethology for what looked like empirical support from observational studies of animal behaviour. The comparisons between newborn animals following their mothers (or the first object they saw) and mother–infant relations, and the conclusions he drew, assumed a common focus on an instinctual basis of behaviour. While Anglo-US psychoanalysis has been dogged by the mistranslation of Freud's German term Trieb as *instinct* (Bettelheim, 1986), Bowlby's use of 'instinct' reflected his background in psychiatry and zoology as well as psychoanalysis. Indeed, his ideas were always the subject of controversy within the psychoanalytic establishment (Bowlby *et al.*, 1986). Hence the newborn duck's imprinting on, or tendency to follow, its mother became transposed into the concept of a critical period by which the mother–child relationship had to be secured if maladjustment was to be avoided.

As Chapter 1 pointed out, evolutionary ideas are frequently employed to lend legitimacy to existing social relations of inequality. As the title of Elena Lieven's (1981) essay 'If it's natural we can't change it' makes clear, the appeal to biology serves to preserve the status quo. By designating gendered and racialised positions as 'natural', they can be treated as inevitable and even desirable. While the viability of extrapolating from animal behaviour to human (historically and culturally variable) practices is largely regarded as suspect, assumptions about 'maternal instincts' still circulate. Within attachment theory the fact that women bear children has been taken to mean that (only) biological mothers 'instinctually' want to, and know how to, care for their children, thereby pathologising those who do not.

If women who abuse their children are seen as deviant women, they are by definition deviant mothers. Concerns with abusing mothers may seem far from those of attachment, but the discourse of maternal sensitivity and maternal deprivation draws them together. But where this happens, all too often the context in which child survival and neglect takes place is ignored. What has been understood as 'maternal deprivation' in some circumstances has more to do with poverty than with women's 'mothering qualities'. Indeed Scheper-Hughes (1989b) suggests that:

> In circumstances of extreme poverty and competition for resources, selective neglect is often a manifestation of parental interventions on behalf of family survival.
>
> (Scheper-Hughes, 1989b: 187)

From her anthropological study of mothers in a shanty town in north-east Brazil where the infant mortality rate reaches 70 per cent, she argues:

> Within the shantytown, child death *a mingua* (accompanied by maternal indifference and neglect) is understood as an appropriate maternal response to a deficiency in the child. Part of learning how to mother on the Alto includes learning when to 'let go'.
>
> (Scheper-Hughes, 1989b: 190)

It is not that the women in the shanty towns do not care for their children, but rather they have to find ways of dealing with their deaths through protective emotional distancing. Rather than blaming these women or their culture for the effects of poverty, we should recognise that 'infant and childhood mortality in the Third World is a problem of *political economy*, not of medical technology' (Scheper-Hughes, 1989b: 187). In evaluating women's adequacy as mothers and the cultural mores that support mothering (as psychology does), we therefore need to distinguish between an infanticide-tolerant society (for economic reasons) and an abuse-tolerant society. In modern, affluent societies where child survival is not such a struggle (for so many), there has been a shift from promoting the quantity of children to the promotion of qualities within children. In this sense parental investment within the child replaces fertility rate such that:

> Children have become relatively worthless (economically) to their parents, but priceless in terms of their psychological worth: the pleasure and satisfaction they bring.
>
> (Scheper-Hughes, 1989a: 12)

There are risks to the child in terms of the heavy weight of expectation of achievement she now carries, along with the assumption – through the availability of contraception – that all births are intentional. Scheper-Hughes (1989a) also suggests that the reported prevalence of malicious intentional child abuse in the West (and its rarity elsewhere) is also reminiscent of the days when children contributed to the productive economy as seen in parental resentment of the worthless, greedy, consuming child.

Commenting on the context for discussions of mother love and child development (or lack of development) we should note that the psychic and political economy of mother love are not divorced from each other. When Winnicott (1958) outlined his 'Eighteen reasons why a mother hates her baby, even a boy' (with a whole history of the cross-cultural preference for boys and devaluation of girls slipped in here), he included (although he did not of course account for them in these ways) 'reasons' rooted in the competition and insecurity fostered between women that arises from the ways the behaviour of their child in family and public contexts signified their competence and adequacy as mothers. Hence the discourse of 'maternal instinct' gives rise to that of pathological mothering: each requires the other as its converse to maintain it. Both are burdened by the weight of phantasy. Both impose equally impossible demands – of idealisation or devaluation – and with the terms cast in these ways it is difficult for women not to fall foul of these bipolar opposites that constitute each other, or at least not to feel that they do.

DEVELOPMENT AS THE REPUDIATION OF FEMININITY

Attachment is the prerequisite for separation, and failure of separation indicates insecure attachment. These developmental achievements are not neutral with respect to gender. The trajectory of development moves from *attachment*, a stereotypically feminine quality, to a culturally masculine *detachment*. Gendered assumptions enter into the very structure of developmental models, which, it can be argued, treat girls and women as intellectually inferior (Gilligan, 1982). But not only is maturity measured as the masculine capacity to tolerate separation and absence, to go on to chart unknown territories, this exploration marks the differentiation from the first love object, from the mother (Dinnerstein, 1978). There is thus a double repudiation of femininity, as both motor of developmental advance and aspect of personal experience, structured within the achievement of autonomy. This is not a casual by-product of the process, but rather is its delicately orchestrated objective:

> A key to the mental hygiene of early childhood lies in building up adequate self-dependence. Even in infancy this principle of self-dependence must be respected. Not only from the breast must the child be weaned. By slow gradations he must develop fortitudes which lie at the basis of detachment. He cannot always play in his mother's lap; he must in time begin to play in his pen; he must learn to play in an adjoining room, first for a few minutes, later for an hour at a time. If his mother must leave the house, he must be content to watch her through the window, even though it costs him a struggle. In time he must learn to go to bed alone, and later, to school alone.
>
> (Gesell, 1950: 261)

So the process of acquiring self-reliance is seen as akin to weaning, requiring bravery, that is, a manly 'fortitude', and not achieved without a 'struggle'. It is to psychoanalysis that we must turn for some understanding of the costs of 'maturity', but here too the cultural and gendered associations of detached rationality are rarely explored (Broughton, 1988; Walkerdine, 1988). Moreover, by a curious twist it seems that it is mothers who are enthralled to their children, through the mandate to forgo their independence in order to foster their children's transition to autonomy.

MONKEY BUSINESS

In addition to ethological work, the set of animal studies closely associated with attachment theory are Harry Harlow's experiments with rhesus monkeys. Harlow's studies were conducted in the US during the immediate post-World War II period, and shared concerns similar to those of Bowlby and others with the nature of mothering and the production of the normal child. Harlow's studies are generally regarded as providing empirical support for the theory of maternal deprivation with its associated sequelae of affectionless psychopathy and 'cycles' of abuse across generations, as the Stone *et al.* (1973) extract at the beginning of this chapter indicates. The report that infant monkeys separated from their mothers cling to a fluffy-covered object rather than the wire-coated dispenser of food is held to indicate that infants' needs extend beyond nutrition to comfort. The isolated monkeys mutilated themselves and could not relate (or relate sexually) when older to other monkeys. These 'observations' are hailed as proof of the far-reaching and irreversible effects of early adversity. Yet the obsession with maternal responsibility for child (and adult) development precludes the formulation of other questions, such as the supposedly protective influence of rearing these 'maternally deprived' monkeys with other infant monkeys. In these ways mothering has become constituted as the single, absolute condition for normal psychological functioning.

As argued in Chapter 1, psychology played its part in social practices which functioned to maintain and naturalise the divisions between men and women, European and non-European, rich and poor, and humans and animals. Donna Haraway's (1989) analysis of the role of primatology in the history of science demonstrates that the study of apes has played a key role in structuring gender and racial inequalities into modern concepts of knowledge and civilisation. Drawing on Harlow's own writings, she elaborates the underlying themes of his work, arguing that Harlow's laboratory translated metaphorical fantasies about women, childbirth and sexuality into a grotesque, manufactured reality. While, according to one of his accounts, he was inspired by Bowlby's ideas on attachment, Harlow, working in 1950s America, addressed a different social context where women were beginning to work outside the home. At an overt level, his project was humanistic, claiming to demonstrate that contact is more important than primary drive reduction (i.e. satisfying hunger) for the development of relationships, and his work was interpreted as a liberalising measure in reassuring working women that they could still be good mothers. But dispensing with women as mothers invited the possibility of men replacing them. Known as 'the father of the cloth mother', Harlow revelled in his absolute control of his surrogate mothers. Accompanying the realisation of the fantasy of male reproduction were misogynistic insults to women's bodies that were not only verbal (in Harlow's descriptions), but were also structured into its procedures. For example, the early-isolated monkeys, as adults unable to conceive in the usual ways, were artificially impregnated by means of 'an apparatus affectionately termed the "rape rack", which we leave to the reader's imagination' (Harlow *et al.*, 1971: 545). After this, the monkeys entered a new career as what he called 'motherless monkey mothers' within a range of Harlow-reared 'evil mothers'. These supposedly tested the hypothesis that maternal rejection caused psychopathology, and prompted the construction of surrogate 'evil mothers'

> designed to repel clinging infants. . . . One surrogate blasted its babies with compressed air, another tried to shake the infant off its chest, a third possessed an embedded catapult which periodically sent the infant flying, while the

fourth carried concealed brass spikes beneath her ventral surface which would emerge on schedule or on demand.

(Harlow *et al.*, 1971: 543)

As Haraway notes, the sadism here is metaphorical rather than (or as well as) literal: the violence lies in the representation and interpretation of what is done, rather than (only) in the infliction of pain.

In Harlow's studies we see comparative psychology looking to the natural world to verify ideology, and thereby constructing the 'natural' in its own image. Nowhere is this more evident than in Harlow's 'nuclear family apparatus', a complex set of interlocking cages modelling what he held as the ideal living arrangements. He even claimed that offspring reared within this environment were intellectually advantaged, which, as Haraway comments, no doubt pleased his professional middle-class audience.

There can be nothing 'natural' about rearing animals in cages and warping their habits and reactions, and there can be no grounds from this for comparison with human dynamics and relationships. But I would argue that the frequency with which these studies are cited not only arises from attraction to what Haraway (1989: 233) calls the 'heroic masculinistic narrative of self-birthing'. It also owes its power to its claims to scientific knowledge which legitimate, even mandate, the setting aside of moral qualms and squeamishness. If anything, these perhaps lead to an even greater investment in finding 'scientific' value and meaning within such work, setting up the chaining of meanings from women and human infants to the 'denaturalised' bodies of rhesus monkeys to enter as 'science' into the discourses of post-war sexual and reproductive politics. The malaise of gory fascination and disgust these accounts inspire is part of what fuels the suppression of the huge leaps of reason, the collapsing together of cultural, historical and species specificity, to enable 'the production of the unmarked, abstract universal, man' (Haraway, 1989: 233) from the study of tortured monkeys.

LOVE AT FIRST SIGHT

If attachment refers to children's affectionate connection with their mothers, the term bonding has been applied to parents' (and specifically mothers') emotional ties to their children. Within both models, it is noticeable that the basic unit of analysis is the individual (mother or child) rather than the relationship. This reflects not only an asocial model which presumes and privileges preconstituted individuals, but also a preoccupation with identifying causes and thereby attributing blame. While the severity of Bowlby's pronouncements about critical periods have been moderated by subsequent accounts (e.g. Rutter, 1982), Klaus and Kennell (1976) brought new life to the notion that early mother–child interaction determined later aspects of development; only for these later researchers the cut-off point was thirty-six hours. They claimed to be able to associate quality of relationship assessed when the infant was 3 days old with a wide variety of social, intellectual and behavioural outcomes, which ranged from permitting wide psychological distance to promoting physical abuse, failure to thrive and even abandonment. Like attachment theory, this drew on ethology, drawing analogies with certain herd-living animals (such as goats) in which post-partum separation can lead to rejection of an offspring by the mother. Although no longer regarded as plausible within psychological research (White and Woollett, 1992), their claims about the possible consequences of separation for mothers and babies due to particular hospital practices or admission to special care baby units have dramatically affected neonatal care.

The work has been criticised on a number of methodological grounds, and the original studies have not been replicated (Svejda et al., 1980). At one level there is an issue about whether this really matters, since the changes in practice, such as the greater involvement of parents, have been generally welcomed. However, studies of early mother–child bonding fail to acknowledge that different mother–baby pairs might react to separation in a variety of ways, especially in circumstances where there is some question of developmental abnormality or even survival (Richards, 1981). Moreover, they fail to consider the role of parental beliefs about separation before resorting to a biologically ordained sensitive or critical period. It should be recalled that a mother using 'natural childbirth' methods has a very different childbirth experience from that of a woman who has major technological intervention and drugs. In each case the perceived significance of separation might well be different. What we see here is that developmental psychology plays a part (albeit indirectly) in creating the phenomena it sets out to explain, and creating unnecessary anxiety for women who, for example because they have had a caesarian section, are unable to take advantage of the supposedly unique opportunities the first few hours of mother–child interaction offer.

Psychology both draws upon and contests medical authority. The significance attributed to early experience underlies the recent moves away from childbirth dominated by medical technology. On the other hand, this emphasis on early experience can also bolster the legitimacy of the medical profession at a time of criticism of, and challenge to, the medicalisation of childbirth (Arney, 1980). More importantly, it provides a pseudo-scientific basis to justify social policy. Arney (1980) discusses Frailberg's book Every Child's Birthright (1977) which identifies 'diseases of attachment', creating a panoply of (maternally) deprived individuals ('bondless', 'hollow' and with 'unbound aggression') on whom the social problems of violence and crime can be pinned. Bonding theory recalls and fulfils a familiar agenda.

All the characteristics of the literature under review here were present in the IQ literature years ago – the claim that criminality and mental defectiveness result from one's early development or biological heritage, the claim that social dysfunctionality also results from it, the presumption that admittedly limited evidence is definitive and provides a ground for policy, the concern over 'cures' and the presumption that responsibility for treatment devolves onto the state or its agencies.

(Arney, 1980: 563)

(PRE-SCHOOL) LESSONS

Links between early experience and later development have been spectacularly difficult to establish. Criticisms focus on sample selection of atypical populations already labelled as deviant, whether prospectively, in following up children in care or who have suffered trauma (as in the early separation studies), or retrospectively, in looking backwards into the family history of convicted criminals or child abusers. Despite these methodological and theoretical inadequacies, the concept of bonding (like the concept of attachment) lives on, and is even thought to be conveniently assessable by means of retrospective questionnaires such as the Parental Bonding Instrument (e.g. Gamsa, 1987), which earthshatteringly establishes 'care . . . as the major parental dimension' (Parker *et al.*, 1979: 8). Addressing a conference on drugs on 17 November 1992, the English Princess Diana recently advocated parental affection as a preventive factor in drug abuse. She drew on the theory that children 'deprived of affection' suffer a lack of stability that makes it more likely that they become vulnerable to drug addiction. In her account, 'hugging' is portrayed within a medical model, with unforeseen medico-moral powers:

> hugging has no harmful side-effects. If we all play our part in making our children feel valued the result will be tremendous – there are potential huggers in every household.

The exhortation is to mobilise a hitherto unrecognised resource, but, whatever our feelings about the importance of affection for children, we should be wary of how this neglects State responsibility for the provision of resources. In these ways ideologies of attachment and bonding both exonerate the State and provide scapegoats to account for the outcomes of seemingly thwarted affections in the form of socially inappropriate activity.

Moreover, enormous effort and resources go into early intervention programmes such as *Head Start* in the US which claimed to 'compensate' for social deprivation and provide enriched environments, thereby proffering visions of greater equality and opportunity. Disappointment over the effects of these projects has made subsequent interventions focus more explicitly on babies and toddlers and set out to make mothers more sensitive and responsive. The problem with these projects is not only that, in identifying deprivation, the locus of the deficit tends to revolve around the child's mother, culture and class, but also that the evidence on long-term effects is unstable, with early indications of success more attributable to the optimism of the 1960s than to any specifically educationally enriching feature of the programme. We should be wary of a simplistic application of developmental psychological research in early intervention programmes:

In the first place, it reinforces the political preference to urge single strategy and (relatively) inexpensive educational solutions to complex social and economic problems (Lazerson, 1970). Second, it risks perpetuating the idea that the impact an educational intervention makes on an individual can be understood in isolation from the context in which it occurs. Thirdly, it fails to recognise that there may be features of experimental projects that it is difficult, even impossible to reproduce in a national social programme (including the fact of being experimental and by definition only being available to a particular group of children).

(Woodhead, 1988: 446)

If there are difficulties in linking research with social policy, then the cultural practices on which research is based render general application even more problematic. Most research on the 'effects' of day care has been conducted in the US where there is no system of maternity or paternity leave, nearly all nursery and pre-school provision is privately funded, there is heavy dependence on relatives for the care of young children and public provision is reserved for those deemed inadequate or especially in need. All this means that there are wide variations in quality of childcare and major inequalities in access to childcare (Hennessy *et al.*, 1992). These may well be reflected in the character of the questions asked within day-care research, and in the kinds of results it produces. This body of work therefore has little relevance to countries with more flexible work and leave arrangements and where public provision of childcare is more extensive. Once again we have a clear instance of how the US domination of psychological research imposes an inappropriate agenda and, in this case, presents the care of young children outside the home in an unnecessarily pessimistic light. There are

three themes, continually repeated during the history of child-care facilities: social innovation through interventions in family upbringing; the importance of the first years of childhood; and the (ambiguous) position of women.

(Singer, 1992: 14)

In a period when more women than ever before are bringing up children alone, the scope for vulnerability to these themes is increasing rather than decreasing. But the increasing demand for female labour in industrialised countries through demographic changes in the age structure of populations has forced a re-evaluation of the organisation of childcare that has also brought fathers into the picture.

FURTHER READING

Benjamin, J. (1988) *Bonds of Love*, London: Virago (connects the account here with more explicitly psychoanalytic analyses of power and gender in relationships, with particular reference to the significance of mother–child relations).
Scheper-Hughes, N. (ed.) (1989) *Child Survival: anthropological perspectives on the treatment and maltreatment of children*, Dordrecht: Reidel (this puts debates about child abuse within a cross-cultural context).

Singer, E. (1992) *Child-Care and the Psychology of Development*, London: Routledge (deals with the impact of child-centred approaches on women, in relation to theories of childcare and development).

For accounts providing the empirical re-evaluation of the notion of 'maternal deprivation', see:

Rutter, M. (1982) *Maternal Deprivation Reassessed*, Harmondsworth: Penguin.

Tizard, B. (1991) 'Employed mothers and the care of young mothers', in A. Phoenix, A. Woollett and E. Lloyd (eds) *Motherhood: meanings, practices and ideologies*, London: Sage.

For a very clear account of issues in childcare provision and research literature, see:

Hennessy, E., Martin, S., Moss, P. and Melhuish, E. (1992) *Children and Day Care: lessons from research*, London: Paul Chapman.

SUGGESTED ACTIVITIES

Depending on the positions and interests of the group, it is often fruitful to discuss local resources for childcare provision, both currently and historically. This might involve finding out about the range of childcare options used by those who are currently parents of young children, and asking older relatives and friends. If difficulties are encountered in finding out about statutory provision then this itself is a resource for discussion (as an issue about accessibility). In particular, questions such as the following could be addressed:

* what factors enter into a parent's decision in determining her childcare arrangements?
* what contemporary and historical variability emerges?
* if more than one person is involved in parenting a child, who takes responsibility for these arrangements?
* how accessible are available childcare services – in terms of price, hours covered?
* what theoretical frameworks are drawn upon to inform this structure?
* how do parents conceive of their relationships with those with whom they share the care of their children?
* how do non-parental carers of children talk about their relationships with the parents of the children they care for?
* to what extent are these accounts informed by developmental psychological concepts and theories (such as 'bonding' and 'attachment')?
* to what extent does developmental psychology address (as a research topic or as a theoretical issue) the affectional relationships non-parental carers develop with the children they care for?

Chapter 7

The rise of 'fathering'

The recovery of some form of initiation is essential to the culture. The United States has undergone an unmistakeable decline since 1950, and I believe that if we do not find a third road besides the two mentioned here, the decline will continue. We have the grandiose road, taken by junk-bond dealers, high rollers and the owners of private jets; and we have the depressed road, taken by some long-term alcoholics, single mothers below the poverty line, crack addicts and fatherless men.

(Bly, 1991: 53)

Alongside the child, developmental psychology constituted the woman as mother as its object of concern and intervention. But its gaze has currently shifted to include men, men as fathers. This chapter explores why and how this has happened, and evaluates the adequacy of the models by which fatherhood is investigated. Moreover, irrespective of whether the 'new man' is old or new, real or fictional, the paradigms for studying him could certainly do with an overhaul. The philosophical and methodological limitations of this work go beyond the study of fathers to throw into relief more general research assumptions and practices.

MOTHERS, FATHERS AND CHILDREN (AND PSYCHOLOGISTS)

Fathers are a relatively recent addition to the developmental psychological literature. In part this derives from the dominance of attachment theory in Britain with its Kleinian psychoanalytic inflection. While attachment theory was a radical departure from Kleinian psychoanalysis, especially in abandoning the notion of unconscious phantasy, nevertheless they share a common tendency to eclipse the father figure and focus on early mother–child relations, rather than analysing the oedipal triangle of mother, father and child (Riley, 1983). Schaffer's (1971) synthesis of research in his *The Growth of Sociability* not only reflects these themes but also refers to the 'scientist' as male too. The basic orienting question for the book is:

How does the infant learn to distinguish among different human beings so that he [sic] is able to recognise his mother as familiar and strangers as unfamiliar?

(Schaffer, 1971: 30)

Here we have the familiar situation where the mother is designated as the primary caregiver, with everyone else by implication falling into the category of stranger. The definition of mother extends beyond the biological childbearer to include any woman continuously involved in childcare (an ambiguous improvement). Correlatively, the child is specified as 'he', which can be interpreted in one of two ways: either as a reflection of stereotypical assumptions by which the mother–child couple is portrayed as reflecting the man–woman couple, or, when represented as the 'generic he', as offering an asocial model of child that implies gender is a detachable variable rather than a constitutive feature of subjectivity. While the latter alternative is simply inadequate, the former also clearly renders girl-children invisible and, more than this, eclipses the significance of gender in childcare. For it is in relation to a woman that a child first experiences feelings of power, vulnerability and especially total helplessness – within prevailing childcare arrangements (Dinnerstein, 1978). Clearly this observation holds different significance for the positions of boys and girls respectively in terms of the meanings gender holds.

The same point may also apply where men are the primary caregivers. It should be noted that the choice of terms in the extract above does not arise from the state of empirical findings at the time nor from the author's personal belief that only mothers 'mother' children. Schaffer was one of the first researchers to challenge the notion of 'monotropy', reporting that babies do form attachments to more than one person and can be equally attached to their fathers, and can even at times exhibit their most intense attachment to them (Schaffer and Emerson, 1964).

By the mid-1970s, although there was more embarrassment and equivocation, the basic assumptions remained unchanged. Taking the Fontana 'Developing Child' series as an index, Daniel Stern in *The First Relationship* (1977) offers an apologetic footnote on the first page for retaining gender stereotypical terms (baby as 'he', caregiver as 'she') in the interests of 'easier and clearer reading'. Schaffer's (1977) book *Mothering* ties itself into some knots in trying to make 'mothering' a gender-neutral term:

Our concern will primarily be with the description of mothering in the child's earliest years irrespective of who actually carries on this process . . . mother may be thought of as anyone with responsibility for the child's care over a prolonged period.

(Schaffer, 1977: 30)

Nevertheless, the baby is still 'he'.

By the 1980s it was no longer possible to ignore the changes taking place in family organisation and childcare, and this was eventually reflected by the publication within the series of Alison Clarke-Stewart's *Day Care* (1982). By this stage we see the strategy of mere *inclusion* of fathers into child rearing (by generalising the term 'mother') has been surpassed by notions of *complementarity*:

> The parent's role includes being a dispenser of love and a disciplinarian, a verbal stimulator, a sensitive responder, a provider of materials and a choreographer of experiences for the child.
>
> (Clarke-Stewart, 1982: 93)

(Incidentally the child is still 'he'.) No prizes for guessing which parent provides which of these two main parental qualities, stimulation and responsiveness, identified as affecting children's development (p.92). Clarke-Stewart goes on to welcome research now addressing the specificities of paternal contributions to childcare, arguing that:

> While his role in providing affection and discipline may parallel hers, the father is more likely to be a special playmate, who engages in exciting, physical games and active rough and tumble. This contributes to the child's sociability. He also provides psychological support to the mother and thus affects the child's development indirectly through her.
>
> (Clarke-Stewart, 1982: 93–4)

The last comment could come straight from Bowlby, and, as we shall see, attention to the complementarity of parental roles works quite nicely to reassert traditional gender roles.

Finally responding to the popular interest in, and burgeoning popular literature about, fatherhood, the Fontana series published Ross Parke's *Fathering* in 1984. Nowadays, however, with the baby as the icon of the caring, green 1990s, it has become glamorous, even mandatory, for men to be portrayed with children. At the inception of the new Ministry for Children in Norway, headed by a man (because it was considered that this would ensure it was taken more seriously), he posed for photos bare-chested and bearing (in his arms) *two* babies (*Guardian*, 21 May 1991)!

ACCOUNTING FOR 'FATHERING'

As discussed in Chapter 5, the earlier literature was more concerned with fathers' absence than with analysing the developmental consequences of active paternal contributions to child rearing. The single-parent family was stigmatised as necessarily having problems, and it is only recently that any more diverse or positive picture has emerged. Even this has been within the popular rather than the psychological literature (e.g. Renvoize, 1985; Shapiro, 1987), and has predominantly focused on middle-class women (cf. Campbell, 1984; Phoenix, 1991). In part this change of popular and academic focus arises from general social and structural changes in industrialised countries. Among the reasons put forward to account for the new preoccupation with fathering, Lorna McKee and Margaret O'Brian (1982) include the increase of women in paid employment, the greater number of single-parent families, especially male-headed households, and the increase of (especially male) unemployment. Other factors include the development of a (small but vocal) male liberation movement (mainly in the US), the continued privatisation of the nuclear family which locates childcare solely within the home, and cultural support for child-centred approaches which inform ideas about parental responsibilities and duties towards children. Above all, this development is very much linked to the impact of the women's movement which, in calling for a redistribution of gender roles, has produced a general shift in women's conceptions of childcare and domestic labour.

However, there are two, contradictory, interpretations of men's increased interest and participation in childcare. On the one hand, it is hailed as a progressive move that men are taking a more equal share; on the other, these developments could be seen as reactionary in the sense that men are competing with women and taking over the one sphere where women have held some limited power and acknowledged expertise (albeit with the 'help' of the professionals). Developments in child custody legislation mean that the inclusion of men is at the expense of women. Lynne Segal (1990) notes the contradictory anxieties about men, children and families, with the importance currently attributed to fatherhood at a time of unprecedented 'discoveries' of child sexual abuse and domestic violence. Similarly, Suzanne Moore (1988), commenting on the general apparent erosion of gender boundaries within fashion and the media, has coined the term 'gender tourism' to describe the asymmetrical 'exchange' of gender roles: while some men venture into culturally feminine spheres there seems to be little reciprocal movement towards secession of male privilege, thus leaving the patriarchal structure of power relations intact.

METHODOLOGICAL INADEQUACIES: GUILT BY ASSOCIATION?

If men as fathers have become visible, there seems to have been little corresponding effort to develop new theoretical and methodological paradigms to theorise this. Developmental psychological studies have tended to research fathering as if it were just like mothering but with little reflection on how appropriate this may be, or indeed whether the fathering work presents any opportunity for more general theoretical reformulation or revision. The research is blinkered in three ways (McKee and O'Brian, 1982). Firstly, it treats fathering as if it were a simple variety of mothering in terms of the tests and procedures used, for example by investigating father–child instead of mother–child attachment in the 'strange situation'. Secondly, research issues have simply been transferred from mothers to fathers. So, the preoccupation with the effects of separation is now applied to father–child relationships, and the work on women's experience of pregnancy and childbirth (e.g. Oakley, 1980) is now paralleled by studies of men's experience of these, without considering that there may be other interesting questions to address, concerning, for example, the impact of a partner's pregnancy on other aspects of a man's life.

Men are now at the sharp end of the inadequate models developed to evaluate women as mothers. Just as single mothers were constituted as a 'social problem', so now lone fathers are classed as 'motherless' families. But, by contrast, gender identity and sex roles is one area where fathers as well as mothers have always been studied (e.g. Roberts *et al.*, 1987; Shinn, 1978), reflecting the homophobic worry that boys brought up by single mothers might be less masculine or become gay through lacking a male role model.

The third limitation structuring the research (McKee and O'Brian, 1982) is its cultural bias in definition of family organisation. Within the burgeoning fathering literature, there has been limited or little consideration of any family organisation outside the nuclear family, apart from one which is undergoing temporary change (separation, divorce). The research has tended to address only minor aberrations from the Western, nuclear blueprint, instead of engaging in wide cross-cultural study and multicultural research within the same country. For example, the Australian sample studied by Graeme Russell in *The Changing Role of Fathers?* (1983) is reflected on the book's cover where we see the child and father (both of whom are white) standing on the doorstep waving goodbye to executive attired mother, complete with that icon of the middle-class professional, the briefcase. The change under investigation here goes no further than a simple role exchange.

INTERPRETING THE ACCOUNTS

These problems could be regarded as part of the legacy of ethological observation as the main research method in developmental psychology (Lewis, 1982). This approach is inappropriately tied to evolutionary and biological concepts through the ethological tradition, and specifically through attachment theory. This leads to a tendency to lapse into biological explanations of similarities (of, e.g., gender-specific ways of relating to neonates) and differences. Observational research assumes that the act of observation does not change what it observes, a view even theoretical physics has revised, while human indeterminacy is of a different order still. In particular, the extent to which observations conducted in homes reflect typical circumstances is questionable.

If we return to Clarke-Stewart's (1982) account of complementary patterns and roles offered by mothers and fathers, a range of other possible inter-pretations can be put forward. In the first instance, it is difficult to sustain such global generalisations when the style and amount of parent (both mother and father) –child interaction varies according to the child's age and gender. Lewis (1982) reports work suggesting that what parents think the study is about affects how they interact with the child: if they think the research topic is play, they play more with the child, if they think it is investigating language they will talk more with her. In determining whether such observations constitute 'objective' measures of typical behaviour we have to consider how the parents construe the investigation.

Alternative readings of the finding that mothers interact less with their child when the father is at home might be that a mother sees it as an opportunity for him to be with the child, or that she knows that she will be observed by the researcher at some other time (during the day), or that she knows that the researcher is interested in father–infant interaction, or even that she is tired from looking after the child all day. This could also explain the report of different styles of play exhibited by mothers and fathers respectively. Mothers who have done, or know they are going to do, childcare all day may have less energy to engage in the 'rough and tumble' in which fathers are reported to indulge. While these multiple readings highlight the indeterminacy of infant action, and ambiguity of so-called 'observations' (Bradley, 1989), there is some support for the last interpretation from Pedersen *et al.*'s (1982) study which reports that employed mothers played more with their children than mothers at home. This highlights how developmental psychological explanations can essentialise social differences arising from gender roles and inequalities through treating the knowledge-generating procedures of the discipline as neutral, context-free descriptions.

THE POVERTY OF THE PSYCHOLOGY OF PATERNAL CARE

To summarise so far, the limitations of theorising about mother care have correspondingly been exported to accounts of paternal involvement in childcare. There are three forms this has taken. Firstly, there is the inclusion model which assimilates fathering to mothering. The second position asserts the 'equal but different' complementarity of maternal and paternal roles, an account which falls into biologically pre-given sexual divisions. The third approach investigates role reversals, circumstances where men stay at home and look after their children while women work. As we have seen, not only is this a rather restricted representation of departures from traditional childcare and family arrangements, it also reasserts the normative status of the roles it deviates from, through the very discourse of role reversal which constitutes the reversed forms as an aberration.

As we have seen, the impoverished range and atheoretical quality of fathering research can be seen as arising from both the methods used and the motivations which prompted the research questions (Richards, 1982). Research on fathers has developed in response to the feminist attack on psychology for both its exclusive preoccupation with mothers and its support for the idea that childcare is only women's concern, and it also reflects the increasing (attention to the) involvement of men in childcare. In addressing these challenges, developmental psychological work has simply extended mothering to include fathering in a wholesale way without engaging in theoretical adjustments, reflections or reformulations.

INVOLVING FATHERS: MEDIA MYTH?

Whatever their role in developmental psychology, fathers are certainly figuring more prominently in popular culture. But the extent to which this greater representation actually provides or supports changed roles for men as fathers is unclear. Betty Parson's book *The Expectant Father* (1983) discusses the impact of a partner's pregnancy for men's lives in terms of learning to tolerate meals not being ready on time and surfaces not quite as polished as usual – scarcely indicating a more equitable division of domestic responsibilities. The fact that the UK magazine *Parents*, for example, addresses most of its articles to mothers casts doubt on the gender-neutrality of its title, although this may well be a reflection of its readership. In the late 1980s childcare magazines started to include articles on or about fathers, but often in ways which confirmed men's peripheral role. While the September 1989 issue of *Parents* boasts a feature on fathers, this turns about to be a fashion spread of men and children who have been whisked off to a department store; the September 1989 issue of *Practical Parenting* carries an article on 'How to turn your man into a father' which is full of useful tips and tricks on luring him into the nursery, serving thereby to reaffirm both his reluctance and his marginal position, and constituting her as somehow already endowed with childcare knowledge. This is not to deride the positive aspects of acknowledging and supporting men's contributions, but the patronising tone often does more to emphasise traditional roles than to encourage change. Indeed the media predilection for depicting man with babies typically refers more to men's earning capacity or proprietorial relations over, rather than emotional involvement with, children by advertising cars or bank accounts (Burman, 1991).

Moreover, despite the increasing attention to, and representation of, men with children, the extent to which this is actually reflected in changed childcare roles has been questioned. If the 'new man' is a media construction, it is now being accompanied by, or replaced by, the 'new lad' (the militantly reconstructed male chauvinist) (Kershaw, 1991; O'Hagan, 1991) or even the 'wild man' (who seeks reconnection with powerful masculine mentors and models) (Bly, 1991). Even where 'role reversals' have been documented, the endurance of such arrangements is fragile. Russell's (1987) follow-up of his original (1983) study reports the families drifting back to the more conventional division of gender roles. Even where parental leave and benefits for infant and childcare are not gender-specified, as is the case in Sweden, Sandkvist (1987) suggests that inertia and reluctance of both men and women to forgo traditional sources of identity (and privilege) mean that these measures are not widely taken up. Further, studies of unemployed men in industrialised societies who are in a position to assume equal or even primary responsibility for childcare suggest that this rarely occurs. With work currently so central to cultural definitions of masculinity, both unemployed men and their wives seem to regard responsibility for childcare and housework as too great a threat to male gender identity (Morris, 1987). Where women take on the role as primary wage-earner in the event of their partner's unemployment, some recent work (Wheelock, 1990) suggests that housework and childcare can be more equitably shared, but systems of state benefits combined with women's low rates of pay often make it uneconomical for women to engage in paid work. Even in dual-earner families when men do participate in, and express commitment to, equal household and childcare work, it is widely reported that women do the work of remembering and planning what there is to do, and women are more likely to take time off work when children are ill than their male partners (e.g. Horna and Lupri, 1987; Lewis and Cooper, 1991).

RESEARCHING AND INTERPRETING PATERNAL INVOLVEMENT

The difficulties in conducting and interpreting research on fathers' involvement in childcare provide important lessons that have a wider significance for developmental psychological practice. In a review, Lorna McKee (1982) criticises the widespread use of survey methods, highlighting the problems in analysing 'frequency data' based on standardised questions. These take as relevant only a narrow range of tasks, ignoring the permeation and interplay between childcare and housework. Secondly, different tasks are treated as if they are equivalent, thus rendering it impossible to assess whether, for example, one parent tends to change nappies more than another, or treating playing with the child as if it were of equal significance with bathing her. Studies often fail to take sufficient account of the age of the child when assessing extent of paternal involvement, not taking into account how differences within parental roles and contributions may be specific to a particular age range of the child, for example if mothers are breast-feeding. Moreover, most research is based on mothers' accounts of their partners' involvement, thus posing a number of interpretational anomalies. Not only may what is said be different from what is done, but also class differences enter into what is likely to be reported. While working-class men have traditionally played a much larger role in assuming childcare and household responsibilities (because their wives have had to work), they are much less likely to admit to this (Lumnis, 1982). Equally, Brannen and Moss (1987) suggest that women's uncritical and contradictory descriptions of their partners' roles may arise from ambivalence about gender and work roles which lead them to overestimate men's contributions.

Research on fathers can throw light on more far-reaching and often unquestioned research practices. Investigating parental practice has usually involved women being assessed, observed and interviewed by male researchers, or by female researchers authorised by male-dominated institutions. In their study of lone fathers, O'Brian and McKee (1983) inadvertently departed from the power relations structured within more typical research. They report that the fathers seemed to have difficulty being placed in the subordinate position of being interviewed, and particularly being interviewed by women. The men employed various strategies to challenge the researchers' authority, ranging from refusing to address the questions, to treating the interview as a counselling session or even in some cases as an opportunity for sexual overtures and harassment. The disjunction between gender and research relations within this study provides insight, through their divergence, into the power dynamics within more typical developmental research. Where power relations of gender and research roles converge (as when male interviewers interview women), the specificity of each may be obscured. Beyond highlighting interviewees' capacity to resist and define alternative agendas within the research, what this study illustrates, then, is that developmental psychology cannot treat the research relationship as having no impact on the research outcome, and that the gender of both researched and researcher plays a relevant structural role. When, as in this case, a study is set up in an unfamiliar way, we become aware of the factors influencing more familiar studies. If this study draws attention to power relations in research because the dynamics of power were no longer coincident, what implications does this have for other work in which the power of the researcher is so multiply structured as to have passed unexamined? In particular, the designation of the prototypical childcarer as female, the child as masculine and the psychological researcher as masculine can no longer be regarded as arbitrary or innocent.

SEPARATIONS AND CONNECTIONS

What issues of general significance emerge from the study of fatherhood? The critique of the reliance on observational methods can be taken further as conveniently reflecting a fantasy of researcher detachment that avoids having to address the emotional complexity of the researcher's own reactions and ambivalences around children and childcare (Richards, 1982). The inadequacy of extrapolating a model of emotional attachment from mothers to fathers raises questions about its suitability as a general model to characterise the diversity of mothers' (as well as others') relationships with children. And the attention to the power relations structured within, and sometimes infringed by, research relationships indicates the necessity for the researcher to be located clearly within the research enterprise, both in terms of the construction of the research material and its account.

Finally, the evaluation of parental roles and practice should promote a reconceptualisation of the definitions and relationships between mothers, fathers and children. Different parenting practices give rise to different children; definitions of childhood exist in relation to those of gender and gendered arrangements. Attention to the variability of these definitions invites a number of implications. The current focus on children's rights can work to further infantilise or confirm infantilisation of women by promoting children's rights over women's. The purported development of new forms of masculinity that emphasise caring and sensitivity can also reassert in new guise much more traditional patriarchal themes where men are portrayed as supplanting, rather than sharing with, women (Burman, in press). From this it is clear we need to see definitions of children, mothering and fathering as interconnected. But it is also necessary to see these as separable so that the categories do not collapse into one another.

The recent North American film *The Hand that Rocks the Cradle* is more concerned with portraying the dire consequences that follow when a woman departs from her rightful role as full-time wife and mother (the central character almost loses the love of both her baby and husband) than with addressing the real changes in the distribution of affectional relations that accompany shared childcare and more equal forms of parenting. The film is about the disasters that befall a family who employ a nanny to look after their two children. The woman whom they choose (who turns out to hold this family responsible for the loss of her own) is consumed by such obsessional jealousy that she attempts to murder the wife and replace her in both the husband's and children's affections. The popularity of the film indicates its expression of widespread fears and phantasies set in circulation at a time when more women than ever are seeking to change traditional childcare arrangements through crèches, childminders, nannies (i.e. primarily through the employment of women) or shared childcare between men and women. While increased paternal participation in childcare indicates a challenge to the psychic patterning of traditional parenting relationships, the cultural representation of this, as exemplified in this film, is in terms of the very traditional theme of women competing for the love of men and children, rather than in terms of the changed responsibilities of men. In terms of the film genre, all that is new about this is the addition of 'tug-of-love' over children within the more typical narrative of seduction and (in)fidelity. But the anxiety generated by sharing childcare and the emotional investments made by *all* the carers (i.e. not just the parents) are clearly very current preoccupations. These more complex issues are rarely considered within the developmental psychological literature.

The last three chapters have explored the representation of contexts and caring relationships within developmental psychology. Not only has the 'discipline' been shown to promote and inform popular and professional practice in families and childcare, its research practices also both reproduce and obscure social inequalities within the deep structure of its knowledge production processes. Five key themes have emerged from our story so far, and will arise again in slightly different forms in later parts of this book. The first of these concerns the way the investigation of action in developmental psychology has been structured by the technology – of testing, of observation, of measurement in general. The demand to provide standardised, quantifiable measures produces or constructs the research object as abstracted from social relations.

Secondly, the primary focal object of developmental psychological inter-vention (and its associated panoply of practices) is not children, but mothers – or rather 'the mother'. Here we can note that it is significant that the limitations of the paradigms investigating adult–child relations are attaining recognition only when they are being applied to men. Just as *The Hand that Rocks the Cradle* displaces a struggle between men and women for the love of children into a competition between women (primarily over a man), so we can see how the evaluation and objectification of women through the regulation of mothering produces women as subjects as well as objects.

Thirdly, as earlier chapters have argued, these discourses of regulation rely upon assumptions about the relevance of evolutionary theory to human popu-lations in more or less overt ways.

Fourthly, as discussed in more detail in Chapter 5, behind the scientific objectivity that structures developmental psychological research lies a set of phantasies of control that betray legacies of fear and insecurity at the same time as derogating women's designated powers of mothering. Here psychoanalytic theorising has something to offer in excavating what is passed over, or absent, within psychology: in this sense psychoanalysis is the repressed other of psychology.

Fifthly, the abstraction of 'the child' and 'the family' as the units of analysis within developmental psychology reflects a failure to theorise the conditions that give rise to the psychology of the context that they inhabit, and in particular make possible victim-blaming explanations where mothers are treated as responsible, for example, for the outcome of the distress caused by poverty.

So far in this book we have been dealing with accounts of children's early development and relationships. But contexts of care are, within current developmental discourses, inseparable from those of communication and education. The rest of this book takes up these issues to focus on areas generally characterised as language and cognitive development.

FURTHER READING

Burman, E. (1991) 'Power, gender and developmental psychology', *Feminism and Psychology, 1, 1*: 141–54.

Burman, E. (in press a) 'What is it? Masculinity and femininity in cultural representations of childhood', in S. Wilkinson and C. Kitzinger (eds) *Feminism and Discourse*, London: Sage.

Chapman, R. and Rutherford, J. (eds) (1988) *Male Order: unwrapping masculinity*, London: Lawrence & Wishart.

Lewis, C. and O'Brian, M. (eds) (1987) *Reassessing Fatherhood*, London: Tavistock.

SUGGESTED ACTIVITIES

Collect together a selection of contemporary images of men from magazines, advertisements, newspaper articles and childcare literature, and consider:

• what gender-relevant qualities they reflect;
• the extent to which the current focus on men constitutes a reiteration or a transition from traditional gender themes;
• what relation is being posited between the model of child and the model of man;
• what tensions and contradictions does the current imagery betray?

Part III

Developing communication

A concern with methodological issues combines with conceptual and political problems in discussions of language development, with Chapter 8 focusing on the theoretical burden carried by accounts of language, Chapter 9 investigating claims for a specific language code that promotes language learning and Chapter 10 moving beyond the discussion of difference and variability to draw attention to power as a structural dimension of developmental psychological research.

Chapter 8

Language talk

[L]inguistic diversity is an asset. It provides an opportunity for pupils to gain first-hand experience, knowledge and understanding of other cultures and perspectives. It also helps to prepare pupils for life in a multicultural society by promoting respect for all forms of language. Variety of language is a rich resource which schools should use as they implement the National Curriculum.

(*Linguistic Diversity and the National Curriculum*, circular 11, National Curriculum Council, March 1991)

David Pascal, the [National Curriculum] council chairman has signalled that he not only expects teachers to correct children who fail to use Standard English in any lesson or in the playground, but also that they should use Standard English when talking to each other.

(*Guardian*, 1 April 1993)

Research on language is one of the most vibrant and theoretically dynamic areas in developmental psychology. The process of children learning to talk, of entering language, poses in miniature the wider questions of social development. Moreover, some critical psychologists (and those in other disciplines) look to these developmental psychological accounts as the route to elaborate a socially and materially based theory of mind. As we shall see, the research does not always live up to this expectation. In failing to do justice to the variety and complexity of what it means to talk, not only does the research reproduce the familiar division between individual and social that it set out to transcend, it also maintains social and educational inequalities. This chapter reviews the forms which research on early language development has taken, focusing particularly on current functional approaches, and raises problems with these traditions. As we shall see, the same themes identified in Parts I and II about the relations between the structuring of developmental psychology and the regulation of women arise in particular ways within child language research.

TURNING TO LANGUAGE

The 'turn to language' within the social and human sciences has brought about an attention to issues of interpretation. Social constructionists such as Harré, Shotter and Gergen challenged positivist psychology to recognise the constructed basis of its 'data' by focusing on the accounting procedures of both psychologists and their research 'subjects' (Harré, 1983). But, paradoxically, while these developments precipitated a 'crisis' in social psychology (Parker, 1989), they have brought new credibility and invigoration to developmental psychology: social psychology's 'crisis' has boosted developmental psychology's status and profile. Now, as a new variant of the developmental myth (which sees what comes earlier as causally related to later events), psychology looks to parent–child communication in the hope of finding a solid grounding for social relations. As we shall see, in a bizarre way, in portraying adult–child interaction as the prototypical forum from which to elaborate psychological theories of social relations, social constructionism has thus brought about a new respect for empirical developmental psychology, with little reflection on the contexts and assumptions of its production. While this pretends to provide a socially and materially based model of psychology, it actually legitimates inadequate and oppressive psychological theories.

At the outset we should note that textbook accounts of developmental psychological child language research have not reflected the preoccupations of the recent research literature. They describe the sequence from babbling to the emergence of the first words, to the use of single word and gesture combinations to convey sentence-like meaning ('holophrases') and the emergence of condensed word combinations that display a rudimentary or 'telegraphic' grammatical structure. However, a restricted analysis of the role of language emerges from these accounts. If acquisition of language is taken to mark the graduation from infancy into early childhood, the role of language as the constitutive medium for the rest of development is ignored. As a topic, therefore, language appears within textbook chapters or subsections on early childhood, as if, once they have 'cracked the linguistic code', children's language learning consists of a simple accumulation of grammar and vocabulary. Seen in this way, the significance of language is limited and static. This view suppresses attention to language development (after all what is it that develops?), and divorces language from its contexts of use. It also fails to theorise qualitative shifts in the structure and use of language in later childhood (such as those arising from becoming literate), and it ignores variations in use arising from social positions and relations. Variation therefore becomes identified with departures from a standard, a standard which is itself a false construction.

FOUNDATIONS AND FORMALITIES

In part the preoccupation with acquisition derives from the legacy of both biological and structuralist approaches to language. In many respects the difficulty of locating language development research in relation to other disciplines instantiates the general problem of the place of developmental psychology. Explanations put forward for language and its course of development draw upon neurology, biology, linguistics, history, sociology and anthropology – to name a few. Rather than choose between competing explanations, as in most of the language debates, a more appropriate question is to resolve what it is developmental psychological accounts of language seek to explain. If we are interested in the specific patterns individual children exhibit in learning to talk, then no single theory or disciplinary model will suffice, nor can they simply be combined in an additive way.

Chomsky's structural analysis of language emphasised the creativity and generativity of (children's) language use which, he argued, could not arise from mere imitation of linguistic role models. Chomsky distinguished between the surface structure of the grammatical features of specific languages and (what he called) the deep structure of what he regarded as a universal grammar that underlies and is presupposed by all languages. It is this deep structure that, according to Chomsky, makes possible the acquisition of specific languages through transforming or realising the universal deep structure into a specific linguistic form. But Chomsky treated the child as a separate, isolated symbol manipulator, making it so difficult to envisage how the momentous achievements of language could occur that he invoked an innate mechanism (a Language Acquisition Device) to account for it. His claims that this was biologically pre-programmed and was specific to language have been challenged on both counts (see below). Most developmental psychology textbooks (including those reviewed in Chapter 4) outline Chomsky's (1959) critique of Skinner as the specific form in which the heredity and environment debate over language development has been played out.

What Chomsky offered was a formal model of the structure of language. He was not, however, suggesting that this could be taken as a psychological account of how children learn to talk. This conceptual confusion, made within much developmental psycholinguistic research, is tantamount to a variety of psychological essentialism, whereby form is treated as (an empirically investigable) property of mind. As Michael Silverstein (1991) notes:

> Noam Chomsky has himself frequently been at pains to point out the incoherence of assuming that the formalist 'linguistic organ', to repeat his metaphor, has anything to do, in realtime psychological processual terms, with language production/comprehension as studiable by empirical means of observational and laboratory psychology. Yet, of course many others have . . . attempted to study linguistic competence, or its development in children, by direct means without understanding the cluster of commitments that place

such competence, as a conceptual construct, beyond the realm of the normal evidentiary modalities of psychology.

(Silverstein, 1991: 151–2)

His argument is therefore that formal models of language structure have no direct bearing on the understanding of how children develop and exhibit these features, and the attempt to base a psychological investigation on this conceptual foundation appears misconceived (see also Sinha, 1989).

Increasing awareness of the limitations of formal, structural models of language has prompted the emergence of approaches which focus on the functions of language in context. But before we join the rush from structural to functional approaches (which themselves retain elements of these problems), we should recall that the problem is not formalism in itself but rather it is psychologists' failure to appreciate the limits of its applicability. What structuralist accounts do offer is an analysis of the specificity of language as a representational system which goes beyond mere substitution for, or reference to, objects to set up new possible domains of meanings. They pave the way for according language a privileged status as a conventionally agreed, public, symbolic system which not only represents but also communicates (and, social constructionists would add, *constitutes*) meaning. Moreover, regularities noted in the structure of language learning across cultures may be due to communicative universals rather than biology. Specific and less helpful legacies of Chomsky's work include a focus on structure rather than context and the separation of language from general communicative processes.

ACTIONS SPEAK LOUDER THAN WORDS: FROM STRUCTURE TO FUNCTION

Critics of the formal, structural models of language and their associated claims of innateness treat the emergence of language as having continuities with non-linguistic developments, also highlighting prelinguistic precursors to language. By these accounts, meaning is not uniquely linguistic but arises from action. This seems a more promising route for a more socially based theory of individual language development. These so-called 'functional' approaches, called functional because they focus on language use (rather than structure), draw on a number of theoretical resources which include aspects of the work of Piaget, Vygotsky and some influence of 'ordinary language' philosophy.

Firstly, they refer to Piaget's (1953) account of sensorimotor cognition which relates communicative abilities to the development of more general cognitive structures and changes. Children's abilities to engage in purposive behaviour, understanding of cause–effect relations and means–end relations are all required for language (to want to communicate, to appreciate that words can produce effects, and to use words as the tool to produce those effects, respectively). Hence it is argued that the entry into language draws on other representational abilities, such as deferred imitation (reproducing a behaviour in another context – which is required for the learning of words) and object permanence (maintaining a representation of an object without external stimulus – necessary for remembering the word label).

Secondly, accounts highlight how in learning to talk a child needs not only to use a particular label to refer to a particular object, but also to use conventional labels or words in order to participate in a language community. Language is, after all, not only a symbolic system, but, in order to function communicatively, its signs have to be shared and understood. Work like Carter's (1978) documents the route by which children initially exhibit variable vocalisations which are linked to specific gestures, and later come to use the same vocalisation no longer tied to a particular action. This conventionalisation of sounds relies on their increasing decontextualisation.

In tracing the specific continuities between activity and the emergence of language, Lock's (1978) analysis of the changing meaning and use of sounds and gestures suggests how they come to be increasingly separated from the action or event they initially accompanied, thus paving the way for their use as symbols. He illustrates this through the example of a child raising its arms. As a response that was once a simple association elicited by a wide variety of cues, this comes to function as a gesture which has some detachment from the immediate context of its exhibition, and ultimately functions not in simple anticipation of being, but as a *request* to be, picked up. In these terms, the developmental path is correspondingly seen as a move from intention to convention via the transition from action, to gesture, to symbol.

Thirdly, accounts which highlight the emergence of language as arising within and from action emphasise how language is used to do things. The 'ordinary language' philosophy of Austin (1962) and Searle (1972) points out that language is not only used to name or label things, but also has non-descriptive functions (such as excusing or commanding) which constitute events, or 'speech acts', in themselves. When we speak we not only utter words, but in so doing our words constitute 'speech acts' and as such produce particular effects within the person(s) addressed (such as feeling pleased when being complimented) (Austin, 1962). Applied to early language development, this has been used to suggest that a complex social as well as linguistic knowledge is involved in learning to communicate. Learning to speak is also learning how to *mean* (Halliday, 1975), with all the semantic and pragmatic, as well as syntactic, understanding this involves. In particular, Bates *et al.* (1979) suggest that this speech act model can inform the exhibition and interpretation of children's early language. Like their gestures, children's utterances are initially *treated* as intentional, that is, as intended to produce effects. By this kind of model, it is only later that children understand the use of vocalisation to affect the behaviour of others.

Useful as these functional approaches have been in moving away from idealised or context-free models of language, they nevertheless retain some of the latter's guiding assumptions which they simply supplement rather than revise. In particular, the mapping of linguistic form on to psycholinguistic function and the failure to analyse the context of the production of the linguistic material under study invite the criticisms that they simply lapse into the same problems as exclusively formal models but in an inadvertent way. Moreover, the very term 'functionalist' harks back to an evolutionary framework that invokes biological (and social) adaptation and instrumentalism that is at odds with the ethos of most of this work. Concluding his critique of contemporary forms of 'functionalist developmentalism', Silverstein (1991) warns against the incoherence of a 'developmentalist "functionalism" mixed with non-developmental formalism' (Silverstein, 1991: 152). He comments:

> The irony may be that, in contrast to the mysterious pre-experiential, *sui generis* formal structure of committed formalist developmentalism, 'functionalism' of this sort always seems to appeal to mysterious, pre-experimental formal-functional transparency, commonsense naturalness, and analogy.
>
> (Silverstein, 1991: 179)

HEARING VOICES?

Emphasis on the emergence of language through activity, continuity of linguistic and prelinguistic development, and the general character of the prerequisites for language as common to all representational processes sets the stage for broader discussions of the relationship between language and thought. This issue also connects with questions about the individual–society relation and the social construction of subjectivity. In particular, textbook coverage presents this in terms of the debate between Piaget and Vygotsky over the status of 'egocentric speech'.

Despite his tendencies towards formalism in other areas (which is itself a source of other problems; see Chapter 12 and Rotman, 1978), Piaget is called upon by functionalist child language researchers seeking to locate language within the context of child action and interaction. While his views on the status of language shifted over time and were sometimes contradictory (Flavell, 1963), Piaget is generally seen as having regarded language as reflecting (rather than more actively constituting) more general cognitive and representational processes. In this his views differ from those of Chomsky: while for Chomsky language and thought are independent, Piaget's ideas are used to treat cognitive development as the precondition for language development. Development consists of individual action on the world which gives rise to cognitive structures and thus representation, including language. Language is therefore simply one of various representational systems. In contrast, Vygotsky theorised language and thinking as originating separately but as coming to control each other. He saw language as fundamentally communicative (rather than solely action-oriented) and therefore social. As Cole and Cole put it in their Vygotskyan-informed textbook:

In Vygotsky's framework, language allows thought to be individual and social at the same time. It is the medium through which individual thought is communicated to others while at the same time it allows social reality to be converted into the idiosyncratic thought of the individual. This conversion from the social to the individual is never complete, even in the adult, whose individual thought processes continue to be shaped in part by the conventional meanings present in the lexicon and speech habits of the culture.

(Cole and Cole, 1989: 296)

The two theorists offer correspondingly divergent interpretations of young children's speech. Piaget regarded young children's speech as egocentric, or unadapted to the communicative context. His model of the egocentric character of young children's thinking was based on his analysis of children's speech (Piaget, 1926), and he treated egocentrism as an inability to take into account the perspective of, or interests of, others, which in turn confirmed his view of the unsocialised character of the child. By contrast, Vygotsky understood 'egocentric' speech as functioning as an intermediary between activity and thought, as an external aid or prop to problem solving. In one celebrated example, a child who was drawing a picture of a car when the pencil broke commented 'It's broken' and went on to draw a broken car. Vygotsky interpreted this as indicating that egocentric speech had modified the course of the activity and therefore plays a more integral role:

The child's accidentally provoked egocentric utterance so manifestly affected his activity that it is impossible to mistake it for a mere by-product, an accompaniment to interfering with the melody.

(Vygotsky, 1962: 17)

Thought, far from existing separately from speech, is rather a development from it as 'inner speech'.

The older children in our experiments behaved differently from the younger ones when faced with obstacles. Often the child examined the situation in silence, then found a solution. When asked what he was thinking about, he gave answers that were quite close to the thinking-aloud operation of the pre-schooler. This would indicate that the same mental operations that the pre-schooler carries out through egocentric speech are already relegated to soundless inner speech in the schoolchild.

(Vygotsky, 1962: 17–18)

BRIDGES AND BYWAYS

Vygotsky has been taken up by developmental psychologists largely due to increasing recognition of the abstracted and asocial character of Piaget's model. In some senses, the functions played by Vygotsky's work to warrant more 'social' accounts of development are not unlike those played by that of G.H.

Mead. Put (over)simply, for Piaget development is from the 'inside out' – a movement away from non-verbal (what he called 'autistic') thinking, first to egocentrism and then to inner speech (as thought). In contrast, for Vygotsky development is from the 'outside in', that is, from the social to the individual. The individual is therefore the end rather than the starting point of the process of development. As a Soviet developmental psychologist, albeit one very much in touch with and influenced by European psychology (Valsiner, 1988), Vygotsky was working within a theoretical framework which challenged the individualism of Western psychology, and treated the individual as constructed through the social. Vygotsky's cultural-historical perspective emphasises the differential meanings and values of biological and environmental factors according to the specific context, and here context is understood as including the historical development of culture (Vygotsky, 1978a).

This emphasis on the socially mediated character of development contributes to Vygotsky's current popularity with social constructionists such as Harré and Shotter (e.g. Cole and Cole, 1989; Harré, 1986; Shotter, 1973). Despite hopes of building a thoroughly social model of the individual, the full implications of Vygotsky's ideas have not yet been reflected in developmental psychological theories. This is primarily due to the conservative readings of Vygotsky's work, which treat it largely as an educational technology, with the Vygotskyan notion of 'zone of proximal development' (what a child can do with help as indicative of what she will shortly be able to do unaided) being used to inform theories of instruction (e.g. Newman et al., 1989). Although it can be used in more radical ways (Newman and Holzman, 1993), in part this exacerbates already existing tendencies within Vygotsky's work, due to the tendency to reduce the social world to the inter-individual, with its focus on small group, or dyadic, interaction. As James Wertsch (1991) comments:

> What is somewhat ironic for someone interested in formulating a Marxist psychology, he made precious little mention of broader historical, institutional, or cultural processes such as class struggle, alienation and the rise of commodity fetishism.
>
> (Wertsch, 1991: 46)

The arguments about the limitations of infancy research made in Chapters 2 and 3 are just as relevant to discussions of child language research. As we shall see, theorists – whether philosophers, psychoanalysts or social constructionists – who see the roots of social life in the selective analysis of early caregiver–child interaction currently on offer therefore risk screening out some of the most important aspects of its contemporary organisation.

GAME PLAYING AND ROUTINES

Together with the influence of Vygotsky, the work on precursors has led to a focus on the characteristics of action in which children are seen as embedded in that action as well as exhibiting it. The particular focus here has been on how adults support children's language learning. This includes the role of specific contexts in the promotion and support for children's early communication. The influence of these ideas is mainly felt in developmental psychology through Margaret Donaldson's (1978) notion of embedded thinking and 'human sense' and (explicitly drawing on Vygotsky's ideas) through Jerome Bruner's notion of 'scaffolding'. Bruner's work is the one which is best known in developmental psychology in the US as well as Europe.

According to Bruner's conceptual framework, the scaffolding of early adult–child interaction originates in adults' attribution of communicative intention to the child, such that even young infants are treated as if they are conversational partners (Snow, 1977). In addition, the structure of conversation is seen to be prefigured by the structure of rhythmic games many adults play with infants. These set up contingent patterns of interaction which are held to involve, frame and structure the children's actions: from initially simply reacting to the game, the child begins to show anticipation of, for example, being tickled, and finally starts initiating turns. The turn taking that Kaye (1982) saw within infant feeding (see Chapter 3) now takes on a key role in setting up the pragmatic structure of dialogue through the reciprocal roles set up by the alternation between speaker and hearer (Bruner, 1975/6). This reversibility of roles is regarded as prerequisite to the use of deictic terms, that is those aspects of language that can be interpreted only in terms of the context of the speaker, such as 'this/that', 'here/there' and (especially important for communication) the pronouns 'I/you'. Joint activity, as the context in which early communicative interactions take place, forms the basis for joint reference or attention. This is indicated by mutual gaze, and from an early age the following and directing of gaze seems to be a reciprocal system (Scaife and Bruner, 1975). Joint attention and action is said to pave the way for, and is mirrored by, the topic–comment structure that characterises children's earliest words, and this structure forms the building block for the subject–predicate structure of linguistic propositions (Bruner, 1983). Functional continuities are therefore traced between the structure of adult–child activities and the conceptual demands presupposed by language.

But not only are these continuities subject to the claims of implicitly harking back to formalism (as already reviewed), they are also rooted in the assumption that language learning lies in dyadic interaction. As Lieven (in press) points out, the idea that all language learning is a dyadic process is a very particular cultural construction that reflects the Eurocentric and class biases of child language research. While most children learn to talk in polyadic situations (interacting with more than one adult, and with other children), and this may play a much more active role in the process by which children pair utterances with meaning, child language research routinely screens out all language partners other than the mother and child (see, for example, the Hoff-Ginsberg quotation below). While there is little research on the effects of siblings on children's language, Barton and Tomasello (in press) report that young children's language is more complex when their environment includes mother and an older sibling than when they are with mothers alone.

Bruner uses terms like 'routines', 'formats' and 'scaffolding' to describe the regular and rule-bound patterns of caregiver–child interaction which, he claims, enable adults to mark important features of the action gesturally or vocally and eventually to induct children into doing so too. These form established, familiar contexts within which children can first exhibit initial babbling sounds, then more differentiated vocalisations and then standard lexical words. Within this account, play is central to language development, since games provide the context for joint activity with others and 'tension-free' opportunities for the exercise and exploration of abilities. Routines set up shared action formats with clear sets of expectations and actions. These in turn set up a restricted and shared set of meanings that can help to provide references to which more advanced communicative signals are attached.

The context of book reading has attracted particular attention as a valuable context for the teaching of vocabulary. Pictures in early reading books, as two-dimensional representations of three-dimensional objects, are regarded as aids to decontextualisation, and the interactional pattern of query, answer and feedback plus label exhibited by mother–child pairs is seen as a prototypical instructional process (Ninio and Bruner, 1978). The value accorded to this activity has been extended to include not only other aspects of language development but also success in schooling (Tittnich et al., 1990). But here we need to step back to reflect on the terms and claims being elaborated.

LABELLING AND NAME CALLING

Despite the widespread focus on reading as instantiating the principal properties for language teaching, there are difficulties in treating it as the ideal-typical model. In the first place, it is a highly specific activity which has a structure that is not characteristic of adult–child interaction elsewhere. Indeed it was selected *because* of its idealised presentation of labels. It seems that different caregiving contexts (feeding, bathing, playing with toys, reading) all give rise to different patterning of adult–child talk (Hoff-Ginsberg, 1991). As Kevin Durkin (1987) comments:

> Since language acquisition is universal and picture-book reading is culture specific, the causal potential of this situation is uncertain.
>
> (Durkin, 1987: 116)

Secondly, the priority accorded to play divorces language learning from other everyday caregiving contexts, and presents a sanitised and idealised picture of women at home with no commitments other than to devote themselves to extending their child's vocabulary. While child language research follows in the footsteps of the developmental tradition of observation, most work is based on intensive analysis of relatively few 'case' studies, in fact often taking the form of diary studies of the researchers' own children. But far from simply recording what happens in homes, studies isolate the objects of study from their everyday contexts by excluding all parties other than mother and 'target' child, failing to document situations representative even of the participants. For example:

> Because the children in this study were too young and because the mothers did not work outside the home, their spending several hours together at home was not a contrived situation except for the occasional exclusion of an infant sibling who would otherwise have been present.
>
> (Hoff-Ginsberg, 1991: 786)

Thirdly, learning to talk is not the same as learning labels. It has, however, been suggested that children learn words and only later realise that words are names through the insight that actions name objects (McShane, 1980). This therefore calls into question the exclusive importance accorded both to labelling and to the promotion of adult–child interaction around contexts said to aid label learning. This links up with the regulation of women through the extension of criteria for adequate childcare into educational provision (Walkerdine and Lucey, 1989), exporting the discourse of 'sensitive mothering' from affectional to educative domains (see also Chapter 11 for further examples). Rather, we should see the equation of language with naming as a reflection of the formalist emphasis on words as object names and on language as a referential activity, mapping concepts onto objects. What this does is to set up precisely the dualist division between language and thought that it aimed to resolve. Theoretically then this assumption harks back to the priority accorded to thinking by the philosopher Descartes, treating thought as private and divorced from language and social relations. It also presumes that language represents truths, rather than produces its own realities. In this sense the model of language on offer is profoundly and naively realist – unlike the constructionist and discourse analytic work emerging in social psychology (Parker, 1992a; Burman and Parker, 1993). Politically, the fetishism within child language research on language as object rather than relationship can be connected to broader analyses of commodity fetishism within capitalism. Communicative processes are reduced to words which are treated as utterances by individuals, abstracted from their relations of production. These words acquire value as indices not only of children's competence but also of caring and teaching mothers (see Chapter 9). Practically, this research pressurises children by treating vocabulary as the primary index of language development and oppresses mothers by demanding that they should devote themselves to accelerating this.

Fourthly, the reduction of language development to labelling bleaches all emotions out of contexts of meaning construction. To the extent that developmental psychology subscribes to a representational theory of language, it imagines that emotions are irrelevant, and, where it *does* admit their importance, it allows only the 'nice' emotions through. In particular, accounts present an overharmonious view of parent–child interaction. Subtle mismatches are a routine and perhaps necessary feature of adult–child interaction. Mention has already been made in Chapter 7 of the differential evaluation of maternal and paternal communicational demands on children. Durkin (1987) cautions against the tendency of research to produce an idealised, sanitised representation of parent–child interaction. In a similar vein, Ben Bradley (Sylvester Bradley 1983, Bradley 1989) provides examples of the ways in which infant negativity and aggression are screened out of observational studies only to reappear as originating from the mothers. Using a Lacanian psychoanalytic framework, Urwin (1982, 1984) demonstrates how contexts of adult–infant play involve negotiations over and attributions of assertion and pleasure as well as identification:

> these playful interactions also provide the adult with occasions for playing with power and control, producing the baby as all-powerful one minute, and perhaps undercutting this the next, through breaking the baby's expectations, for example. In some instances the interactions may be highly erotic or sexualized. Here one would anticipate that the sex of parent and infant would produce differences, though not altogether predictable ones. The mother, for example, may conjure in fantasy the potential lover who controls or entices her, or project herself as the passive recipient of the desires of another, or as active and potent, a positioning which may not be available elsewhere. As for the baby in the mirror stage, these kinds of interactions act as a support to the adult's own narcissism. This is one of the reasons why relating to babies can be so pleasurable.
>
> (Urwin, 1984: 294)

The variety of fantasies and positionings available within adult–infant interaction make it unlikely that this would be as consistent and stable as current formulations of functionalist-constructivist work assume.

> much has been made of mothers 'interpreting' their baby's actions as if they signalled specific intentions or carried a particular meaning as an explanation for related changes in the babies' communications. . . . But by itself interpretation carries no magical properties. First . . . posing the problem in terms of meaning outside getting inside by-passes the issue of the infant's contribution. Second . . . one would anticipate that adults would normally show more inconsistency, more ambivalence, or contradiction than these studies seem to presume. For example, competing demands on the mother, her conscious and unconscious desires, will affect her subjective positioning and hence the particular discourse through which she reads the baby's behaviour at any one time.
>
> (Urwin, 1984: 298)

Finally, this focus on play moves away from a functional to a competence model since it treats the child rather than the interaction as the unit of analysis, thus illustrating a tendency for socially mediated models to collapse into more traditional socio-cultural evaluation. The focus on conventionalisation and labelling can lead to a suppression of the multiple forms of variation. While class variation in child language and mother–child language is measured against norms which are themselves based on samples of white, middle-class mothers (Lieven, in press), nowhere is the selective and regulatory structure of research more evident than in its treatment of multilingualism.

NATIVE TONGUES: MAKING MULTILINGUALISM PUZZLING

There are two main questions that are thrown up by an attention to multilingual issues: the first is why it is largely absent from mainstream accounts and the second is why it is not treated as a topic of interest rather than as a problem. In contrast to sociolinguistic work (e.g. Chaika, 1982), there is an almost overwhelming assumption within accounts of early language development not only that this is unilinear, but also that children learn a single language. Books with titles like *A First Language* (Brown, 1973) or the journal title *First Language* suggest that children learn to talk one language, or at least one language at a time. Even now accounts of language learning sometimes omit all mention of bilingualism or, especially, multilingualism. More usually it appears as an extra chapter or 'issue' in a text. The editors of a recent volume on bilingual development comment on how little cross-over there is between researchers with a particular interest in bilingualism and those working on language development (Homel *et al.*, 1987). Bilingualism is effectively excluded from research as if it were a confounding variable, with studies littered with comments in sample sections or footnotes such as 'All of the participants were white, native speakers of English; all the families were monolingual' (Hoff-Ginsberg, 1991: 785), and 'All were white, British-born two parent families' (McGuire, 1991: 147), with no explanation about why or how the cultural background or family composition was relevant to the research aims. Moreover, multilingual issues often do not figure even in current books specifically designed for an applied professional audience (e.g. Tittnich *et al.*, 1990).

From this we might suppose that speaking more than one language is unusual. However, whatever the multiple forms and definitions of being multilingual (Baetens Beardsmore, 1982), the majority of the world's population are bilingual or multilingual. Once again we see the Anglo-centric samples of white, middle-class, monolinguals – majorities within their own countries, but a fraction of the world's population – which form the basis of research coming to function as the typical measure of development.

Not only is coverage of multilingualism conspicuous by its absence, but where it is discussed it is often in a negative light. Indeed current research on multi-lingualism is combating a tradition which treated it as a cognitive and educational handicap (cf. Hakuta, 1986). This is no surprise considering the methodological procedures by which these 'findings' emerged. Early twentieth-century studies attempted to correlate bilingualism and IQ (itself a culturally biased test) by comparing monolingual and bilingual performance on verbal tests in the bilingual child's *second* language. Even now, multilingual children are dis-advantaged in assessment contexts which rely exclusively on verbal tests rather than also using non-verbal tests (McLaughlin, 1984).

The negative view of bilingualism arises from the investigation of linguistic minorities within a dominant culture, in which poverty and racism often confound the language issues. As Skutnabb Kangas (1981) makes clear, the linguistic and educational tasks facing those whose home language is that of the majority or minority group are very different, and language-teaching programmes correspondingly should reflect this. For a native speaker of a high-status majority language, learning a second language is an optional extra that current theories consider is best done through immersion programmes. For children whose home language is that of a minority, they have to learn the dominant language in order to have access to educational and employment opportunities. It is not surprising that children who are not yet proficient in the language in which they are learning curriculum subjects fail to achieve to the level of their native speaker counterparts. Moreover, as well as the historical treatment of bilingualism as a remedial educational issue, language difficulties are often confused with communicational problems by teachers (conversely also creating problems in identifying genuine learning disabilities). These factors contribute to bilingualism being seen as a 'special educational' issue, which is reflected in the over-representation of cultural minorities in education sectors associated with low academic achievement (CRE, 1992). In turn this both draws attention from the problem of an irrelevant curriculum being responsible for minority children's educational difficulties and reinstates cultural dominance:

> Developing from the notion of cultural deprivation, the immigrant children's special needs in education soon became the acceptable approach to cope with their alleged cultural and linguistic deficiencies. Gradually public attention was diverted away from the content of the curriculum and its dubious relevance to non-English children and directed towards evidence for their presumed cultural limitations and linguistic handicaps. The assumption was that the discontinuity between these children and their school was the result of the malfunctioning of the children themselves, not the school.
>
> (Tosi, 1988: 82–3)

Current theories take the position that disadvantaged cultural minorities should be taught through the medium of their home language, thus supporting and maintaining their cultural background, as well as facilitating the transfer of linguistic and reasoning skills from one language to the other. But, as the tensions between theory, policy and practice in the quotes at the beginning of this chapter suggest, even now multilingualism is often portrayed within assimilationist and compensatory models as a necessary evil to facilitate transition to the majority language. (For critiques and opportunities of the National Curriculum see Conteh, 1992; Savva, 1990.) It is in this context that Anglo-US developmental psychology textbooks continue to discuss bilingualism in terms of the educational disadvantage of minority children, with specific concern expressed at levels of provision for, and low rates of success of, English language programmes.

The complexity of the issues raised by multilingualism are rarely acknowledged. Discussions are often just in terms of bilingualism, yet rarely if ever is one an absolutely 'balanced' bilingual, or 'balanced' in all spheres (and what assumptions underlie this drive towards equilibrium?), since factors such as frequency and contexts of use, as well as cultural and familial identifications enter the definition. The relationship between methods of instruction and status of the speaker as part of a linguistic minority or majority has already been mentioned. But in some circumstances the meanings and relative importance accorded to bilingualism are not connected with majority or minority status. Treatments of multilingualism should be seen in their historical and class contexts. While currently most discussions of multilingual issues in Europe and the US are cast within a political framework of assimilation of minority groups (in terms of aiming either to promote or to prevent this), historically it has been cultural élites who have been multilingual while the colonised or subordinate groups have been denied access to other languages as a means of social control (as has happened recently in South Africa). To take a (less extreme and) contemporary example, in Catalunya at the moment the regional state administration are repudiating Spanish as their first language and promoting Catalan, which is seen as expressing resistance to rule from Madrid (Torres, 1992). In general, questions of power are integrally linked with those of rights to language, and the fact that Anglo-US dominated psychological research assumes a monolingual language learner itself speaks volumes about legacies of colonialism and imperialism – of both the territorial and the cultural varieties.

Given the association between language and cultural identity, and the history of colonialism (in which erosion of indigenous languages played a role crucial to the maintenance of political control), there is clearly an obligation on language researchers in general to dissociate themselves from that tradition and address properly theoretically informed questions which the study of multilingualism demands. More recently, surpassing a grudgingly corrective model, positive views are emerging of the role and importance of being bilingual, in terms of more flexible cognitive and problem-solving skills and more general benefits of being less tied to a particular world-view (Skutnabb Kangas and Cummins, 1988). Far from treating bilingualism as a problem, some researchers have subjected *mono*lingualism to scrutiny:

> Monolingualism is a psychological island. It is an ideological cramp. It is an illness, a disease which should be eradicated as soon as possible because it is dangerous for world peace.
>
> (Skutnabb Kangas, 1988: 13)

This disease metaphor has recently been taken up by the Instituto Central America to promote language schools with the slogan 'El monolingualismo es curable' ('Monolingualism can be cured'). Interestingly, this carries different implications for different audiences. While it functions as an invitation to Europeans and North Americans to learn (Latin-American) Spanish, it is also an exhortation to speakers of indigenous languages to learn international languages so that they can participate in the world scene directly.

SPEAKING WITH FEELING

Consideration of multilingual language development therefore illustrates a set of general issues relevant to, but tending also to be eclipsed by, accounts of language development. Recognising language as a source of cultural or national identification invested with great emotional significance may, and should, inform the analysis of the origins and functions of individual differences in children's speech. Moreover, in spite of Bruner's benign notions of 'scaffolding', the initial context for learning language can also involve emotionally highly charged and conflictual situations. Roger Brown (1973) reports from his longitudinal study of the language development of a child, Eve, that she first used the time adverbials 'after', 'then' and 'first' after they were explicitly directed towards her in negotiating her request that she be allowed to drink milk from her baby sister's bottle. Further, it was only a considerable time later that she used these words in other contexts. Lieven (1982) discusses this account as highlighting how language learning takes place in particular contexts and that early language use displays that history. The conclusions she draws are that there is no single route to learning language, and that it is a continuous process. Children differ in the ways they construct speech and what they use speech for.

Related to this, it is also clear that the cultural context in which the child lives enters into the structure and style of, as well as the actual, language she speaks. Urwin (1984) too argues that descriptions of language development are so focused on whether or when a child has achieved possession of a particular linguistic or grammatical structure that they fail to attend to the emotional significance of the development under consideration. The cognitivist interpretation of a child's extension of her linguistic repertoire is assumed to be determined by the salience of the objects or actions they name. But, more than this, common first words like 'more' or 'gone' 'are precisely those which are particularly likely to mark the child's own control within predictable practices' (Urwin, 1984: 312). Salience here necessarily takes on emotional meanings that remain untheorised within current accounts. It is clear then that a more differentiated approach to language development is necessary, one that attends to contexts of language use as well as structure. To this end we now turn to the research investigating talk addressed to, as well as exhibited by, children.

FURTHER READING

Bruner, J. (1983) *Child's Talk: learning to use language*, Oxford: Oxford University Press (a very readable exposition of Bruner's ideas).
Lieven E. (1982) 'Context, process and progress in young children's speech', in M. Beveridge (ed.) *Children Thinking through Language*, London: Arnold (a clear and helpful summary of research trends in developmental psycholinguistics).

Skutnabb Kangas, T. and Cummins, J. (eds) (1988) *Minority Education: from shame to struggle*, Avon: Multilingual Matters (applies the debates about language and cultural dominance to education in a varied and useful collection of papers).

SUGGESTED ACTIVITIES

Taking the 'anti-linguicism manifesto' elaborated in Chapter 1 of Skutnabb Kangas and Cummins (op. cit.), develop a structured series of questions to be addressed as individuals or in small groups:

- to what extent are or were language issues addressed in courses you are taking or have taken?
- what is the effect of the presence or absence of these issues?
- whose language is the medium of instruction?
- what is the relationship between the language of instruction and cultural assumptions permeating the theory?
- what is the relationship between language use and structural positions of disadvantage?

Chapter 9

Discourses of caregiving talk

When you give your child a bath, bathe him in language.

(Bullock, 1974: 58)

This chapter reviews the research literature which investigates the role of the contexts in which children learn to talk. As we shall see, this domain provides a key arena in which the main themes structuring language research are played out. Firstly, the obsession with the speed of development at the expense of theory: it is an unexamined assumption that the earlier a child speaks or exhibits a particular construction the better. The second theme to be considered at some length in this chapter is the privileging of particular language styles which imports the structure of evaluation and regulation of women we encountered in the literature on 'attachment' (Chapter 6) into the arena of child language development. Thirdly, related to this, we see a polarisation set up between those adult caregivers (almost exclusively defined as mothers) who are considered to promote child language development either adequately or inadequately (again subject to this dubious assumption about rate of development) and with the corresponding pillorying of the latter (deemed 'insensitive') mothers.

It is a commonly held view that children benefit from the speech they are exposed to within the course of caregiving. The fact that many adults in many places modify their speech to children has given rise to the pervasive assumption that this must aid language learning. However, research has produced no clear answer to the question of what it is about the speech directed to children that is helpful. Methodological and interpretational limitations of research give rise to an account of language development that is oversimplified and insensitive to analysing the precise role specific features of the linguistic environment play in the promotion of language. These absences not only obscure an understanding of how the speech directed to children relates to how they acquire and develop language, but the research also sets up an unwarranted negative stereotype of caregivers who are routinely designated as deficient in their supposedly language-promoting qualities. This negative evaluation extends beyond individuals to the rating of class and cultural language variation. As we shall see, this insensitivity to variation and its significance has conceptual implications for an adequate study of language, as well as major educational and political effects. In this chapter I present a critical review of this research, taking issue with the assumption that there is a single model of how to talk with children. I will argue that issues of difference, discourse and practice necessarily enter into the evaluation of appropriate communication.

BABYTALK

Research from the 1960s onwards has documented systematic differences between speech directed to children and speech between adults. This takes the form of shorter sentences, simplified syntactic forms, well-formed utterances, use of higher pitch, exaggerated intonation and slower speed. This talk addressed to children is also characterised by redundancy, with frequent entire or partial repetitions (Snow, 1972), is closely tied to the immediate context (Snow, 1977) and exhibits particular features that have been interpreted as functioning to engage children in, and support their, talk. In particular, they are regarded as helping the segmentation and learning of words, through repetition and familiar word-frames identifying word boundaries, and mapping ideas onto language by talking about what is accessible and elaborating on what the child says (Cross, 1977).

Indicative of ideological presumptions about who looks after children and who is responsible for their development, this child-directed speech style has been dubbed 'motherese', a term which continues to appear in current textbooks (e.g. Bukatko and Daehler, 1992; Mitchell, 1992) despite increasing recognition that mothers are not necessarily children's sole or major caregivers and that these modifications are not confined to mothers, or even adults, since older children use them towards younger ones (Dunn and Kendrick, 1982). Even when accounts shift to the less loaded term 'child-directed speech', research is based almost exclusively on mothers' speech to children; the change in terminology has not reflected any fundamental reorganisation of research procedures or questions.

As an adaptation to children's limited linguistic proficiency, this speech style appeared to offer an alternative account for language learning that dispensed with the need for Chomsky's innate language acquisition device. This was because the designation of babytalk as a simplified speech register appeared to challenge his claim that the linguistic models to which children were exposed were too degenerate to enable language development. However, the mere prevalence of speech modifications to children does not in itself imply that these are helpful, or why they are (if they are). There are problems in demonstrating the value of child-directed speech in teaching grammar, not least because this model collapses into a more radical form of nativism, only this time locating the competence within the mother rather than the child. Instead of postulating an innate facility to learn language within the child, mothers are invested with an 'omniscient' (Shatz, 1982) facility to promote language learning with no explanation as to how this arises. This produces both a fundamentally asocial account of the origins of language development and a consensual and unitary model of social relations:

> The conjecture that the caregiver is innately attuned to the emergent abilities of the infant, and equipped to accommodate her or his behaviour so as to frame input at just the right level of complexity suggests not only omniscience but X-ray vision: since not all linguistic activity and knowledge is overt, the adult must be making skilful intuitive inferences from limited and potentially ambiguous data and elaborating these at just the right time and in just the right way. . . . Such a theory is 'social' only in the limited sense that it represents one party as acting and the other as reacting instinctively: the outcome is operation in unison, and arrival at like-mindedness.
>
> (Durkin, 1987: 109–10)

In addition to these conceptual problems, researchers have tended only to describe features of child-directed speech rather than analyse what it is about its specific features that is helpful. Where this has been addressed, attempting to link frequencies of features of maternal and child speech has confused rather than informed the picture.

'INPUT AND OUTPUT'

Notwithstanding the initial investment in demonstrating the facilitating effects of child-directed speech and some clear ideas about how this promotes word *meaning*, it has become apparent that the research into child-directed speech can say little about how this aids the teaching of specific aspects of language. Most research has focused on grammar, rather than on the broad spectrum of linguistic, pragmatic, discursive and metalinguistic skills involved in language use. Even within this restricted domain, the clear picture painted by early studies has been clouded by reports that speech to children is sometimes more, rather than less, grammatically complex than speech between adults. As Durkin (1987: 128) notes, 'simplification as a strategy is not equivalent to simplification as an effect'. This observation casts doubt on the status of child-directed speech as a simplified speech register.

Moreover, despite Bruner's claims that maternal speech varies in relation to and graduates with the child's language level, studies have also failed to demonstrate such 'fine-tuning'. A conceptual problem with Bruner's 'close-coupled feedback system' (Ninio and Bruner, 1978) is that according fixed knowledge to parents ignores how parental beliefs inform the language addressed to, and therefore the language models available to, children. Furthermore, 'fine-tuning' turns out to be rather complicated to research since global measures relating characteristics of the mother's and the child's speech by calculating the average length of (mothers') utterances (MLU) can be mediated by the feedback mothers receive about their communicative successes or failures with their children (Bohannen and Marquis, 1977). Such broad measures can therefore mask, rather than illuminate, subtle changes in the complexity of speech mothers address to children (Pine, 1992a).

Since such speech is also addressed to foreigners and animals (Ferguson, 1977), it has even been suggested that this style may reflect the effort to communicate with a non-competent speaker rather than a desire to teach language. By this account, these speech modifications may be a by-product of a restricted set of semantic relations associated with, but not specifically concerned with, syntax. Indeed, speech directed to children arises within activity and from the desire to communicate, rather than for the sole purpose of language teaching.

'EFFECTS'

The attempt to explore the effects of adult speech modifications to children has produced an inconclusive and inconsistent literature. In part this arises from a set of methodological difficulties that express more far-reaching limitations in the way in which language development has been conceptualised. In the first place, there may be no basis for inferring causal relations from correlations between particular features of adult speech and particular aspects of language development. After all, the adult could be *responding* to advances in the child's language, rather than solely promoting those advances. The use of simple correlational models is also inadequate, since this does not take into account how specificities of speech addressed to children may no longer be relevant once children have progressed beyond particular linguistic stages. Moreover, there is no reason to suppose, as correlational models do, that adult speech modifications should have a linear relationship to language development (Bohannen and Hirsh-Pasek, 1984). Even if an effect is found, this may arise from features that are only indirectly associated with the input, such as other changes over time that are then reflected within talk to children.

A further set of issues highlights the connection between methodological procedures and the status of available models. The theories to account for adult speech modifications are *post hoc*, working back from correlation between maternal and child speech features to speculation about what function the maternal characteristics play, and while this does not render the research meaningless, it does mean that it should be interpreted with caution. The models also presume that any effects of child-directed speech on child language will remain constant with the child's level of linguistic ability. Clearly, there may be constraints on when a child can make use of available linguistic resources and support (through their frequency or salience). Reflecting the general move towards acknowledging children as contributors to the structure of the context in which they grow up, research has shifted to exploring how this context is used by the child within the process of acquiring and developing language.

'USES'

A further general problem in interpreting how children use the language they are exposed to is that the relationships reported between talk addressed to, and exhibited by, children can be explained in a number of ways. So while maternal expansions are regarded as beneficial to child language development in terms of repeating what has just been said (by mother or child) and thus reducing the processing load for the child (e.g. Cross, 1977; Wells and Robinson, 1982), it is unclear exactly what it is about such 'recasts' that is helpful. Possible ways 'recasts' could promote language include: following on from what the child says; maintaining the topic of what the child has been talking about; expanding the utterance using words the child has used; reformulating the child's utterance by adding to or correcting it; or it may simply be a specific indication of a more general conversation-eliciting style of maternal speech. Furthermore, these functions are not mutually exclusive, since they may be determined by more general changes in relationships between mothers and children whereby mothers modify the way they talk in accordance with children's language growth. While Farrar (1990) was able to demonstrate specific relations between how mothers adjust their speech to children and the children's acquisition of grammatical elements, he suggests that this effect is specific to a particular point in the child's linguistic development and only relates to the acquisition of particular grammatical structures rather than being generally facilitative. The broader issue this kind of study raises, therefore, is the need to refine both theoretical models and methodological procedures in order to analyse both the features of adult speech considered predictive of linguistic growth and the structure of that developmental process.

Concluding his review of caregiver talk research, Pine (in press) calls for a more sophisticated approach to research analysing the relationship between child-directed speech and language acquisition that moves beyond the documentation of general frequency effects to more detailed analyses of what it is that individual children hear and say, and how each child's linguistic system changes within the period under investigation. This demands a more qualitative and fine-grained approach to the study of maternal speech effects. It also requires examination of the assumptions behind what makes a good language learning environment, and why. In particular, while current models offer some suggestions about how child-directed speech may involve children in talk while reducing communicative and processing demands (Snow, 1977), it is unclear whether these characteristics of child-directed speech arise from specifically communicative pressures or rather whether they reflect a particular culture-blind model of the language-learning child.

STYLES AND STEREOTYPES

Since the research on child-directed speech is based on mothers' speech to children, it should come as no surprise that this latches into the wider discourse of 'sensitive mothering'. In terms of language development, maternal *in*sensitivity has been equated with directiveness and intrusiveness. In a classic study, Nelson

(1973: 69) distinguishes an 'object-oriented, question-asking, relatively concise style' (seen as 'sensitive') with a 'behaviour-oriented, intrusive, discursive style' (seen as insensitive). In a similar vein, McDonald and Pien (1982) contrast a conversationally oriented style with a behaviourally regulatory style. Julian Pine (1992a, 1992b) takes issue with these simple positive/negative classifications, arguing that they do nothing to inform the understanding of children's language learning, and that moreover they reflect what is no more than a stereotype of 'good mothering'. Three particular problems can be noted.

Firstly, they confuse 'child-centredness' with a particular language-oriented style of interaction. But since there is no reason why asking questions should be a necessary index of maternal sensitivity, this gives rise to some rather bizarre contradictions:

> Thus a mother who 'orders her child around' (Nelson, 1973: 68) is seen as being 'intrusive', whereas a mother who insists on her child answering a long series of 'What's that?' questions is not.
>
> (Pine, 1992a: 5)

It is clear that both question-asking and behaviour-controlling can be done in a more or a less 'sensitive' way. This means there is no necessary relationship between 'maternal sensitivity' and 'directiveness'. Therefore

> the tendency to view question-asking positively and directiveness negatively would seem to reflect the value placed in our culture on particular kinds of language-oriented, as opposed to behaviour-oriented, forms of activity and to have little to do with the child-centredness or otherwise of the mothers concerned.
>
> (Pine, 1992a: 6)

Secondly, as Pine points out, the way the notion of 'maternal sensitivity' is operationalised implies a stability in the structure and significance of mothers' interactional behaviour irrespective of the age or stage of the child. Diverse aspects of mothers' speech, such as directives, imperatives and conversational redirections, are collapsed together within the category 'maternal directiveness', thus treating as equivalent devices which direct children's attention and those which regulate their behaviour. It would seem unlikely that asking questions would serve the same (mal)functions for a 1-year-old as for a 3-year-old child. Questions directed to 13-month-old babies might well act as prompts and aids to structure children's responses rather than as 'real' questions. Based on his study of children at the one-word stage of language development, Pine (1992b) suggests that a more appropriate reformulation of McDonald and Pien's (1982) classification might be between behavioural directives and tutorial prompts or test questions.

Thirdly, as well as definitional incoherence and homogenisation over time and culture, there are additional methodological and conceptual difficulties in relating child language characteristics to 'maternal sensitivity'. Nelson (1973) introduced a classification of 'referential' and 'expressive' mothers which she regards as arising from differences in functional characteristics of mother–child interaction, specifically between maternal direction and children's referential vocabulary (knowledge of word labels) when they have a repertoire of fifty words. The differential valuation of children who use more object words ('referential') and those who use a larger number of phrases ('expressive') betrays a cognitivist orientation which equates language with labelling (see Chapter 8). Moreover, claims made for referentiality as an index of language development are now being disputed. Lieven and Pine (1990) and Pine and Lieven (1990) argue that such claims arise as an artefact of studies which use cross-sectional designs (comparing different aged groups at the same time) rather than longitudinal designs and use age rather than linguistic level as the yardstick of comparison. If we recall that so-called referential-nominal children over-whelmingly come from the upper-middle classes of Western industrialised societies, then it becomes apparent that class and cultural assumptions are struc-tured into a seemingly disinterested developmental measure.

More than this, the dimension of 'maternal sensitivity' which was originally supposed to determine the child's level of *emotional* security (or 'attachment') has now been rendered into a measure of *linguistic* adequacy. The regulation of mothering has extended beyond the domain of caring for children into promoting their linguistic and educational progress. Yet nowhere has it been established that *rate* of language development bears any relation to later linguistic or educational competence – this is simply an unanalysed assumption that is overdetermined by the technologisation of development and the drive to maximise and accelerate it (Rose, 1990).

The child-centred approach (both within language teaching and pedagogical practices more generally) thus sets up further means for the regulation of women, as mothers and as teachers (since the overwhelming majority of teachers and nursery workers are women). Collapsing the distinction between play and work as the child-centred approach does (see Chapter 12 for further elaboration) and making all play potentially educative has given rise to the requirement that women convert their household labour into educational opportunities for their children (Walkerdine and Lucey, 1989). This takes to ridiculous lengths the principle of learning through 'direct' experience which keeps women constantly busy constructing interesting and 'stimulating' activities, as well as caring for their offspring. An article on 'Tips for talking to toddlers' suggests:

Sing songs and say rhymes.
Introduce books as early as possible – home-made scrap-books and magazines as well as picture books. Look at the pictures and ask questions.
Talk as you work and give a running commentary at least some of the time you are pushing the pram.
Visit railway stations, ferries, markets, rivers, airports so that vocabulary is extended.
Just talking is not enough, particularly if the parent is just pontificating.
(*Independent on Sunday*, 19 May 1991)

LANGUAGE AS CULTURAL PRACTICE

In some ways the research on syntactic development illustrates clearly the inappropriateness of attempts to formulate general models of language learning. Such evidence that does relate forms of speech addressed to children with the emergence of particular forms is highly qualified and specific to the particular language being learnt by the child. To take an example, there is a debate over exactly what it is about binary choice questions (questions to which the answer is either yes or no) that contributes to the emergence of auxiliary verb forms in children's speech. Newport *et al.* (1977), who first reported this association, suggested that these questions may be helpful by making auxiliary verb forms more salient because they are placed initially within questions (such as 'Can you?' 'Do you?'). This, however, can scarcely be relevant to languages that do *not* place auxiliaries at the beginning of questions or have no auxiliaries at all. Similarly, the practices held to best induct children into language reflect culturally specific ideas about what it means to learn to talk.

Bambi Schieffelin and Elinor Ochs (1986) draw on anthropological and socio-historical (Vygotskyan) approaches to challenge the abstraction of language development from general cultural practices, and to explore how cross-cultural perspectives inform the understanding of language learning as itself constituting, as well as encoding, cultural practice.

> [A]ll societies do not rely on the very same set of language-socialising procedures. Indeed although prompting a child what to say appears widespread, expanding children's utterances, using leading questions, announcing activities/events for a child, and using a simplified lexicon and grammar to do so are cross-culturally variable.
>
> (Ochs, 1986: 6)

Those studies which highlight the prevalence of child-directed speech even across cultures (e.g. in Japanese, Korean, Israeli, Mandarin Chinese, as well as US and European cultures) are almost exclusively of academic or middle-class backgrounds. As Lieven (in press) notes:

> This raises the question of whether we are dealing with the effects of higher education or of some ideological homogenization of the upper middle classes in advanced industrial societies.
>
> (Lieven, in press)

Even where adult speech modifications are found or reported, they do not always take the phonetic or prosodic form identified in the 1970s literature (such as Snow and Ferguson, 1977).

Ochs (1983) reports from her study of language socialisation in Western Samoa, where children have a variety of caregivers and siblings provide the most active direct care, that mothers tend to address older siblings in order to direct the care rather than addressing the children who receive it. Hence Samoan children do not expect a direct maternal response to their indication of need. Moreover, the organisation of status hierarchies determines speech adaptations, so that adults, as higher-status people, do not adapt their speech to their children. There is little opportunity here for the supposedly universal babytalk register to occur, and instead children are given explicit instruction and direction about how to speak. What this highlights is how the notions of sensitivity and responsiveness so prevalent within the developmental psychological and psycholinguistic literature are themselves cultural practices. Even the tendency to accord personality, individuality and intentionality to young babies also emerges as specific to Western cultural beliefs:

> It is important to realize that when an American mother responds to her infant in a particular way, she is doing so not because of *innate biological* patterning, but because she is acting on cultural assumptions about qualities and capacities of young children.

> (Ochs, 1983: 188)

In a similar vein, Bambi Schieffelin's (1983; 1990) study of Kaluli children in Papua New Guinea highlights how their explicitly instructional style of language induction follows from cultural beliefs about the entry into language marking the boundary between inhabiting the world of animals and spirits and that of humans. Sound play is discouraged because it is seen as animal-like, and this is taboo. Learning to speak is regarded as marking the child's departure from the land of spirits to join human society. Accordingly, children are prompted into language through explicit demands to imitate model utterances, and since high cultural value is placed on being able to produce well-formed speech, immature forms are devalued as 'soft' and socially inappropriate, rather than interpreted as steps towards linguistic competence.

This should make us cautious of the strong claims made for the value of a topic-expanding style since so many children learn to talk in its absence or with a more directive style. Lieven (1984, in press) argues that the variation in cultural practices and corresponding child strategies for language learning may offer important insights for approaches to language delay and disorders. Although they may not display the features that figure within the literature, she points out that these cultural practices do all provide some support and scaffolding, whether through talk or activity, through which children can construct semantic and syntactic relations. She suggests that specific cultural practices may provide the equivalent of those features attributed to the (supposedly) child-directed speech code. Taking the example of the Kaluli practice (reported by Schieffelin) of holding a baby up facing away and 'speaking for them' in a high-pitched voice, she argues that this apparently instructional mode may nevertheless provide a strategy for promoting the segmentation of the stream of language and attribution of meaning by drawing children's attention to segments of speech that they can identify and memorise, and, ultimately, reproduce. She also comments on Schieffelin's report that, although mothers do not display child-directed speech, they do exhibit adaptation to their children's communicative status, but by organising the children's focus of attention rather than responding to it (as in the topic-expanding style). The repetition and exhortation to imitate 'may well give the child the same sort of segmental and syntactic information which, it has been argued, sequences of child topics and their expansions by adults provide' (Lieven, in press).

The lesson here is that, when investigations go beyond being fixated on measuring the prevalence of a style to the analysis of what functions it is held to play in language development, then it emerges that similar functions can be identified in other, more common, forms of speech to children. It also demonstrates just how ludicrous and unjust is the negative evaluation of class and cultural practices structured within child language research.

Moreover, cultural practices enter into not only the rate but also the nature of the language spoken. Indeed, what counts as using language is itself culturally variable (Schieffelin, 1979).

> The important generalization is that although children the world over will ultimately assume the basic communicative roles (speaker, addressee, referent audience), societies differ in the developmental point at which and the situations in which it is appropriate for children to assume particular roles, these differences being linked to their attitudes about children and their communicative competence.
>
> (Ochs, 1986: 8)

In Shirley Brice Heath's (1983) ethnography of three different English-language communities in mid-America, within the African-American community she calls 'Trackton', children are rarely addressed until they can speak, their babbles or first words are rarely noted or encouraged, but they are continuously surrounded by an intensely verbal culture of talk, activity and story-telling. This corresponds to the community's cultural beliefs that children cannot be taught, but have to learn for themselves. These children 'break into' language, first by imitating the ends of words, and then they vary and repeat these oral 'chunks', adding other parts and playing with the sounds. These children go on to exhibit an analogical and imaginative approach to language use, in contrast to the nearby white 'Roadville' children who are taught to talk with an emphasis on accuracy and labelling. While the 'Roadville' children had a better grasp of narrative sequence, they lacked the 'Trackton' children's imaginative ways with language. Not only is the *process* of language development therefore not unitary, but language use is itself diverse.

CULTURAL PRACTICE THROUGH LANGUAGE

Language learning is not divorced from other socio-cultural meanings of growing up. It is not only integral to participation within social life, but is also a major tool for conveying cultural knowledge about social relations. While much research has been devoted to the process and promotion of children's language learning, the issue of what else children learn through language has been eclipsed. Yet the very forms and variety of the language children learn to talk encode structural meanings about the world they (will) inhabit. Analyses of caregiver talk in playgroup and nursery settings, even those with an explicit commitment to gender equality, indicate the pervasive asymmetrical use of gender-specified descriptions. Browne and France (1985) report that, in a British nursery, girls gained approval for their appearance and behaviour (as 'pretty', 'sweet natured', 'neat and tidy'), while boys were praised for their activity ('tough', 'brave', 'big', 'strong'). When girls exhibited the assertive behaviours deemed appropriate for boys who could stick up for themselves, they were called 'proper little madams'. While such double standards are probably so familiar to us as to sound banal, we cannot ignore how children absorb social as well as linguistic categories from what we say to them. Moreover, teaching girls to be good rather than clever (as the gender-divided language suggests) has been identified within processes of devaluing girls' educational achievements (Licht and Dweck, 1987; Walkerdine et al., 1989).

At more general methodological as well as theoretical levels, it is important to attend to the particular forms of language to which children are exposed and the particular practices within which children are reared. Schieffelin (1990) notes in her research with the Kaluli that it is not surprising to find a marked absence of the forms associated with men and with public, formal speech in the children's utterances, since it is women who are primarily involved in childcare. An equivalent lesson for the US and European research is that close attention to the structure of adult–child interaction suggests that some deviant characteristics of child speech, which have been treated as evidence of immaturity, arise as a reflection of the speech addressed to them through parental efforts to present simplified linguistic forms (Durkin, 1987).

The cross-linguistic research presents a catalogue of misinterpretations and misattributions of deficit to children or adult-language-teachers and cultures owing to the failure to analyse the language the child actually hears (rather than a formal grammar of the language). This is especially important given the different structural demands of different languages. For example, Gopnik and Choi's (1990) claim that Korean children learn labelling later than English children due to a greater emphasis in the Korean language on verbs is now being disputed as arising instead from the differing practices of English and Korean mothers who place differential emphasis on naming objects rather than the social routines involved in playing with them.

A further example of the consequences of the cultural and linguistic insensitivity that can enter into cross-linguistic research arises from work which attempts to relate language acquisition to cognitive development. In Clancy's (1989) study of Korean children she reports that 'wh'-questions (that is, why, what, where interrogatives) did not appear in the order that would be predicted according to their supposed cognitive complexity; and by contrast the children seemed to be using 'how' much earlier than would be expected. However, attending to the language that the children actually heard (the 'input') indicated that Korean mothers were using the word translated as 'how' in English in ways that would suggest it should actually be translated as 'what' (both the above examples cited in Lieven, in press). Once again we see features of social and linguistic context have been mistaken for properties of child development.

DIVERSITY, DEFICIENCY AND DOMINANCE

Basil Bernstein's terminology of 'restricted' and 'elaborated' codes to describe class-related language variations still circulates as a theory of linguistic and cultural deficit, despite his protestations in popular as well as academic publications (e.g. Bernstein, 1970) that the deprivations contributing to educational inequalities are social and not linguistic. Even in introducing a volume of Bernstein's research, Michael Halliday (1973) was compelled to dispel this misreading. Similarly, even where it is resisted, the ethnographic and anthropological work discussed above is transposed into a deficit or disadvantage model. While Brice Heath (1986) grapples with the tricky issue of how cultural differences in language practices relate to children's educational progress, her account is concerned with the failure of current schooling practices to recognise, support and differentially engage with the variety and diversity of linguistic styles. As well as addressing the relative strengths and weaknesses of subcultural languages, she therefore problematises the culture of the school rather than that of the children. The fact that references to her work in recent textbooks (Bukatko and Daehler, 1992) and professional handbooks (Tittnich *et al.*, 1990) fail to appreciate this point indicates not only the productivity of the process of popularising of research but also the intransigence of normative assumptions that underlie developmental psychological practice.

Diversity of patterns of language use and development therefore get a bad press within developmental psycholinguistic research. Both academic and popular accounts subscribe to a variety of the 'cycle of deprivation' theory which relates the child's lexical style to the mother's interactional style. Variation tends to be analysed only in terms of the negative evaluation of particular maternal practices. Despite the fact that this classification of maternal practices is erroneous and unhelpful, the devaluation and derision of working-class and minority women for their communicative and interactional styles continues. Mothers have been encouraged to talk to their children in particular, culturally sanctioned ways, castigated for their failure to do so spontaneously, and educational policies and aid have been transfixed by mother–child interaction as *the* route to educational improvement (and national development).

The quotation at the beginning of this chapter is from the Bullock Report, *A Language For Life*, a policy document commissioned by the British Department of Education and Science. This suggests that the 'gap' between home and school can be filled by maternal talk to children, and by this structural inequalities become simply a matter of deficient linguistic style. The resonances of medical and racial hygiene within the metaphor of bathing and cleansing hint at the longer history of the preoccupation (reviewed in Chapters 1 and 4) with surveying the homes and habits of working-class and disadvantaged groups. To a greater or lesser extent the research on maternal style therefore both mirrors and contributes to conceptions of cultural deficiency which, wittingly or unwittingly, fail to recognise that the forms celebrated as superior are those associated with the already privileged, middle-class culture which is then reproduced in schooling (Bernstein, 1973). Culturally mediated differences are postulated without analysing what the nature of the deficiency is supposed to be, without recognising that a deficiency can be defined only in relation to the demands of a particular context. Since contexts and meanings vary, according to a particular style a fixed status as deficient or lacking in some way not only homogenises culturally diverse practices, it also posits middle-class white language norms as universally superior while naturalising the cultural hierarchy.

Social relations influence what is said to and by children, and enter into the standards by which it is interpreted. I have argued that there could be no *one* model of language learning, and that we must attend to *difference*. However, the emphasis on differences can be only half the story, and we must move on to the analysis of how this difference is structured. Hence, for an adequate analysis of language development, questions of power necessarily arise. Yet (with the exception of Urwin's (1984) analysis discussed in Chapter 8) the notion of 'context' employed within developmental psycholinguistic research typically includes no notion of power. While 'conversational control' does arise as a topic, and asymmetrical patterning of adult–child discourse is explored (e.g. French and Maclure, 1981; Camaioni, 1979), this is discussed only in terms of the facilitating features of caregiver speech to set up shared meanings. That this 'facilitation' is also a form of social control is either taken for granted or assumed to be desirable. Just because power relationships, within parenting and within research, are so pervasive as to be taken for granted does not mean that they do not inform both accounts of what children know and how we know what they know. In the next chapter we move from a focus on difference to one on power.

FURTHER READING

For the classic elaboration of 'motherese', see chapters in:
Snow, C. and Ferguson, C. (eds) (1977) *Talking to Children*, Cambridge: Cambridge University Press.

For critiques of this, see:
Lieven, E. (in press) 'Crosslinguistic and crosscultural aspects of language addressed to children', and Pine, J. (in press) 'The language of primary caretakers', both the above in B. Richards and C. Galloway (eds) *Input and Interaction in Language Acquisition*, Cambridge: Cambridge University Press.

On cultural practices and language socialisation:

Schieffelin, B. and Ochs, E. (eds) (1986) *Language Socialisation across Cultures*, Cambridge: Cambridge University Press.

SUGGESTED ACTIVITIES

Taking accounts such as Snow (1972) and more popular variants such as the 'Tips for talking to toddlers' discussed above, explore these in relation to assumptions about gender, class and culture, such as:

- who are they addressed to?
- how do they address their audience?
- is the promotion of language linked to later developmental achievements and, if so, of what kind?
- to what extent is having children at home considered an educational rather than a caring activity?
- what demands does this pose?
- how necessary is this?

For a critical commentary on these assumptions, see Walkerdine and Lucey (1989), Lieven (in press) and Pine (in press).

Chapter 10

Language and power in developmental research

Speak roughly to your little boy
And beat him if he sneezes
He only does it to annoy
Because he knows it teases.

(Lewis Carroll, *Alice's Adventures in Wonderland*)

Those have most power to hurt us, that we love.

(Francis Beaumont, 1584–1616, *The Maid's Tragedy*)

In this chapter, I will address the consequences of taking power relations as central to developmental psychological and psycholinguistic research, and focus on four examples of research. These illustrate not only different approaches to the study of children's language use and functioning but will also be used to advocate the following claims. Firstly, we need to understand the power relationships in which children are positioned in order to interpret appropriately what children say within developmental psychological studies. Secondly, children *express* their developing understanding of relationships through language. Thirdly, children *use* alternative positionings made available to them through language to contest and change their social position. Fourthly, analysing the power relations that underpin developmental psychological research can, when acknowledged, work to aid rather than obscure the interpretation of children's actions and interactions.

This attention to the contexts in which developmental psychological research is constructed shows how the study of children's knowledge or 'abilities' is not separate from issues of language and power, but turns out to be inextricably intertwined with them. The conception of power here is not as a property to be possessed or exercised by one individual over another, but is a position set out within relationships; in this case relationships structured by the history of psychology and the positions elaborated (of professional surveillance) within discourses of scientific research. These are reinscribed within the current material practices of intervention that developmental psychology informs and legitimates (educational and clinical psychology, health visiting, social work) (see Henriques *et al.*, 1984; Parker, 1992a). Attending to power is not to treat it as a by-product of specific instances or utterances. Rather, discourses structure what can and cannot be spoken. Discourses construct the objects they discuss, and produce varieties of subjectivities that inhabit the frameworks of meaning they delineate (Foucault, 1972). So far this book has been concerned with the ways developmental psychology participates in institutional discourses that elaborate specific positions (of expert professional, recipient of service), and that in particular produce children and families as its subjects. In applying this perspective to the study of child language, we have seen in Chapters 8 and 9 how discourses of maternal sensitivity regulate women. In this chapter it will be argued that the power with which discourse is invested is not so much a matter of the way language is used, but rather, as we shall see, that power structures the selection, production and investigation of language.

BEYOND THE SENTENCE

In exploring how children learn, use language and are positioned within power relations intimated by language, we have to move beyond definitions of language in terms of syntactic and even semantic structures, to address the broader structuring of meanings that language plays a key role in expressing and maintaining. In other words, we have to extend the unit of study beyond the traditional domain of linguistics, the sentence, to wider linguistic and textual practices, that is to discourse.

Developmental psycholinguistic researchers have come to recognise that more than grammatical knowledge is required for competent language use. Moreover, meanings do not arise from sentences in isolation, but through referential systems that are connected both to each other and to the social practices which they describe and constitute. Part of what it means to learn to talk is to know the rules by which talk is organised. Children therefore need to know more than linguistic rules to participate in the negotiation of meanings. Since language use is connected to the performance of roles and relationships, and talk is the forum in which these are mediated, resisted, played out, children require some awareness of the rules by which social relationships are regulated.

But while the studies reviewed in this chapter arise from distinct and contrasting theoretical and methodological perspectives, they share three common assumptions. Firstly, they view meaning as determined by particular contexts, circumstances and relationships that hold at the moment of utterance, rather than as specified according to pre-existing and context-free rules. Secondly, the notion of power that informs these studies is one that does not accord children and their interlocutors a fixed or unique position. Power is not an absolute attribute or possession wielded by one party (for example, an adult) over another (the child). Rather, one's status or power position exists only in relation to others, indeed some would argue it constitutes that relationship. Thirdly, it follows from this *relative* notion of power that one is not uniquely positioned within relationships, but that multiple positions are made available through varieties of discursive practices. Hence, while part of being an adult is, within some discourses, to be accorded a (relatively) more powerful position than that of a child, children can draw upon discourses of, for example, parental duty and responsibility to exercise considerable control over others.

RESTRICTED RIGHTS TO TALK: THE SILENCE OF THE LAMBS?

In the first place, an adequate analysis of children's talk demands an understanding of power for the interpretation of what children say. Harvey Sacks (1972), using conversation analysis, discusses a piece of child's talk in terms of what its form indicates about the structuring of social interaction and the speaker's position within this. He uses conversation analysis to draw attention to the shared social knowledge we bring to bear in interpreting social behaviour, highlighting the work of interpretation done by competent communicators. Within this framework the selection of a particular linguistic form can be seen as the product or realisation of social meanings and categories.

As an approach, conversation analysis derives from ethnomethodological work in sociology which explores how we come to understand, account for and make comprehensible particular pieces of social interaction. An ethnomethodologist focuses on the ways language is used to conduct and correspondingly constitute forms of social organisation. A conversation analyst explores how conversation is organised in turns, how particular choices of linguistic form constrain the turn-taking sequence and what the particular pattern of openings, closings, conclusions, hesitations and repair devices indicates about the nature of the relationship between interactants. In other words, this is a sociolinguistic approach to language, but one which is not tied simply to documenting frequencies of occurrence or variation of linguistic forms. Rather, conversation analysts take a piece of text and attempt to tease out generalisations or rules that describe how the talk is organised (often producing a description that is much longer than the texts they investigate).

One text that Sacks (1972) uses to explore adult–child relations is this: 'The baby cried. The mommy picked it up', said by a 2-year-9-month-old little girl. Sachs sets out to show that not only are the two sentences connected, but that they qualify as a story. He argues that shared knowledge about social organisation enters into the topic frames by which talk is interpreted, so that mention of a baby invokes the expectation of a mommy. It would therefore be redundant for the child to have said '*Its* mommy'. Moreover, Sacks argues that, when taken in the context of children's restricted rights to talk, this reduced fragment of conversation can qualify as a story, and, further, that the elliptical nature of the story is itself an index of the child's limited access to what he calls the 'conversational floor'. Rather than adopting conventional story markers such as 'once upon a time', she introduces her story by 'announcing a problem', a conversational device that allows parties to commence talking in circumstances where they would otherwise be flouting social norms. (Consider 'It looks like rain' said at a bus stop to initiate talk.) Announcing the 'problem' of the baby crying therefore constitutes an appropriate 'ticket' to start talking. From opening the story with the problem, the mommy picking up the baby is an appropriate end or resolution to the 'problem' given current norms about the role of women and their capacities to satisfy babies' needs. In this context of limited space to talk, Sacks argues it would therefore be superfluous to add 'and then the baby went to sleep', which would have been a more explicit story ending. Hence the recognition of the power asymmetries within which children are positioned brings about a re-valuation of the status and function of what they say. Furthermore, the structural forms of power relations themselves arise from generalised frameworks of meaning and organisation such as familial discourses.

While it may seem far-fetched to invest so much interpretation in such a little text, the overall significance of this example lies in the attention to speakers' rights to talk, the opportunities available for taking the conversational floor and the implications these have for the psychological evaluation of the quality and quantity of what children say. As a further illustration, Sacks discusses the characteristic opening question used by children: 'You know what?' This is one of a curious class of questions that properly invites another question ('What?') as its answer. Moreover it is the initial answerer rather than the questioner who has the 'reserved right' to speak again after the other speaks. This may seem a paradoxical device for children to use to promote their access to the con-versational floor. However, not only does the child speak again through the obligation to reply to the 'What?' question, she is also answering an 'open' question, in the sense that the asker does not know, but the child *does know* the answer. The child can then go on to talk about whatever she deems to be an appropriate answer through meeting the obligation of replying to a question.

Sacks takes the prevalence of 'You know what?' questions in children's talk as indicative of children's restricted speaking rights: by using this device thay can ensure that they will be allowed to speak again (through the obligation to answer the question 'What?'). What this pattern of turn taking suggests is that children have rights to *begin* to talk but they may continue only if requested. This device guarantees them some space to talk within the conventions of the structure of conversation. Hence the structure of language is used to secure, albeit limited, conversational access by children. An understanding of children's status and speaking rights therefore enters into the form and structure of what they say.

LEARNING ONE'S PLACE

Children also indicate through the language they use their developing *awareness* of the power relationships within which they (and others) are positioned. Children's sociolinguistic skills of interpreting and adapting their talk to particular contexts has been used to assess their social as well as linguistic understanding, as in Elizabeth Slosberg Andersen's (1990) research with children who were invited to display their understanding of gender, professional and caregiving linguistic registers through playing out scenarios with puppets. Much work in this area has focused on children's use of markers of politeness. Ervin Tripp *et al.*'s (1984) year-long observational study of four families with two or more children aged between 2 and 8 investigated children's developing understanding of power relations within their families through the analysis of what they call 'linguistic control acts'. In analysing the structure of talk addressed to parents, siblings, child visitors and researchers, they noted that children's 'effective power', or the ability to get compliance from their addressee, was dependent on many factors. Although typically accorded a low-status position, within the familial context children could exert some power, particularly in securing compliance from caregivers when requesting goods and services constructed as due to them by virtue of discourses of parental obligation to care for children.

Ervin Tripp *et al.* (1984) also analysed how the form of requests reflected both the esteem with which the addressee is endowed by the speaker and the speaker's evaluation of the 'costliness' of the request. A developmental pattern was documented of increasing variety of forms in which to express deference, ranging from overt forms (such as 'Please'), to justifications (where the speaker attempts to present a rationale for their request or bases it on common-sense norms rather than naked assertion of power), to more indirect forms of allusion or hinting, where the goal of the request is not made explicit (as where 'It's very cold in here' functions as an indirect request to put the fire on). This covert form expresses the greatest esteem for the speaker by according him or her the choice of ignoring the implicit request. Ervin Tripp *et al.* also analyse examples of children rapidly moving from more to less explicit forms of request as they are forced to revalue its 'cost' to the addressee. The authors report the following interaction in which Patty, an adult female researcher, was addressed by Saul, a 3-year-old boy:

S: Hey, I'm hungry
P: Didn't you eat your breakfast?
S: No, I didn't. I just go to bed, and I want to eat. I'm hungry
P: You're hungry
S: Could you get me something to eat?
P: No I can't. You have to ask your Mom
S: Well, Momma won't give me something
P: (laughing) Well, why not?
S: Because he he [sic] won't fix me anything
P: Doesn't she usually?
S: No. Do you have a lot of cake at your house?

(from Ervin Tripp *et al.*, 1984: 133)

In this extract the differing formulations used by Saul reflect his changing evaluations of the 'cost' of his request. Initially this was expressed as a direct demand ('I'm hungry'), then it became clear that this was a request that Patty was not going to comply with immediately. Saul moved then to justification ('I want to eat. I'm hungry'), and then to a polite formulation ('Could you get me something to eat?') and finally resorted to a very indirect hint ('Do you have a lot of cake in your house?'). Once again issues of power are central not only in the use of deferential forms, but in the expectation that Patty as a *female* researcher would respond to demands cast in terms of need and nurturance.

As the example above illustrates, in the display of flexibility in the forms and strategies used in relation to the cost of their requests, young children also demonstrate their awareness of gender-specific roles and responsibilities through the differential forms of their requests to their parents. Less polite imperatives were directed to mothers and more appeasing explanations to fathers. This reflects culturally sanctioned expectations that mothers function to meet the demands of children, especially if these are expressed as 'needs'. Children correspondingly used assertions of want and helplessness to make their mothers comply. The authors comment on the utterance of a 7-year-old boy who said 'If you don't give [me] some now, I won't want any later'. In order for this to function as a threat, we must presume that mothers have some investment in their caregiving role, at least in the form of being seen to fulfil their role as proper mothers. Correlatively, mothers were noted as being more co-operative to the requests of girls than boys. Moreover, it seemed that girls used a greater range of strategies in dealing with demands made of them while not complying any more frequently than boys; girls ignored requests as much as they refused or complied with them. What this study indicates is, firstly, that gender issues are highly salient within routine parent–child interaction (to both parent and child) and, secondly, that gender enters into the forms of language expressed by and directed to children. This awareness of discourses of gender can be regarded as but a specific example of the ways social meanings, including those which mark power asymmetries, inform the contexts and the products of children's talk.

CHANGING PLACES?

Not only do children express their awareness of asymmetries and roles through the forms of language they use, they also draw on alternative discourses to change their positioning. Walkerdine (1981) analyses some astonishing material where two 3-year-old boys verbally sexually harass their female nursery school teacher in response to her criticism of their behaviour towards another (girl) child. Walkerdine discusses this in terms of the boys' assuming the position of men within language in relation to which the teacher, as a sexually objectified woman, is positioned as inferior. They therefore counter their relatively power-less position as pupils in relation to her authority as a teacher by using the male discourse which positions women as passive and powerless. What this illustrates is that not only are there a range of possible positions made available by alternative discourses structuring social relations, but these positions are competing and contradictory. In this example the multiplicity of positionings functions as a resource by which the inferior status arising from the configuration of one discourse can be resisted.

In Burman (1992a) I describe how I set up a role play within interviews I was conducting with children by which I asked them to interview me. Intended as an attempt to create a more egalitarian structure within my research, at one point I found myself constrained by the very discursive structure I had set up to answer questions that demanded a degree of personal disclosure I found most un-comfortable. (It should also be noted that this was a situation in which I, like many other researchers, routinely placed children.) When Anna asked me if I had a 'boyfriend', not only was I unable to avoid answering the question without challenging her conversational control and thereby departing from the fragile 'role play' I had set up, but I was also unable to define my own terms to talk about relationships and friendships. The pressure for my compliance arose from my own presentation of the interview encounter as voluntary and collaborative. Not only was I forced to position myself within the discourse of compulsory hetero-sexuality (Rich, 1983), but the requirement to speak arose from those immediate and wider discursive structures of the role play and the research interview that had authorised me to set up the research encounter in the first place.

Even though this arose within an interviewing relationship within which I was positioned as more powerful, within adult–child and experimenter–subject relations, I could not therefore depart from the structure of talk which positioned me as subordinate and under obligation to respond. My child 'interviewer' was able to use the discursive structure of the interview encounter to assert control over conversational topic as well as turn.

In *The Mastery of Reason* (1988), Valerie Walkerdine discusses how casting a psychological assessment within the framework of a task or game (as develop-mental psychologists often do) presents a misleading representation of the struc-tural power relations of experimenter and child. In particular, the kinds of questions typically asked of children within such investigations draw upon pedagogical discursive practices, such as asking children pseudo-questions, that is questions where they know that we know the answers. She argues:

> What is a game, and how are the roles of the participants defined? How far does a device designed to lessen the effects of a powerful experimenter, by 'putting the child at ease', also serve to render the power invisible, by dis-claiming its presence, while making the child an object of an evaluative reading from a different discourse? It could be argued that, rather than helping, it is dishonest and disingenuous.
>
> (Walkerdine, 1988: 54)

In the instance reported above I was required to adhere to the subject position of 'respondent' I had assumed through my obligation to respect the rules of the pseudo-egalitarian structure I had set up. This is an interesting example precisely because it demonstrates how the partial but not complete coexistence of experi-mental and 'game' ('playing interviews') discursive practices can give rise to contradictions and divergences of subject positions of the kind analysed above. But this exceptional instance, itself brought about by a particularly assertive little girl, highlights the much more pervasive situation where the teaching/ experimental discourse so invades and informs pseudo-collaborative psychologist–child interaction that, in the terms typically formulated, we cannot determine by which rules and roles the children are playing. This raises questions not only about the ways children read or understand the more covert mani- pulations of psychologist–child assessment, and the delusions of democracy that psychologists playing games with children may harbour (see also Chapter 12 for a critique of notions of democracy in education), but also links in with the fantasy of non-intervention and untainted scholarly purity with which observational work is often invested:

> it is important to note the positive effectivity of the experimental discourse in positioning me as 'experimenter' and the children as 'subjects'. This provides a set of rules, of regulations of practice, the interpretation of the practice, the interaction itself, in which certain things are done, said and then read. . . . Like the classroom, the experiment produces a discursive practice in which evidence is read, and a regime of truth produced; in that sense, then, the dichotomies objective/subjective take on a different significance. Similarly, those criticisms of experiments which treat observational data as more 'natural' or 'ecologically valid' fall into a trap, which fails to engage with the positive effectivity of the discursive practice in which any performance is produced.
>
> (Walkerdine, 1988: 51)

FIXING INTERPRETATION

In addition to being a means of expression of, and intervention within, social relations, language is also the forum in which linguistic understanding is investi- gated. We have already seen how gender and cultural assumptions are repro- duced both within language and the study of language. It is time to look more generally at the intersection between contexts of talk and the constitution of children's talk as a research object.

The analysis of 'discourse' both as method and as theoretical 'perspective' has had considerable impact within social psychology (Parker, 1992a; Parker and Shotter, 1990), and offers useful critiques of developmental psychology (see e.g. Davies and Harré, 1990; Henriques et al., 1984). The recognition that social meanings are inscribed within language means that language is productive, as well as reflective, of meaning. While language constitutes meaning, this meaning is not only a free-floating linguistic array but is also irreducibly tied to material- political structures. Indeed the very concept of discourse disrupts the idea of 'language', since it is not reducible to the merely linguistic. Requests from teachers to have dreams interpreted, to have their labelling of a child as 'damaged' ratified, anxious questions from mothers after their children have taken part in some developmental psychological study of 'Did she do all right?', all these are routine indications of, elements of, the contradictory but privileged discourses, or sets of expert knowledge, with which developmental psychological researchers are credited. This book has already described the discourses that structured the emergence of developmental psychological practice and the consequences of these for its terms of enquiry, in particular in constituting 'the child', 'the family' and women (as mothers) as focal objects. The positions these (clinical, scientific) discourses delineate overdetermine and structure current developmental psychological practice. As the above examples illustrate, they structure the ways in which developmental psychological researchers are perceived when they go into schools or homes. They fuel the power of evaluation and regulation with which researchers are invested.

Issues of power correspondingly enter into the discursive structure by which developmental psychological research is constituted and interpreted. They inform the production as well as the interpretation of what children say. As discussed in earlier chapters in this book, some current critiques of developmental psychology have highlighted how the dominant discourses which portray children as inherently benign and mothers as facilitative of development thereby suppress or fail to see the ambiguity and indeterminacy of, especially infant, action and interaction (Bradley, 1989; Urwin, 1984). The power of the discourses therefore works not only at the level of determining the agenda for research questions, but also in selectively structuring the 'evidence'. One kind of strategy to explore the ways power has entered into the structure of developmental psychological research is to recover the multiple meanings that have been obscured. On the other hand, an analysis which attends to the diversity and ambiguity of interpretations of children's talk and activity can simply work to celebrate the multiplicity of interpretations without clearly theorising the constitutive effects of power.

Within the role-play part of the study from which the example above was drawn, another child, Ravi, moved from asking me questions (about how I arrived at the school and where my bicycle was) to make the comment 'Sometimes bicycles get stolen'. I interpreted this statement as an offer of an issue he wanted to talk about, and the lexical indeterminacy of the statement not only as indicating his awareness that he was deviating from the role-play structure but also as constituting an indirect request to abandon it. In this context the role play was dispensable, or at least positioned as enframed within, or constituted by, a set of broader structural power relations which accorded me the right to accept or reject his offer. The important point to note about this is that in terms of my original, quite typical, developmental psychological research question the indeterminacy of Ravi's statement could be taken to indicate a failure of understanding rather than comprising a specific discursive negotiation. 'Sometimes bicycles get stolen' is a syntactically and semantically anomalous statement, with maximum lexical markers of uncertainty – of time, person and number. On a purely linguistic reading it can generate at least three possible sets of interpretations, as friendly advice, as a veiled threat and as a request to narrate a specific past experience. But the ambiguity it expresses qualifies not the certainty of what has happened or might happen, but the tentativeness of the request. The uncertainty does not concern whether or not a bicycle has been stolen, or whose bicycle has been stolen, but rather whether it was permissible for him to talk about *his*. Questions of power have here entered the linguistic structure of what is said as well as how it is interpreted (see Burman 1992a, 1993).

While this example harks back in some ways to Sacks' analysis, described earlier, of the fruitful ambiguity of seemingly indeterminate syntactic forms (such as 'D'you know what?') as a means to gain permission to speak, its significance can be developed in two ways. Firstly, taking such issues seriously demands a careful scrutiny and revaluation of the contexts in which received wisdom about children's knowledge and abilities is arrived at. Secondly, despite the multiple readings and referents that can be drawn from Ravi's statement, an attention to the structural effects of power relations within the adult–child, experimenter–child encounter can work to disambiguate, or fix, interpretation. Discourses, including those constituting developmental psychology, are more than linguistic. Language may constitute the material world, and may even comprise the totality of our understanding of it, but the discursive arrangement of meaning arises from material-political structures. There may be no unadulterated 'truth' of what children are 'really' like or 'really' know, but rather our task is to be better able to interpret and recognise how the context of investigation structures that which we 'discover' or document.

In the past three chapters I have described moves to set up more socially based accounts of language development and use (which have largely failed within more traditional approaches); drawn attention to the importance of issues of difference which are usually suppressed or devalued within mainstream models, but which actually demonstrate the impossibility of a single model of the language learner or language teacher; finally this chapter has focused on power relations, as structuring differences between children, parents and researchers. Drawing attention to these power relations is not (only) a matter of highlighting the ways children are oppressed and how they manoeuvre within these relationships. For these are not simply local aberrations or abuses, but form the material and discursive structures within which, and in relation to which, developmental psychology functions. The realms of signification developmental psychology elaborates, of 'sensitive' mothers, of 'damaged' or even 'whole' children (see later), of scientific research and clinical evaluation (read disinterested façade masking manipulation and exploitation?), are firmly connected to the historical and current professional-political practice of developmental psychology.

FURTHER READING

The following texts specifically address adult–child, and in some cases specifically psychologist–child, relationships:

Burman, E. (1992a) 'Feminism and discourse in developmental psychology: power, subjectivity and interpretation', *Feminism and Psychology, 2, 1*: 45–60.

Davies, B. and Harré, R. (1990) 'Positioning: the discursive production of selves', *Journal for the Theory of Social Behaviour, 20, 1*: 43–63.

Walkerdine, V. (1981) 'Sex, power and pedagogy', *Screen Education, 38*: 14–21, reprinted in *Schoolgirl Fictions*, London: Verso, 1990.

Walkerdine, V. (1988) *The Mastery of Reason: cognitive development and the production of rationality*, London: Routledge.

SUGGESTED ACTIVITIES

Tape (ensuring informed consent) some adult–child interaction, of the sort that happens at teatime. Use this as a resource for:

a) engaging with the issues raised by doing transcription, of which those raised by child language pose in miniature the wider questions about selectivity and interpretation in the transforming of an auditory representation into a written one. For material on this, see:

Ochs, E. (1979) 'Transcription as theory', in E. Ochs and B. Schieffelin (eds) *Developmental Pragmatics*, New York: Academic Press,

and more generally:

Tedlock, D. (1983) *The Spoken Word and the Work of Interpretation*, Philadelphia: University of Pennsylvania Press.

b) discussing the variety and complexity of the power relationships being elaborated, in terms of what broader sets of meanings (of, e.g., gender or parental or child responsibilities) they instantiate.

c) If the taping is not being conducted in the home of the person who is taping, and he or she is present:

- how is he or she addressed or included within encounter?
- if they are not present, then why not (and what fantasies of non-contamination of data are being maintained)?
- does this remove the process of interpretation?
- how is the purpose of the enterprise discussed, and what does this indicate about the position of the psychologist/student/researcher?

Part IV

Cognitive development
The making of rationality

This final part analyses the significance of Piaget's contribution as a major intellectual figure and resource for developmental psychology. Chapter 11 explores how cultural issues mingle with those of method in how and why his ideas were taken up; Chapter 12 considers the impact of the educational applications associated with his ideas; and Chapter 13 moves from the cognitive developmental account of moral development to reflect on the moral status of developmental psychological practice, and this book within it.

Chapter 11

The production of Piagetian psychology

He's researching surface texture, differentiating between colours, and developing his audiosensory perception. He thinks he's playing with a rattle.

(for Duplo, *Parents* magazine, December 1984)

The name most associated with developmental psychology, indeed in popular accounts almost synonymous with it, is that of Jean Piaget. No nurse, social worker, counsellor or teacher will complete her training without learning about his stage model of cognitive development. This is somewhat surprising when we consider that Piaget's primary interest was neither in psychology nor in education. It is useful when reflecting on perceptions of the contribution of Piaget's work to recall the variety of disciplines he worked within, and across. So, while his role in education, psychology and philosophy of science is well known, the fact that he also held professorships in sociology from 1939–52, and before that from 1925–9 (jointly with psychology and philosophy of science), is largely forgotten. He was also a member of the International Psycho-Analytic Association, was in analysis for some time and even wrote on developmental psychology and psychoanalysis (Piaget, 1919), but most Anglo-US psychologists are unaware of this.

Despite this, Piaget remains the dominant *psychological* resource for professionals who want to know how children think. This is irrespective of other possible contenders (Vygotsky, for example – see Chapter 8). The current academic climate largely downplays Piaget's importance (the March 1990 special issue of *The Psychologist*, magazine of the British Psychological Society, on 'Research Trends in Developmental Psychology' contained no mention of his work). However, features of both the model and his questions live on. Indeed, it could be argued that it is precisely because Piaget's influence on developmental psychology has been so profound in structuring the form of the discipline that it is largely invisible.

Impressive as Piaget's work was, its popularity (and subsequent fluctuations in popularity) is not simply a response to its intrinsic worth. This chapter explores the role and impact of Piaget's work, treating this not (only) in terms of the achievements of an individual man. Rather, his work provides a case study in evaluating steps in the process of formulating, taking up and interpreting a set of ideas. The movement from theorist to inscription in practices is complex. Piaget's guiding preoccupations reflected the cultural and historical contexts that his work also came to inform. Especially within Anglo-US readings of his work, aspects incongruent with the dominant empiricist culture are ignored or treated as flaws. As we shall see, some of these selections and suppressions provide useful indications of themes and functions that structure contemporary developmental psychology.

OF MOLLUSCS AND MEN: PIAGET AND DEVELOPMENTAL PSYCHOLOGY

Piaget has been held responsible for a number of specific contributions to developmental psychology. He is credited with the recognition that children's thinking is qualitatively different from that of adults, that different ways of thinking predominate at different ages and that these correspond with progressively more adequate ways of organising knowledge. Hence his status as a stage theorist, and the association of his name in education and welfare practices with the apparatus of ages and stages (e.g. Burns, 1986), despite the fact that notions of stage sequences were in wide circulation by the beginning of the twentieth century. His work is generally portrayed as humanist, countering the mechanistic accounts of child learning and training put forward by behaviourism, and emphasising children's active involvement in, and construction of, their learning environment (Gardner, 1982; Ginsberg and Opper, 1979). Piaget's focus on the organisation of knowledge and the elaboration of rules governing this organisation places him firmly as the exponent of the wider intellectual movement of structuralism within developmental psychology (Broughton, 1981a).

His emphasis on adaptation reflects the backcloth of evolutionary theory, and he was instrumental in importing this theory into psychology. As the celebrated story goes, he started out working on environmental adaptations in molluscs and went on to apply the same concepts of assimilation, accommodation and adaptation to the development of logical thinking. But not only did he combine the disciplines through the transitions in his working life, he also set out to link biology and philosophy through the study of the development of the child. Piaget was the creator and architect of 'genetic epistemology' (the study of the origins and growth of knowledge) as an expression of his interest in the developmental construction and organisation of thought. The overarching questions that prompted this model arose within the same late nineteenth- and early twentieth-century concern to uncover 'truths' about the nature of thinking which informed the development of social anthropology, psychiatry and criminology.

A further factor in the popularity of Piaget's model was that it presented a model of development in interactionist terms at a time of dissatisfaction with the 'empty vessel' environmental determinism of behaviourism as well as the rationalism and innatism of genetic determinism. Offering a model that drives development from the concrete to the abstract, he traced a trajectory from early reaction patterns to primitive habits to rational, logical thought. Piaget's work also paved the way for the cognitive approach that has come to dominate psychology for the past three decades, with his influence seen most particularly in cognitive science and artificial intelligence (Boden, 1979; Papert, 1980). In terms of methodology, Piaget attempted to counter some of the spurious assumptions of empiricism that guided standardised testing methods through his 'clinical' or 'critical' interviewing procedures, although this aspect has been eclipsed within the selective incorporation of Piaget's work within Anglo-US developmental psychology.

PIAGET'S QUESTIONS

Although the consequences of this are rarely understood, Piaget's project of genetic epistemology meant that he was interested in children only insofar as they instantiated, and provided a forum for investigating, general epistemological questions about the origins and growth of thought. There are several implications of this. Firstly, his preoccupation with the general knower or 'epistemic subject' rather than individual children means that he was not primarily a 'psychologist'. Irrespective of whether there is a specific domain of the psychological, Piaget intended to work in psychology for only a brief period before returning to biology or philosophy. His interest lay in providing a general account of the emergence of knowledge, rather than a specific analysis of how and when individual children exhibited this. Interestingly, despite holding many professorships in psychology and education within his lifetime (including in experimental psychology) in France and Switzerland, he had no formal qualifications in psychology, and when in 1976 he wanted to present his book on the equilibration of cognitive structures to the University of Geneva (where he had worked since 1929) as a thesis for a doctorate in psychology, the university officials refused on the grounds that his work could not be contained within one discipline (Gruber and Vonèche, 1977: xiii).

Many of the debates around the status of Piagetian research arise from the failure to appreciate that Piaget was not a psychologist nor primarily interested in the psychological implications of his work. Nevertheless, genuine difficulties do arise in determining how to turn the Piagetian epistemological project into a psychological one. Through his exclusive focus on the abstracted epistemic knower, Piaget blurred the distinction between individual and socio-cultural context. As Venn and Walkerdine (1978) put it:

> For Piaget, the individual subject is an exemplar, the typical representative of the species. He subscribes to the Lamarckian idea of cumulative assimilation,

whereby the characteristics of individuals over time are resorbed into a single intellectual organism. Thus the processes, including those of cognitive development are the same in all single individuals, so that one need only study any exemplar and generalise.

(Venn and Walkerdine, 1978: 79)

The Piagetian model is therefore unable to theorise cultural and historical change in relation to the development of knowledge. Moreover, since the content of thought is accorded less importance than its (generalisable) structure, the emphasis on action is eroded in favour of a tendency towards increasing abstraction and idealisation:

for Piaget the development of thought becomes 'indifferent to' the actual content of thought and the material base, although constructed out of it. He speaks of action on the concrete as being the basis out of which the operational structures are constructed, but his account is in the end unsatisfactory because he is more concerned with the results of abstraction as indicators of the way the mind works. . . . He is not dealing with scientific knowledge as such.

(Venn and Walkerdine, 1978: 87)

Hence Piaget depicted a subject who is irrevocably isolated and positioned outside history and society (Riegel, 1976; Broughton, 1981b).

Having introduced some of the key aspects of Piaget's project and preoccupations, we can now turn to the ways these have been taken up and drawn upon to warrant particular psychological and educational practices. The popular equation of Piaget with developmental psychology threatens to ignore the conditions under which Piaget's work became so well known, and in particular its continuities with other bodies of theory which facilitated its assimilation into Anglo-US psychology. The child-centred approach with which his work is so heavily identified pre-dates his appearance on the British and US intellectual 'scene' (Walkerdine, 1984). Moreover, Piaget's association with the current practice of developmental psychology, with a repertoire of conservation tasks cast as standardised assessments, seriously misrepresents his own methodological approach, ignores the debates about method that dogged Anglo-American debates with Geneva-based researchers and does not adequately account for the processes which transformed single case studies into experimentally administered tests (Burman, 1994). This selective incorporation is not so much a misreading as an opportunistic utilisation of techniques to fit into the already burgeoning 'technologies of the social' to which developmental psychology contributed.

TERMS OF THE DEBATES: CONTINENTS AND CONFLICTS

Clashes over methods have played a major part in debates about the status of Piagetian theory, disputes that have been overdetermined by broader cultural and geographically informed differences in aims and epistemological framework. Put briefly, Piaget's investigations with children took place as the social sciences were moving from informal observation and experimentation to developing standardised forms of assessment, a tendency that Piaget, in general, vigorously opposed. His 'clinical method', or, as he later called it, 'critical examination', is a flexible semi-structured interviewing technique, involving several investigations across a variety of problems that is designed to provide a profile of each child's thinking. While Piaget's early investigations relied primarily on interpreting children's reports and opinions, his investigations increasingly became based on children's actions as well as what they said about the result of their actions. This approach contrasts strongly with standardised experimental techniques in its emphasis on treating each encounter with a child in its own terms to 'take account of the whole mental context' (Piaget, 1929: 19).

It is significant that Vygotsky, while critical of Piaget for his neglect of attention to language and culture, regarded Piaget's method as his most important contribution. From their very different perspectives, what they shared was an understanding of the participation of the researcher within the experimental task. Hence Vygotsky depicted developmental research as indistinguishable from teaching and instruction contexts. In other words, the context for discovering what children know is inseparable from teaching them. He saw empirical research as linked to the practical promotion of children's psychological functioning in future situations. The experimenter is therefore an active participant in the context of a study, aiming to help children construct new means to solve the problems posed to them (Vygotsky, 1978b). As with Piaget, the 'dependent variable' within Vygotsky's method is the experimenter's observation of the process by which the solution is reached. This model of the research process is a far cry from mainstream British and US developmental work in which the variables under investigation are located firmly within the child (rather than constructed in relation to the child) and the context of investigation is seen as neutral or invisible.

Hence a number of false oppositions have structured and polarised the Anglo-US interpretation of Piaget and Geneva-based Piagetian research. One issue that fuelled the industry of Piaget critique was based on a misrendering of the conservation task to sever the children's judgements from their explanations, with dispute over which of these was the more accurate index of children's knowledge (e.g. Brainerd, 1973). A similar literature was devoted to splitting action from account (that is, what children said from what they did), giving rise to debates about whether verbal or non-verbal measures are the most appropriate (Miller, 1976; Siegel, 1978; Wheldall and Poborca, 1980). Inadequate as these treatments were, what they did correctly highlight was the ambiguous role of language and neglect of social relations within Piagetian research. Whatever their insensitivities to the subtleties of Piaget's theoretical edifice, the debates about 'décalage' (which for Piaget has a complex theoretical meaning, but which is interpreted by Anglo-US researchers simply in terms of within-subject and between-subject variation) do question the structural character of the model. Studies which demonstrated that children (e.g. Donaldson, 1978) and adults (McCabe, 1987) performed inconsistently, or that their performance could vary dramatically according to slight modifications of task characteristics, challenged the idea of the successive emergence of distinct and coherent structures of thinking.

Broad differences of interpretation that are focused around methodological issues are also reflected in contrasting approaches to the concept of development. While Piaget was committed to a qualitative model of development in which stages came to play a key role, the preoccupations that motivated, in particular, the US research concerned the acceleration of development, as typified in the 'training studies' which try to teach children to do Piagetian-type problems at ever earlier ages. Piaget scornfully termed this the 'American question'. This development also challenges the qualitative and structural features of the model, replacing Piaget's temporally ordered sequence of development with a much more malleable motion of learning (although accounts varied according to whether they proposed that the period of time between stages was compressed or called for stages to be disposed of altogether). However, in recent years there have been indications of rapprochements on this issue (e.g. Karmiloff Smith, 1979).

A final area of misconception that spans both theory and method concerns the aims of Piagetian investigation. Piaget's ideas and research are often treated as investigating and determining whether or not a child 'has' a particular concept. Critiques of Piaget have largely set out to show that under different circumstances children can demonstrate possession of the qualities associated with the concept at ages earlier than those indicated by Piaget – the so-called 'early successes' Donaldson (1978) and others describe. However, Piaget was less concerned with what children knew, and more interested in the status of their knowledge (Piaget, 1929). His interest in mapping the growth of logic onto children's thinking led him to develop a taxonomy of children's reponses to explore whether children regarded their opinions as necessary or contingent. This is an interest more in 'propositional attitude' (Russell, 1982), or the status children accord their judgements as knowledge, or belief, or opinion, than in concept acquisition.

CONTINUITIES AND RESOURCES: MODERNITY, SCIENCE AND GENDER

My account may seem to imply that Piaget's concerns were far removed from those who have taken up his work, especially in Britain and the US. I have focused so far on points of tension to highlight the process and problems of this selective incorporation of Piaget's work. However, there are also important points of convergence that clarify how and why particular selective readings of Piaget came to occupy so important a position within Anglo-US developmental psychology and its associated educational and welfare practices. In particular, the amenability of his ideas for incorporation within apparatuses of social regulation together with a common commitment to science and progress brought together these diverse traditions in the name of modern improvement.

In general, developmental psychology is a paradigmatically *modern* discipline, arising at a time of commitment to narratives of truth, objectivity, science
and reason. It shares its origins with psychology and the modern social sciences
generally in the late nineteenth century, when scientific discoveries and developments were revolutionising Western Europe at every level from sanitation to
railways, to factory production, to the triumph of science over religion. As
already discussed in Chapter 1, developmental psychology participated in the
post-Darwinian theorising which linked individual change and growth with
evolutionary outcomes (Riley, 1983). It was in this context that Piaget formulated
his project of 'genetic epistemology', attempting to apply biological concepts of
adaptation, environmental pressure and change to humans, which he specifically
identified within the development of the child.

Piaget's commitment to the modern project can be seen in his depiction of the
developing child as a budding scientist systematically encountering problems in
the material world, developing hypotheses and learning by discovery and activity
(Piaget, 1957). Here the individual is the unit of development, rationally re-
solving obstacles presented by, and within, the material world. Logic, epitomised
within 'the scientific method', is cast as the pinnacle of intellectual development.
This produces a model of thinking which treats the individual as prior and
separate, and celebrates activity and discovery – qualities which also carry
colonial and gendered nuances. As the quotation at the beginning of this chapter
indicates, science, itself a gendered practice, becomes imported into representations of children such that the quintessential developing child is a boy (see
also, e.g., Burman, in press; Walkerdine, 1988; Walkerdine *et al.* 1989). Such
assumptions are made and remade manifest in current advertising for 'educational' toys, where, as well as depicting the learner as a scientist, 'he' (*sic*) is also
an astronaut:

> His space top's heading for Venus (It's just to the left of the fridge). It's
> countdown time for intrepid astronauts.
>
> (*Under Five*, December 1990)

And as a construction engineer:

> Fisher-Price understand that no major construction job is complete without a
> chicken on top. Even the simple act of picking up one of the blocks helps a
> baby learn how to grip. Once he's mastered that he'll try stacking them up.
> This is good too – it develops his eye/hand co-ordination. And even if he
> knocks the whole lot down, it's still educational. (It shows a baby he's in
> control and gives him his first feelings of independence.)
>
> (for Fisher Price in *Practical Parenting*, September 1988)

Notice how being destructive or making a mess is sanitised ('if he knocks the
whole lot down, it's still educational') so that any protesting mother is positioned
as impairing motor ('developing eye/hand co-ordination') and emotional
development ('shows a baby he's in control and gives him his first feelings of

independence'). Texts such as these are permeated by a tone of indulgence and a requirement to bolster a fragile ego. Parent and child mirror the heterosexual and gender roles of woman and man through the positioning of woman as carer and the developing child as masculine pioneer, or at least woman providing the beneficent gaze by which the illusion of the male(child)'s power and autonomy is maintained. (In Burman, in press a, I explore other investments in the portrayal of mother and child as a heterosexual couple.)

Similarly, modern preoccupations not only permeate the identification of the subject of Piagetian developmental psychology, but also structure the model itself. In Piaget's account, the goal of development is greater adaptation to changing and ever more complex environmental demands. The developmental trajectory of children's thinking follows the 'up the hill' model of science and progress (Rorty, 1980): a hierarchical model of 'cognitive structures' emerges whereby a more mature logic arises from and supersedes earlier and less adequate structures. The developmental path this produces is depicted as common to all, irrespective of culture and history. As such it is thoroughly normative. The clash between Piaget, with his commitment to internal processes of 'equilibration' determining the pace of development, and the social reforming tendencies of 'compensatory education' (associated particularly with the US and the work of Bruner) plays out the contradiction between naturalism and cultural intervention that pervade the modern project generally (Burman, 1992b). The specific shape that these debates take within child-centred education forms the focus of the next chapter.

SCIENCE AND MORALITY

Two further strands associated with modernity are exemplified within the Piagetian model (and not only the Anglo-US misreading of his work). The model is committed to the project of human emancipation (improving the condition of human life). As argued in the last section, the modern commitment to progress imposes an enclosed, self-sufficient, autonomous individual.

Secondly, as well as treating scientific rationality as the pinnacle of psychological development, Piaget follows the modern project in his faith in science as promoting well-being and peaceful coexistence as opposed to Social Darwinism, war, competition and so on. In common with others of his time, Piaget, developing his ideas in Europe between two world wars, was deeply concerned to envisage how morality and reason could prevail over what he saw as biological doom and destruction (Piaget 1918a, 1933).

> Science is one of the finest examples of the adaptation of the human mind. It is the victory of mind over matter. But how has this success been achieved? Not merely by accumulating knowledge and experience. Far from it. Rather by constructing an intellectual co-ordinating tool by means of which the mind is able to connect one fact with another. This is what we need socially . . . a

new mental instrument at once intellectual and moral, for in such a sphere the two things are one.

(Piaget, 1933: 7)

In addition to his commitment to science, Piaget's religious background within liberal protestantism and active involvement within the student Christian activity testify to a lifelong preoccupation with (and commitment to) reconciling faith with religion and finding a rational basis for morality. Many of his earliest writings were on this theme, including his semi-autobiographical novel (Piaget, 1918b). Vidal (1987) argues that Piaget's motivation to find the roots of morality in social coexistence derive as much from his early rejection of metaphysics and his search for a rational and objective basis for religion, as from a desire to refute innatism in developmental psychobiology. Moreover, this was explicitly associated with accounts of disorder and upheaval in the political sphere. While this rhetoric does not appear in Piaget's accounts of children's thinking, Vidal argues that they formed part of the motivation for his investigation of children's thinking, along with the general project to psychologise metaphysics.

LIBERAL PARADOXES

In these ways, Piaget's model of individual development is deeply imbued with liberalism. The transition from egocentric to socially adapted thinking is explicitly formulated in anti-authoritarian terms:

Every progress made in the different moral and social domains results from the fact that we have freed ourselves from egocentrism and from intellectual and moral coercion.

(Piaget, 1933: 22)

In advocating 'new', 'child-centred' educational approaches, Piaget subscribed to the liberal view of education as the key to greater co-operation, and cautioned against the dangers of imposing a particular set of values or political philosophy, unable to acknowledge the imposition of the particular politics he advocated. As for other social reformers, childhood for Piaget became a topic of interest as the site of intervention for a particular social project, namely the promotion of peace and harmony. The challenge of educating children involved recognising adult faults of self-centredness and subjection to social coercion, as well as children's condition.

Childhood, I believe, will furnish an explanation of our difficulties and failings. At the same time, however, it will teach us how to do better than we have done, showing us the reserves of energy that exist in human beings and the sort of education that will enable us to rise above our present level of development.

(Piaget, 1933: 13)

In these sentiments Piaget subscribed to Enlightenment philosophical beliefs that children can teach us what society can be like, can testify to the potential which participation in society has drummed out of us, harking back to the romantic notion of the child as 'father to the man'. While children testify to the malleability of human nature, to the violence of coercive society, they also demonstrate the achievement of modern Western society in relation to 'other' cultures who are seen as closer to nature. In this sense there is a paradoxical conception of childhood at work, whereby experience, culture and action both mitigate and afford biological forces. If war is natural, for example, then we need society to protect us from destruction. While Piaget's view was more sophisticated than this, his only recourse was still simply to invoke reason and love as equally inherent in human society (Piaget, 1918a).

OTHER TRACES: CULTURAL CHAUVINISM

Like most other modern accounts Piaget's theoretical framework privileges masculine and Western forms of reasoning, stigmatising and dubbing as inferior the irrational. Piaget himself invited comparison across history and cultures to illustrate the value of Western 'progress':

> If we begin to lose faith in humanity, in the possibilities of progress of which mankind is capable, there is nothing that will so reassure us as to look back at the past and compare society today with those so-called primitive peoples. . . . Such a comparison is enough to show us not only how plastic mankind is, and how easily human nature can be transformed by its social environment, but also how this transformation is essentially the result of education. We will realise in fact that the primitive is intellectually and morally even more the slave of self-centredness and social coercion than we are liable to be.
>
> (Piaget, 1933: 21)

As already noted in earlier chapters, such child–primitive comparisons were commonplace in nineteenth-century anthropological, psychoanalytical and psychological theorising. What they indicate is that in its single-minded march to true maturity such a model is unaware of, and resistant to, recognising the cultural and historical origins and specificities of its own project. Even if current comparisons between Western and non-Western societies were not intended by Piaget, his ideas and educational innovations were certainly taken up and interpreted in these ways, as in this popular account for training teachers:

> One of the great changes in American life is that we are struggling to be decent to children [. . .] This is a new idea. In many parts of the world children are [. . .] children. Like sticks. Or lower class. Or second class. But gradually, in America particularly, but elsewhere too, our conscience is being heard: Citizens are people . . . women are people . . . natives are people . . . workers are people . . . Our country has been one of the first to take the next step:

Children are people. This is a step to feel proud of. We have begun to ask ourselves: 'What is a child after?' The question complicates life, but it is a sign of our decency that we have begun to ask it. You have every right to feel good about what you do.

(Hymes, 1955: 138–9, punctuation in original)

Piaget was a prolific and original theorist, but his guiding preoccupations were also very much rooted in the modern celebration of science and reason as the panacea for social inequalities. Now in an era where science and industrialisation have brought pollution rather than sanitation, unemployment rather than work, new industrial disease and exploitation of labour rather than health and leisure, and small- and large-scale destruction of the planet, it is less clear that science has so much to offer. This chapter has indicated something of the cultural and intellectual context of Piaget's work, focusing on the selective interpretation of his work with differences in methodology reinscribing pre-existing agendas in fulfilling social demands to classify and test children. Unless we have a clear understanding of Piaget's ideas we will be unable to tackle the real problems in his work. Some indications of the misconceived gender and cultural assumptions underlying this model have also been mentioned, and they will be taken up further in the next chapter, which specifically addresses the educational impact of Piaget's ideas.

FURTHER READING

For a coherent analysis of the assumptions underlying Piagetian theory, see:
Broughton, J. (1981a) 'Piaget's structural developmental psychology I: Piaget and structuralism', *Human Development, 24*: 78–109.
Broughton, J. (1981b) 'Piaget's structural developmental psychology III: logic and psychology', *Human Development, 24*: 195–224.

For a radical critique of the contemporary forms of cognitive developmental psychology (which is almost as true as when it was first published), see:
Riegel, K. (1976) 'The dialectics of human development', *American Psychologist*, 698–700.

On the links between Piagetian psychology and modernity, see:
Burman, E. (1992b) 'Developmental psychology and the postmodern child', in J. Doherty, E. Graham and M. Malek (eds) *Postmodernism and the Social Sciences*, London: Macmillan.

On Piaget himself, see:
Gruber, H. and Vonèche, J. (1977) *The Essential Piaget: an interpretive reference and guide*, London: Routledge & Kegan Paul – a very valuable compilation and synthesis of Piaget's work.
For more (critical) biographical analysis, see:
Vidal, F. (1987) 'Jean Piaget and the liberal protestant tradition', in M. Ash and M. Woodward (eds) *Psychology in Twentieth Century Thought and Society*, Cambridge: Cambridge University Press.

SUGGESTED ACTIVITIES

1 On Piaget and the issue of accelerating development, read and discuss: Clarizio, H. (1981) 'Natural vs accelerated readiness', in H. Clarizio, R. Craig and W. Mehrens (eds) *Contemporary Issues in Educational Psychology*, Boston: Allyn and Bacon, and on the consequences of orienting instruction to the individual child's 'learning needs', see Kepler, K. and Randall, J. (1981) 'Individualization: the subversion of elementary schooling', in Clarizio (ibid.).

2 Drawing on the extracts reproduced in Gruber and Vonèche (op. cit.) from Piaget's novel *Recherche*, his other early writings about the relation between science and moral issues, and including 'Biology and war', explore the relations (and tensions) between science and social emancipation, through such questions as:

   • what role does reason play in Piaget's view of society?
   • what incompatibilities does Piaget struggle with in his analysis of the relations between science and emotions? Between science and humanism? And between science and religion?
   • what model of society does Piaget elaborate, and what are its consequences? How adequate is a model that takes as its unit separate individuals? What scope is there for the analysis of structural power relations and differences? How does this model relate to models of market forces and relations?

Next, use the same questions to interrogate one of the early articles Piaget published in English for a popular audience elaborating his ideas, 'The child and modern physics', *Scientific American, 197*: 46–51.

Chapter 12

Piaget and child-centred education

You will make mistakes sometimes, but gearing your effort to the needs and interests of children is worthwhile. No matter how you keep score you can know in your heart: Yours is a democratic, a reasonable effort. Your children will increasingly feel right; each day as they live will be more satisfying. You can hardly ask for more than that.

(Hymes, 1955: 139)

The one thing we have to avoid then, even while we carry on our old process of education, is this development of the powers of so-called self-expression in a child. Let us beware of artificially stimulating his [*sic*] self-consciousness and his so-called imagination. All that we do is to pervert the child into a ghastly state of self-consciousness, making him affectedly try to show off as we wish him to show off. The moment the least trace of self-consciousness enters into a child, goodbye to everything except falsity. . . . The top and bottom of it is, that it is a crime to teach a child anything at all, schoolwise.

(D.H. Lawrence, 1973: 194–6)

This chapter takes up themes conventionally associated with Piaget's work to explore their inscription and development within 'child-centred' approaches to education. Child-centred pedagogy plays out the conflicts and internal contradictions of both emancipatory and normative tendencies. These tendencies are prevalent in, but by no means exclusive to, Piaget. This child-centred pedagogy subscribes to a naturalised, individualised model of childhood which confirms social privileges and pathologises those who are already socially disadvantaged.

'Child-centred' education enjoyed its heyday in terms of explicit inscription within educational policies in the post-World War II period, reaching its apotheosis in Britain with the Plowden Report (1967). It continues to be influential in approaches to infant and primary (elementary) education. However, as time goes on, conceptual incoherence as well as failure to challenge social inequalities have brought about criticisms from both sides of the political spectrum (for different reasons), the effects of which are now seen in the return towards more structured aproaches to education.

'PROGRESSIVE' EDUCATION

Although Piaget came to be the key theorist cited in the development of the new 'progressive' education of 1960s and 1970s Britain and America, its conceptual roots lie in the work of various European eighteenth- and nineteenth-century philosophers and educationalists such as Jean-Jacques Rousseau, Johann Pesta-lozzi, Friedrich Froebel and, in the early part of this century, Maria Montessori and the psychoanalysts Susan Isaacs and Margaret Lowenfeld (Singer, 1992). The philosopher John Dewey has also been an important resource, particularly in the US. While there are clearly major differences of approach between the different theorists, broadly speaking all subscribed to a 'child-centred' approach in the sense of advocating that education should be oriented towards children's interests, needs and developmental growth and informed by an understanding of child development. This approach contrasts with an educational approach emphasising performance in terms of the achievement of standard forms of accreditation, with a fixed curriculum divided into specific disciplines, and with formal teaching methods. While these are the theorists commonly cited to account for its origins, it was the set of technologies it gave rise to and its associated practices that make it important, and important to developmental psychology and the whole landscape of education.

In part, the emergence of 'progressive' education was a response to the 'payment by results' schemes of the first elementary schools of the 1870s onwards. In these, funding for the school depended on the achievement of pupils (thereby setting up a disincentive to have less able pupils within the school), with a corresponding instrumental and vocational model of education as the (measur-able – thanks to psychologists) acquisition of skills. A second factor in the emergence of child-centred pedagogy was the reaction to rote methods of teach-ing, such as repetitive drills. A third reflection of this development was the rejection of a (behaviourist) model of the child as empty vessel simply absorbing and reacting according to external contingencies. Associated with this was also the emphasis on 'love' and, 'nature', which also coincided with the introduction of women into teaching (see Walkerdine, 1984). As we shall see, the above three factors position the emergence of 'progressive education' as a key expression of individualism. Moreover, within the post-World War II period the call for educa-tional provision oriented to a child's needs and interests became synonymous with the creation and maintenance of a democratic, 'free' and open society which could foster independence of thought and action.

Central tenets of the child-centred approach are indicated by five key terms: readiness, choice, needs, play and discovery. 'Readiness' means that the child must be ready to learn, with learning concerned with social and emotional, as well as cognitive, development. 'Choice' highlights how learning should be directed towards the individual interests of the child, and that the child should dictate the timing and content of the learning process. In terms of 'needs', children are seen to have fundamental needs, the failure to meet which gives rise to later (both individual and social) problems. (In this sense child-centred approaches have continuities with mental hygienists in laying claim to a rhetoric of 'prevention' of different types of ill-health.) The focus on 'play' suggests that learning should be voluntary, enjoyable, self-directed, non-goal oriented, functional for emotional well-being and that the general opposition between work and play should be broken down. The promotion of autonomy was seen as central to fostering curiosity, confidence and competence, in which play functioned as the guarantor of freedom and independence. Finally, the role of 'discovery' highlights that learning takes place through individual, personal experience.

In this model, education was conceptualised as the external realisation of an inner potential, with the emphasis on the uniqueness of each child giving rise to a demand that learning should be 'relevant' to her needs and interests. The process of learning was valued over the topic or content of what was learned, and the commitment to learning by doing rather than being told meant that the teacher's active role was defined as structuring the environment provided for the child. The extract below takes Piaget as the originator of child-centred education to arrive at the following definitions of a teacher's role:

1 The teacher is an analyst in the sense that he [sic] analyses the unit to be presented in terms of what will provide for optimal intellectual, social and emotional (including attitudinal) development.
2 He manipulates the environment in that he selects certain material and plans certain experiences which he believes will promote the outcomes desired.
3 The teacher becomes more a guide, expert, advisor and group leader, in the broad sense, in what is essentially a flexible and fluid teaching-learning environment.

(McNally, 1974: 127–8)

While the first of these points reflects the child-centred approach's claim to deal with the 'whole child', the second and third highlight how the teacher's intervention occurs in the form of provision of context rather than instruction or regulation of the child.

DILEMMAS AND AMBIGUITIES OF PRACTICE

As a statement of teachers' commitments to the educational development of their charges, the child-centred approach expresses some important sentiments. However, some difficulties have emerged in translating them into practice. In the first place, a teacher attempting to conform to these precepts encounters an untenable conflict between the mandate for non-interference to promote independence, and her institutional position as responsible for children's learning. How can she oversee the individual development of a class of thirty children? Various studies of both accounts of, and implementation of, 'progressive' education (Billig *et al.*, 1988; Sharp and Green, 1975) have highlighted how teachers positioned themselves as both responsible for, but helpless in, moulding children's development (thereby inducing great guilt, Walkerdine, 1988). The designation of intervention as tantamount to authoritarian repression meant that teachers could not criticise or regulate children's behaviour. In her analysis of a situation where a teacher was verbally abused by her 3-year-old male pupils using sexist language, Walkerdine (1981) argues that the teacher's subscription to a romantic, child-centred model of children's needs meant that she treated the expression of aggression as natural. By this designation, not only could she not blame the children, but she could assert her authority only at the expense of inciting later personality and social maladjustment. As Lowenfeld, the influential psychotherapist and educationalist, put it:

> The forces of destruction, aggression and hostile emotion which form so powerful an element for good or evil in the human character, can display themselves fully in the play of childhood, and become through this expression integrated in the controlled and conscious personality. Forces unrealised in childhood remain as an inner drive, forever seeking outlets, and lead men to express them not any longer in play, since this is regarded as an activity in childhood, but in industrial competition, anarchy and war.
>
> (Lowenfeld, 1935: 324–5)

A second set of problems arises from conceptual incoherence within child-centred approaches. Apart from the general uncertainty about how to recognise when a child is 'ready', and how to determine a child's 'needs', it would seem that middle-class children are more 'ready' than working-class children since they are more prepared and familiar with the skills needed to engage with schooling. The uncritical commitment to 'readiness' therefore maintains unequal treatment of children, since teachers devote most of their time to the 'ready' and most able children, that is, those they define as most able to benefit (Sharp and Green, 1975). In terms of the claim to dissolve the play–work opposition, this opposition is nevertheless reinstated within the distinction between time-wasting, therapeutic and 'productive' play, with children directed accordingly. Moreover, the glorification of play as functional, voluntary and co-operative soon turns out to be idealised, since this ignores the coercive, cruel and dangerous aspects of many forms of 'play', both in the form of personal hobbies or institutional school activities (Sutton Smith and Kelly Byrne, 1984). Both on analysis and in practice, therefore, the child-centred approach dissolves into intuitions, *ad hoc* judgements that advocate the meting out of educational provision in unequal ways, and undermine the authority and efficacy of the teacher as structuring and responsible for what children learn.

Not only is the pedagogy difficult to apply, it is also worse than unhelpful. In the first place it denies the teacher's power relation with the child (Edwards and

Mercer, 1987). Moreover, subscription to a child-centred philosophy sometimes acts as a mask behind which teachers mark their professional distance from parents and disguise a firm control that holds in practice (Sharp and Green, 1975). Secondly, it strips the child of the aid of the teacher through the teacher's efforts to foster autonomy – in this sense reproducing one of the differences between Piaget- and Vygotskyan-informed educational approaches (Moll, 1990). Thirdly, concern has been generated about how children can be isolated through the attempts to promote learning tied to individual need (Kepler and Randall, 1981). The rest of this chapter draws out the origins and significance of these limitations.

AUTONOMY AND INDIVIDUALISM: FREE THINKERS?

Child-centred approaches perpetuate a model of learning that accords with a liberal model of society – as composed of rational, freely choosing, isolated, equal individuals (Sullivan, 1977). With its connotations of separation and detachment, so close is autonomy perceived to be to the maintenance of a liberal, 'free' society (seen as best promoted by home care), that proposals for day-care provision set out in the Child Development Act 1971 were vetoed by the then US President Nixon on the grounds that this threatened the traditional (North) American family and (North) America's tradition of individualism. This claim motivated Carol Speekmann Klass's (1985) case study of a day-care centre, from which she concludes that, far from encouraging children to be more collectively oriented, day care seems to produce autonomous children capable of self-directed activity who are not dependent on adult authority.

There are tensions between the priority accorded to individual development and the egalitarian impulses of US individualism. In its positive hue, individualism carries connotations of self-reliance, self-improvement, independence of thought and non-conformity. But it is also associated with self-interest, competition and abdication of personal responsibilities in favour of economic forces, specifically the vagaries of the market. The progressive strands of individualism within modern Western societies, such as equal rights and social reform movements, coexist with, and are rooted within, the development and expansion of capitalist free-market economies.

Treating the individual as the unit of social, educational and economic activity perpetuates rather than challenges social inequalities. The focus on individual children masks patterns of difference based on gender, class or culture. Indeed, it is noteworthy that in Sally Lubeck's (1986) comparative study of two nurseries (one a predominantly white pre-school, the other a Head Start Center with black children and teachers), the latter exhibited greater group and community orientation. This could be taken to suggest that the pattern noted by Speekmann Klass is yet another reflection of culture-bound research masquerading as 'culture free'. In addition, Lubeck observed different patterns of interaction between the teachers and children which she maps onto different family (nuclear vs. extended) patterns of interaction. She makes some claims about how the pre-school's 'centrifugal' patterning of time and space, with children working away from the group, and activity structured around 'choice', treats children as uniquely different, linking the promotion of individuality and autonomy with receptiveness to change. In contrast, the 'centripetal' force she identifies in the Head Start Center encouraged children to cohere and be part of a group. We should note here that she links collectivity to conformity in a way that reflects Western individualism, and further devalues the cultural group designated as exhibiting these patterns of behaviour:

> By structuring time, space and activity so that children do what others do, while also conforming to the directives of the teachers, the teachers thus seem to socialize children to adapt to the reality they themselves experience.
>
> (Lubeck, 1986: 138)

However, on closer inspection this reality is not a culturally specific pattern of relating, but a response to circumstances of both disadvantage and intrusive monitoring by educational authorities. The institutional pressures she notes as structuring the functioning of the Head Start Center – with officials and inspectors dropping in unannounced at any time, as well as greater administrative demands in the running of a social service programme – could easily account for the teachers' tendency to work with each other, and apart from the children. Minority cultural patterns exist in relation to those of the majority and should be interpreted correspondingly. Otherwise responses to disadvantage are mistakenly treated as intrinsic properties of a static culture.

DEMOCRACY: THE SELF-GOVERNING CHILD

Along with autonomy, democracy is a key term within the child-centred discourse, which, in the post-war period, functioned as the guarantor of anti-authoritarianism. Child rearing attracted attention as the arena in which the foundations of a democratic society could be laid. In the US the White House held conferences on 'Children in a Democratic Society'. Advice to parents and educators spelt out the social merits and benefits of the 'new' approaches. But this celebration of egalitarianism all too often could also take the form of self-righteous cultural chauvinism, with choice and economic freedom equated with democratic participation:

> Little children – preschoolers still at home – get a lot of backing in their urge to grow. In America we like independent little fellows. We admire gumption and an up-at-them quality. We are all for independence [. . .] We don't put long dresses on our babies. We don't bind their feet . . . Boy or girl, the Five is in jeans, free to run and dig [. . .] From an early age we give youngsters an allowance, 'This is your money; spend it as you wish . . .' We listen when children talk, as if they really were people. We give them reasons when we talk, just as if they were human [. . .] In this country you don't have to be

twenty one to vote . . . in families. Children cast their votes from eighteen *months* on, and their vote is counted too.

(Hymes, 1955: 108–10, punctuation in original)

Children are treated not 'as', but 'just as if they were', human. There is something disingenuous and deceptive about these claims to equality, with explicit contrasts with those who do (or did) not equivalently subscribe to equal treatment irrespective of gender and age.

Moreover, child-centred education becomes a compensatory measure that can offset material inequalities, and, further, is located as critical in the production of self-disciplining citizens. Concluding her book *The Self-Respecting Child*, written just as child-centred education was beginning to structure primary schooling in Britain, Allison Stallibrass wrote:

> It seems to me that if children have the opportunity to become competent and self-governing four-year-olds, they are more likely to become competent, spontaneous and self-governing seven-year-olds, even if, at the latter age their environment chances to be inappropriate and stultifying.

It seems an early inculcation of child-centredness forestalls not only later alienation, but also pre-empts less savoury influences: here the threat of coercion (with its connotations of authoritarianism) looms large:

> Even if the school to which a child proceeds at the age of five or eight turns out to be a barrack-square type, he [sic] will be no more unhappy there if he has developed an inner core of individuality through making choices and decisions for himself, than if he has become a soft piece of clay, pliant in the hands of anyone wanting to try to cast him in a common or prematurely adult mould. . . . In any case, State infant schools are rapidly becoming places where such qualities as self-reliance, initiative and spontaneity are welcomed, and a sheep-like conformity discouraged.

(Stallibrass, 1974: 259–60)

What is left unspecified is precisely what it is that children may be moulded towards (although the reference above to 'common' should alert us to the devaluation and pathologisation of working-class values). This allows us to leave unexamined the assumptions about the nature of individuals and their relations with society that the child-centred pedagogy maintains. Moreover, while democracy is celebrated as central to child as well as societal development, this shifts to become less a feature of social structures and more an evaluation of family life:

> Throughout the preschool years there is an intimate interaction between the psychologies of the child and of the parent. Democracy is a way of life which demands attitudes of tolerance and fair play. If we wish to lay the basis of such attitudes in young children we must begin with the education of adults. The adults in their own behavior must furnish the models and intimations of the

democratic way. . . . Democracy is a mature virtue, a product of gradual growth, which embodies obedience, self-control, self-direction.

(Gesell, 1950: 310)

While self-control and self-direction are central to the child-centred pedagogy, it becomes apparent that obedience is a covert outcome of it, since children are considered to be more willing to obey rules if these appear to arise out of their own deliberations and choices. While the overt exertion of authority would smack of totalitarianism, its covert application in the name of the betterment and protection of society is seen as laudable. Hence, notwithstanding the cultural value placed on freedom, it becomes clear that the child-centred pedagogy is just as coercive as traditional approaches but in more subtle ways, and that underlying the model of the romantic, natural, innocent child lies an image of children as destructive, asocial and therefore threatening to the social order (Walkerdine and Lucey, 1989).

THE HOME AND THE SCHOOL

Not only can groups be stigmatised but child-centredness can lead to individual-ised interpretations of what are really socially structured inequalities. The com-mitment to an optimistic and meritocratic view of education as self-realisation and as the key to social mobility renders invisible the role of the school in perpetuating inequality. Since it fails to accord any importance to the role of teacher and school as agents, the focus is on the home background. The only available explanation to account for pupil failure or under-achievement is therefore in terms of individual or cultural deficit – blaming the child or the family (Fuchs, 1973; Sharp and Green, 1975). Indeed, so influential were the ideas about educational achievement as the outcome of a maturing inner potential that it is only relatively recently that research has demonstrated that features of school organisation and functioning do have an impact on children's educational achievement in them (Rutter et al., 1979; Smith and Tomlinson, 1989).

Child-centred approaches therefore tend to subscribe to notions of com-pensatory education and cultural disadvantage or deprivation by assuming that there is something wrong or missing in the child's background. They link easily with a social pathology view of the background from which the child is drawn. Correspondingly, pupil success is seen as due to appropriateness of the pedagogy but pupil failure is attributed to home background. Despite a rhetoric of parent participation, parents are disparaged for failing to uphold 'progressive' educa-tional ideals if they demand more structured approaches. This liberal model also assumes children come to school with equal access to educational opportunities. It ignores the role of the school as perpetuating middle-class norms and values which therefore advantage middle-class children. By being blind to cultural differences, and treating all children as the same, it thereby denies and perpe-tuates the inequality of their starting positions. In his review of (and plea for) child-development programmes within Third World countries, Robert Myers (1992) cautions against this dominant model, which within a Third World context all too often means the devaluation of indigenous cultures and values in favour of Western-based educational ideas:

> Conceptualising the entry into school as a 'transition' *from* home *to* school puts undue emphasis on school and tends to devalue the home as a place for learning: Our concern, therefore, should be centred on the ability of a child to learn in various environments rather than on learning as if it only occurred in schools.
>
> (Myers, 1992: 211, emphasis in original)

Furthermore, the goal of democracy and the identification of democratic styles of child rearing and education were explicitly linked to longstanding fears about working-class family life.

> Underprivileged children suffer not only in a physical sense. They suffer psychologically. They feel mental insecurity. In crowded and shiftless homes they develop anxieties and perplexities. They see sights and experience shocks from which more fortunate children are in decency spared. Innumerable households still use methods of harsh discipline, chronic scolding, shouting, terrifying threats, slapping, beating. Needless to say, such inconsiderate disregard for the dignity of the individual is inconsistent with the spirit of democracy. In fact, misguided and crude forms of child management are so widespread as to constitute a public health problem, a task of preventive mental hygiene.
>
> (Gesell, 1950: 310)

In the above account it is clear that 'decency' is code for class, and that working-class cultural patterns are pathologised. This is not to condone the mistreatment of children but rather to point out that, notwithstanding the commitment to democracy, measures for promotion of tolerance do not extend to willingness to see value in diversity (Walkerdine and Lucey, 1989).

From the above formulations it is easy to see how the discourse of child-centredness slips into social regulation. Indeed, Gesell went on to urge three main areas of 'social control' for the welfare of the pre-school child: firstly, medical supervision of child development; secondly, parental and pre-parental education in which 'Adult education has come into increasing prominence as a means of social control' (Gesell, 1950: 311); and, thirdly, re-adaptation of the kindergarten and nursery school. He justified his calls to attend less to the achievement of skills such as reading than to differences between children in terms of the pre-school's role in what he termed 'supervisory hygiene' (Gesell: 1950: 313).

In a similar vein, the frontispiece to Strang's (1959) *Introduction to Child Study*, depicts a mother holding a baby and taking two children (girl and boy) into a church-like building. The caption reads: 'The whole family goes to school. Thus schools contribute intimately and intensively to child development.'

Education became the route to intervene in and reform family life – although we could note that only the mother is shown in the picture, thus reiterating how it is primarily mothers who are the site of intervention and evaluation. A focus on the child abstracted from context therefore moves to an evaluation of family life that is divorced from an understanding of social inequalities. Hence education is positioned as the central apparatus of social regulation in the production of the fiction of the democratic citizen.

Even where attempts have been made to recognise social disadvantage, all too often these read as indictments of families instead of social structures (or social services). The influential National Children's Bureau report on educational inequality in Britain, *Born to Fail?* (Wedge and Prosser, 1973), struggles to avoid blaming parents for their poverty and unemployment while at the same time treating lack of parental involvement in children's schooling as an index of parental interest in, or aspiration for, their children (rather than an indication of how schooling fails to engage with child and family). But so powerful is the discourse of familial responsibility that child-centredness, with its failure to theorise social relations, could scarcely avoid being incorporated into it. A recent reminder of the continuity and potency of these themes is the leader of a teachers' union's comments dismissing children of lone parents as 'no hopers' in his address to a union annual conference: 'Peter Dawson, general secretary of Professional Association of Teachers, said that teachers faced the appalling consequences of a million lone-parent families. Schools were being turned into first-aid posts for psychologically crippled children' (*Independent*, 2 August 1991).

THE WHOLE CHILD?

Mearns' (1961) National Children's Home lecture epitomises how normative and punitive moral assumptions enter into a seemingly naturalistic child-centred approach. Written as advice for professionals working with children, his book *The Whole Child* was intended especially for those working in residential settings. In this sense the need to deal with 'the whole child' arose from the demands of total institutional (rather than specifically educational) care. Far from being 'whole', Mearns's 'child' literally breaks down into constituent components. 'CHILD' is an acronym, where C stands for 'care and companionship', H for 'home and habits', I for 'independence and interests', L for 'love and laughter' and D for 'discipline, direction'. Each letter therefore moves explicitly from a seemingly benign discourse of child-centredness to one of overt social regulation: in the name of 'the whole child', the apparatus of moral evaluation is maintained. What this demonstrates is how child-centredness is, albeit in different forms, social regulation, that is, the surveillance *par excellence* of children since it presents itself as 'freely' undertaken. Correspondingly, the model of the 'whole child' exists only in relation to that of the 'damaged' or 'disadvantaged child' (whom we encountered in Chapter 10) that it thereby both produces and regulates.

Familiar themes emerge. Homes are to blame: 'In almost every case of maladjustment the defect has its origin in a home which has failed in some respect' (Mearns, 1961: 28–9). Play and laughter, so central to the lexicon of child-centredness, become literal metaphors of mental hygiene: 'It [laughter] is, moreover a potent disinfectant to destroy the twin germs of jealousy and envy' (Mearns, 1961: 29). Moreover, the channelling of ability and affection come in for particular concern, demonstrating how the individualism of child-centredness leads to resignation rather than support. The account of 'the school years' takes two issues as the focus of interest: intelligence is seen as fixed, as

an hereditary characteristic. Poor environment can retard, even prevent, its proper flowering; but not even the most elaborate education can make any significant improvement in the IQ. The moral here is that *parents must accept a child's intelligence for what it is and expend their efforts not in trying to improve it. . . .*

(Mearns, 1961: 35)

The second key issue for 'the school years' is 'homosexuality', presented within a general section on 'The Handicapped Child'. This is treated as relevant only to men, since 'female homosexuality is not a community problem in this country' (Mearns, 1961: 36). Sexual orientation is cast within a disease model:

In fairness to those who are themselves the helpless victims of the homosexual abnormality, it should be said that many have resisted their impulses and have adjusted themselves to their disability. They remain instinctively and psychologically homosexual, but boys are safe from them, since they are able to canalize their urges in artistic and similar pursuits. These facts do not however lessen the general risk.

(Mearns, 1961: 36–7)

These sentiments are not only homophobic, but they also reflect naturalised and essentialised views of male and female sexuality. It seems that 'the whole child' is endowed with gender and sexual orientation from the beginning, with gender-differentiated sexual drives. Moreover, these exist only as problems to be managed:

Matters are perhaps rather simpler for girls because they are less readily aroused and in most cases have a deeper sense of moral responsibility. Be that as it may, the position is never plain-sailing if the circumstances of temptation are created. Boys are more inflammable, sexually speaking, and they are from the psychological viewpoint, egocentric, self-seeking and demanding. Boys take; girls give.

(Mearns, 1961: 75–6)

The failure to see child development as socially constructed rather than biologically unfolding leads to an ignorance of the ways the models reinscribe particular moral values. Far from being 'whole', with pedagogy 'centred' around her or him, the child of the child-centred approaches is a carefully orchestrated social production with 'needs' and (gender, class, cultural, sexual) qualities designated to mesh with normative conceptions of social arrangements.

FROM PROGRESS TO BACKLASH?

Writing at a key moment when child-centredness had become official education policy in Britian, Garland and White (1980), in their review of the theory and practice of nursery care, distinguished between those nurseries guided by an underlying assumption that the child should ultimately determine what will satisfy her needs (seen as child-centred) and those which positioned the adult in that role (seen as authoritarian). The 'predominant goals' of the former were, in their analysis, the social and emotional development of the children, while in the latter the focus was on cognitive growth and the acquisition of skills. The authors trace continuities in philosophy to the differing traditions from which pre-school care developed. They see the more authoritarian, skills-based style as having its roots in institutions concerned with the care of children of poor and working women, in which the dominant theme was (as discussed also in Chapter 1) one of rehabilitation. They suggest:

> looking back at some of the day nurseries we visited, it is hard not to feel that there existed a continuity of tradition between the dame schools, in which the emphasis was on keeping children out of mischief, and those we saw in which, as we have described, the children were felt to be primitive and irrational creatures to be kept carefully and constantly controlled by the adult world.
>
> (Garland and White, 1980: 112)

It has been the argument of this chapter that, notwithstanding its rhetoric of emancipation and empowerment, child-centred approaches are still associated with those preoccupations with social control and regulation, only with self-regulation regarded as more effective than overt coercion precisely because it gives the impression of freedom and choice. Underlying the playing, autonomous child lurks a model of an aggressive and primitive being whose instinctual impulses need to be indulged in order to ward off later emotional complexes (and social problems) – hence the theoretical basis for the opposition between the two philosophies becomes tenuous. Even the distinction between the focus on building social relations rather than cognitive skills collapses so that the social orientation becomes a means of maximising the cognitive:

> those nurseries who place social and emotional goals first do so because they feel that in terms of the child's longterm success as a cognitive being, a sound emotional being is essential.
>
> (Garland and White, 1980: 111)

Corresponding to the contradictions within the liberatory direction of child-centred approaches and the return to themes of reforming a pre-social, anti-social child, there are problems with confining the educational goal to the promotion of *individual* development. Contemplating how the apparently radical, empowering tendencies of the 1960s 'progressive education' could have transmuted into the instrumentalism and atomistic skills-oriented vocationalism of the 1990s 'conservative revolution in education' (Jones, 1989), James Avis (1991) identifies as the source of continuity its thorough-going individualism.

> Each child and student is categorized atomistically and expected to pursue their own separate and autonomous development. The difficulty here is that there is no grasp of the collective processes or indeed the formation of collective ways of appropriating and using educational forms and knowledge. Education is reduced to the pursuit of individual development. The social processes involved in the production of knowledge are ignored and knowledge is rid of its social uses.
>
> (Avis, 1991: 117)

The fact that 'progressive education' operates with a concept of knowledge devoid of social differences means that not only does it fail to address how knowledge can be used to dismantle structures of oppression, but it thereby also exacerbates those social divisions by naturalising them. As such, from a focus on process it has been reduced to a set of teaching techniques.

What Piaget and the other theorists who inspired 'child-centred' approaches to education share is a commitment to this view of knowledge as arising outside social structures and relations. In some senses the fact that Piaget is taken as the primary source of these ideas (rather than the psychoanalysts) confirms this even further, given his focus on the abstract epistemic subject and his model of the problem-solving scientist. It is this model of learning, as a separate, isolated activity, that sets up the continuities with the current instrumentalist orientations through a conceptual transition from knowledge as process to knowledge as the exercise of techniques.

> we can point to the rash of strategies of curriculum development which are premised on the notion of skills, of the separation of form from content, of, therefore, a crude positivism that enshrines the reification of knowledge in educational practices. The extent to which such an abstraction is consistent with the abstraction of labour as commodity is revealing.
>
> (Venn and Walkerdine, 1978: 71)

But for too long the debates about education have floundered on a set of false oppositions between child-centredness and vocationalism, in which the learning needs of individual children are pitted against the industrial needs of society. Being child-centred meant that the child was abstracted from social relations, fuelling the charge that whims of children were being indulged without due reference to the society in which they lived. Yet beneath the rhetoric of child-centredness we have seen the older themes of social pathology and regulation resurging. The liberalism that child-centredness was supposed to express celebrates freedom and choice, but existing social inequalities structure differential access to choice. Increasingly, parents and children are expected to shoulder more responsibilities in the name of greater participation and democracy, but are actually accorded fewer means to fulfil these. I have explored the role of developmental psychology in legitimising the translation of individualism into normative conceptions of development. Its moral status and conceptions of morality remain to be addressed in the next, last chapter.

FURTHER READING

Billig, M., Condor, S., Edwards, D., Gane, C., Middleton, D. and Radley, A. (1988) *Ideological Dilemmas*, London: Sage, see chapters 4 and 5.

Marks, D. (1993) 'Case conference analysis and action research', in E. Burman and I. Parker (eds) *Discourse Analytic Research: repertoires and readings of texts in action*, London: Routledge.

Sharp, R. and Green, A. (1975) *Education and Social Control: a study in progressive primary education*, London: Routledge & Kegan Paul.

Singer, E. (1992) *Child Care and the Psychology of Development*, London: Routledge, describes the origins and impact of child-centred practices.

Walkerdine, V. (1984) 'Developmental psychology and the child-centred pedagogy: the insertion of Piaget in primary education', in J. Henriques, W. Hollway, C. Urwin, C. Venn and V. Walkerdine, *Changing the Subject: psychology, subjectivity and social regulation*, London: Methuen.

Walkerdine, V, and Lucey, H. (1989) *Democracy in the Kitchen: regulating mothers and socialising daughters*, London: Virago.

SUGGESTED ACTIVITIES

1   Analyse interviews with teachers, either by recording teachers' accounts in local schools or training colleges, or drawing on extracts from Billig *et al.* (1988) (op. cit.) or Sharp and Green (1975) (op. cit.). What are the tensions between a commitment to the needs and interests of children and the statutory requirement to teach skills such as reading and numbers?

2   Explore how the child-centred approach moves from a focus on the child as having needs or problems to the child as being a problem. Here structural legacies of developmental psychology's role and function (see Chapter 1) are currently played out within the domain of educational psychology. Read Marks (1993) (op. cit.) and Ford (1982) for accounts of the relationships between coexistent and competing frameworks of meaning. In particular, consider professional and parental perceptions of the purpose of a case conference in relation to the following questions:

- what is the problem?
- who is the problem?
- what agendas or professional interests are being played out/maintained?
- what is the relationship between a discourse of developmental needs and a school management discourse of removing a 'difficult' child from a school?
- to what extent are ideological or common-sense notions about social conformity and adaptation replayed within 'expert' reports?
- what structural constraints overdetermine the decision-making process?

Chapter 13

Morality and the goals of development

Developmentalism is a beguiling creed, to be a developer of backward lands an
attractive vocation. We all want to see ourselves as bearers of aid, rectifiers of past
injustice. To be sent among a distant nation as a conveyer of progress can only make
one feel good. . . . It boosts self esteem. It is to regain certainty and purpose, to cast
away the ennui and despair of decaying industrial society and to restore bracing
faith in the goodness and charity of one's fellow men and women.

(Morris, 1992: 1)

It has been clear that an underlying project of developmental psychology has
been to produce moral citizens appropriate to the maintenance of bourgeois
democracy, but it has been less clear what notion of morality it subscribes to. This
chapter addresses the treatment of morality in developmental psychology. The
debates and criticisms generated in this area can be regarded as encapsulating in
a microcosm the limitations of current developmental models. While the moral
assumptions permeating models of moral development have attracted some
critical attention, their exhibition within this arena should be understood as only
one particular instance of what is a general problem. In this chapter the moral
status of models of moral development is located within the broader cultural and
political landscape within which developmental psychology functions. The
remaining questions about whether developmental psychology can outgrow
rather than simply process, mature and recycle the conservative and culture-
bound presentations of early twentieth-century privileged men are complex. But
a prerequisite for this is to understand what these theories are and do.

PIAGET'S RULES ON CHILDREN'S GAMES

In *The Moral Judgement of the Child* (1932) Piaget describes his investigations
of children's developing appreciation of morality. He conceived of morality as

systems of rules, and his aim was to understand how we acquire these rules. In line with his paradoxical model of the child both as asocial and as party to insights that civilisation has knocked out of us, Piaget held that most of the moral rules we learn are imposed and enforced on us ready-made by adults. However, he saw in the 'social games' played by children the opportunity to see how these rules are constructed and interpreted by children. By asking children to teach him how to play the game of marbles and asking questions about who had won the game and why, Piaget built up a picture of characteristic ways in which children of different ages both practised and accounted for the rules.

Piaget traced a development in children's play from regularities or rituals that an individual child devises to amuse herself which are full of idiosyncratic habits and symbols, to an imitation of some aspects of what others are doing in terms of rules she has devised but assumes hold generally. At this point, he argued, children may believe themselves to be playing together, but may in fact be playing entirely different games in parallel, without seeing the need for a shared set of rules. This clearly ties in with Piaget's ideas about childhood egocentrism. By about 7–8 years, he claimed, children began to see the game of marbles as a competitive game structured by rules. The success of the game depends on mutual co-operation between players according to collectively upheld rules. By 11–12 years (in what he later termed formal operational thinking) Piaget argued that children are interested not only in rules governing the particular game or version of the game they are playing, but in reflecting upon the total set of possible variations that might be called upon in a given case – in other words a hypothetico-deductive approach characteristic of formal reasoning. At this point we should note that, for Piaget, it is the appreciation and engagement with *competition* that is taken as the indicator of sociality.

This work formed the basis for a wide-ranging exploration of children's moral understanding. He explored children's awareness of rules by asking children such questions as 'Can rules be changed?', 'Have rules always been the same as they are today?' and 'How did rules begin?'. At the second stage (which would be called 'preoperational' in his later work), children's imitation of rules was based on a perception of rules as sacred and unalterable, despite violating these rules in their own play. Once again childhood egocentrism is used to account for this paradox. Piaget identified a developmental progression from *heteronomy*, where the self is undifferentiated from the (social, moral, physical) context, to *autonomy*, where the individual chooses to engage in particular social contracts. He traced a change in approach towards rules from an initial *unilateral respect* (where rules are obeyed due to adult constraint) to *mutual respect* (where rules are social conventions operating to maintain fairness). He went on to pose stories involving minor misdeeds to children, investigating their ideas about responsibility in terms of moral questions he considered relevant to children, such as stealing and lying. The outcome of his clinical interviews with children was that he claimed, in contrast to older children and adults, young children judged the naughtiness of an action by its results rather than by the agent's intentions, that is, the magnitude of the damage is treated as the index of the scale of the misdeed.

KOHLBERG ON PIAGET

Laurence Kohlberg (1969a, 1969b, 1976), a US developmental psychologist, elaborated on and developed Piaget's work on moral reasoning to put forward a series of six stages and three levels in the development and articulation of moral judgement from childhood to adulthood. He based his work on the classification of the kinds of moral reasoning displayed by individuals of different ages when they were confronted with hypothetical dilemmas. The most celebrated 'dilemma' used to elicit the underlying structure of people's moral reasoning was about a penniless man, Heinz, who urgently needs an expensive medicine to save his wife's life, and which the pharmacist refuses to give or supply on credit. Should he steal the drug? Here there is a conflict between the values of property and life. We should pause to note that, in the transition from Geneva to the US and from the 1930s to the 1960s, a process of methodological and taxonomical rigidity has taken place. The ascription of moral level has become a question of classification according to age or stage; from premoralism, to conformism, to individual principled morality.

A number of claims underlie the framework. Firstly, the stages are said to be universal and fixed. Secondly, the sequence is invariant, with variation only in rate of progression or fixation at a particular stage. And, thirdly, each stage is a structured whole, with characteristics of reasoning associated with a stage related together into a total world-view. All this is reminiscent of Piaget's model of the relations that hold between the organisation of cognitive operations. In terms of evidence used to support this model, there is apparently fairly widespread support for the claim that the stages occur in a fixed order (Colby *et al.*, 1983). There is also cross-sectional support, in that higher stages are reported among older subjects. In addition, some longitudinal studies suggest that over a period of years individuals tend to advance to higher stages (Walker, 1989). Even some cross-cultural work lent support, with Kohlberg (1969b) identifying the same sequence of stages (with the stories slightly adapted), in the US, Britain, Taiwan, Mexico and Turkey, and the stages and sequences confirmed in other societies by Edwards (1981). So it seemed as though the arena of moral development had been pretty well sorted out. Or had it?

KOHLBERG'S DILEMMAS

From the 1970s some critical voices emerged which suggested that the sorting process was on a less than equitable basis. It seemed that the ascription of the moral highground was of uncertain validity, of contested value and unfair distribution.

In terms of methodological criticisms, a first problem arises from basing a classification of moral level on verbal reports. Unlike Piaget's early work, Kohlberg's model relies exclusively on what people say about what (other) people should do, based on hypothetical situations. But being more thoughtful, circumspect, taking more factors into consideration does not necessarily mean that people behave more morally. Further, the practice of investigating moral reasoning via hypothetical situations makes the moral problems posed even more detached and distanced. In this context Carol Gilligan's (1982) work on women's reasoning about the real-life dilemma of whether or not to terminate a pregnancy provides a particularly striking contrast.

Secondly, corresponding to the work challenging what is seen as Piaget's rather pessimistic view of children's abilities, there has been some work which seeks to analyse and minimise the linguistic and narrative demands of the task. Stein et al. (1979) reformulated Heinz's dilemma into a story about a lady who had a sick husband and had to steal some cat's whiskers in order to make the only medicine that would save his life. Despite the fairy tale genre and simplicity of the story, they report young children as having difficulties understanding it. They suggest that the children do not draw the obvious inference that the medicine will save the man's life since they cannot maintain the major goal in mind while trying to pursue the subgoals of securing the whiskers and making the medicine. In order to engage with the dilemma, the task presupposes the ability to understand a complex narrative and to think through alternative courses of action, both of which may be more complicated than the process of making moral judgements alone.

Criticisms addressed to the theory rather than the procedures by which it was arrived at also take a number of forms. In the first place, it is claimed that it addresses only a very restricted notion of morality. While this is not the place to go into alternative (such as behavioural or psychoanalytic) models of morality, the Kohlbergian model of morality as moral reasoning cannot engage with issues of moral commitment, and individual priorities or differences of moral salience of particular issues. Nor does it address the subjective experience of feelings of guilt and shame which, as Kagan (1984) notes, children exhibit from an early age. Once again we see that a cognitive developmental model which prioritises rationality cannot theorise its relation with emotions except insofar as emotions are regarded as subordinate to, or at best by-products of, cognition.

The rigidity of representation of morality also fails to deal with domain specificity, familiarity and, further, the reality of the conflicting moral codes and priorities we are subject to (Turiel, 1983; Song et al., 1987). Moreover, not only is this a model which treats talk about moral behaviour as equivalent to moral activity, it also fails to address how accounting for the morality of one's behaviour tends to follow rather than precede the actions. Hence these accounts measure moral rationalisation rather than reasoning (Hogen, 1975).

DOUBLE STANDARDS: GENDER-DIFFERENTIATING RIGHTS AND RESPONSIBILITIES

One of the most influential criticisms of the model is that the stages do not fit female development. Carol Gilligan (1982) points out that both Piaget and Kohlberg derived their stage norms from studying boys and men. She challenges the capacity of the model to express women's psychological development. She reinterprets boys' and girls' accounts of Heinz's dilemma, where in terms of Kohlbergian criteria the girls would be scored as reasoning at a lower moral stage of development. She points out that the girls' and women's reservations about stealing the drug were based on additional considerations arising from an engagement with the context, such as the effect on the wife if the man was imprisoned for the crime and the worry about who would care for her if she fell ill again.

Although it is unclear whether she is advocating improving or abandoning it, Gilligan therefore throws the model of moral development that Kohlberg proposes into question. In tracing a linear progression from undifferentiation or attachment to autonomy, she argues that it subscribes to a model of morality based on individual rights and freedoms of the kind enshrined in Western legal systems, whereas, she holds, women's moral development is characterised by a much more contextualised morality concerned with conflicting responsibilities and care – that is, concerned with responsibilities and relationships rather than rights and rules. She argues that Kohlberg's model emphasises separation rather than connection by taking the individual rather than the relationship as the primary unit of analysis.

Gilligan ties these different conceptions of morality to the different roles traditionally accorded to men and women. Since women define their identity through relationships of intimacy and care, the moral issues women face are to do with learning to assert their own needs without seeing this as 'selfish'. For both sexes, she argues, the issues that we face are to do with the conflict between integrity (separateness) and care (attachment), but that men and women approach these issues with different moral orientations. For men the emphasis is on 'equality', based on an understanding of fairness, equal respect, balancing the claims of other and self. In contrast, women's morality, she claims, is more oriented to issues of responsibility, with recognition of differences in need that an equal rights approach cannot address – an ethic of compassion and care and not wanting to hurt. Gilligan calls for the necessity for these contrasting moral orientations to be seen as complementary rather than one being systematically downgraded, and ultimately for them to be integrated into a more adequate vision of moral maturity. While there are problems with the idealisation of women's qualities within this account (see Sayers, 1986), the value of this work lies in demonstrating the limited application and far-reaching devaluation of women structured within the cognitive developmental model.

CULTURE AND THE GOALS OF DEVELOPMENT

A further serious difficulty with Kohlberg's model lies in the status of the sixth stage, which represents individual moral conviction as the most advanced morality beyond the respect for democratically arrived at and contractually maintained rules (Stage Five). Firstly, few people are designated as attaining the higher points on the developmental ladder (with Jesus Christ, Mahatma Gandhi, and Martin Luther King named by Kohlberg as among the lucky few – among whom he also includes himself!). This raises questions about the theoretical status of the highest point of development. Secondly, some cultures are recorded as not reaching even beyond the second stage. There are clearly methodological difficulties involved in the study of people from one culture by those of another. These are issues that anthropologists routinely address, although some have been known to rely on psychology with disastrous results (see, e.g., Hallpike, 1979). The suggestion that Kohlberg's stages can be related to the 'complexity' of societies (Edwards, 1981) sets up a hierarchy from 'primitive' to 'complex' which simply reflects a Western cultural bias. It may, however, be more accurate to make a distinction between rural and urban societies, with Stage Five reported much less frequently in the former (Snarey, 1985). But this calls for an analysis that connects cognitive/moral development with culture and context.

However, a further issue comes into play when researchers measure indigenous people's abilities and interests by means of a test devised outside their own culture. Here developmental psychology reproduces and bolsters the dynamic of imperialism by offering tools that produce a picture of inferiority and moral underdevelopment through the ethnocentric and culturally chauvinist assumptions that inform both theory and tool (Joseph et al., 1990). Kohlberg later reformulated some of his claims about Stage Six so that it is now seen as an ideal, rather than a necessary, endpoint of development (Levine et al., 1985). This, however, seems to offer a rather cosmetic change which leaves the methodological, and moral-political, problems intact.

In this we can see played out problems common to all developmental psychological theories that claim to hold generally. The postulation of a starting state and an endstate involves the prescription of the endpoint, the goal, of development. We talk in terms of 'progressing', 'advancing' from one stage to the next. But the norms by which we evaluate that development may be far from universal. In particular, as we have seen, the individual autonomy of conscience of Stage Six fits well with the modern, Western ideology of individualism. But this is not the highest point of moral development for all cultures, many of which value obedience and respect for elders and tradition over personal conviction. Kagan (1984) notes that in Japan the guiding principle of social interaction is to avoid conflict and maintain harmonious relationships. With such a different value system and contrasting view of the relationship between individuals, we could expect that a Kohlbergian Stage Six person would be considered aberrant and amoral in according personal principles more importance than societal expectations.

Further, the model of 'man' prescribed in Kohlberg's (and by implication Piaget's) model derives from particular social interests, based on a liberal model of society seen as functioning by means of social contractual arrangements between people (Simpson, 1974; Sampson, 1989). The rationality which is so highly valued in the cognitive developmental model ties in with a bourgeois conception of the individual which either accepts class divisions or denies their existence (Sullivan, 1977; Buck-Morss, 1975). In its celebration of autonomy, Kohlbergian theory therefore partakes of a liberal view that sees society as composed of independent units who co-operate only when the terms of co-operation are such as to further the ends of each of the parties. This also clearly recalls Piaget's definition of social interaction in game playing through competition. Not only does this lead to an asocial view of the individual, in terms of the ascription of pre-social interests, it also sets up a form of conceptual imperialism in its application to cultures which do not share this underlying model. Sullivan treats this model as a case example of the political and conceptual problems wrought by an inadequate theory of the social: thought is severed from action, form from content, the abstract from the concrete and, ultimately, emotion from intellect.

DEVELOPMENTAL PSYCHOLOGY AND THE DEVELOPING WORLD

Some of the methodological and moral difficulties described above have been reflected in the failure of the project of cross-cultural psychology. On practical grounds researchers were forced to recognise that the cultural assumptions held by research 'subjects' about the nature of the task demanded of them did not always correspond with that intended by the researchers. Cole et al. (1971) found that the African Kpelle consistently failed Piagetian classification tasks when asked 'how a wise man' would organise piles of foods and household items together. It was only when in despair the researcher asked how 'a fool would do it' that they exhibited the typical Western classification based on type (sorting similar items together) that had been defined as task success, rather than functional relations that reflected the ways the items were used.

Such examples highlight that the problems are more than mere practical or technical difficulties, and cast doubt on the entire project of developmental psychology. The presentation of a general model which depicts development as unitary irrespective of culture, class, gender and history means that difference can be recognised only in terms of aberrations, deviations – that is, in terms of relative progress on a linear scale. The developmental psychology we know is tied to the culture which produced it. And, while such insights have had some impact within academic psychology, they are maintained in policy and in popular representations of childhood and child development.

The image of the active, natural, innocent child functions within the economy of cultural representations of children in so-called developing countries in ways which castigate poor people for their poverty, lapse into racist assumptions about child neglect and penalise the children of the poor rather than promote their welfare. Claire Cassidy (1989) discusses how, when poverty and ignorance lead to malnutrition in Third World countries, this is sometimes treated by welfare workers as an example of parental neglect. There is a failure to distinguish between culturally normative and deviant forms in evaluating child development in 'other' cultures. In purveying what is advertised as a general, universal model of development, developmental psychology is a vital ingredient in what Jo Boyden (1990) has termed the 'globalization of childhood'. While Western sentimentalised representations of children are rooted in the attempt to deny children's agency (notwithstanding the claims of child-centredness) and prevent social unrest, the key dimensions that have come to structure Western organisation of childhood are being inappropriately imposed in 'developing' countries. The division between public and private has been central to Western industrialisation, but it should be recalled that poor people have less privacy, and that street children may have none at all (although see Glauser (1990) for an analysis of the distinction between children *of* the street and children living *on* the streets). But Western conceptions of children as unknowing, helpless and in need of protection from the public sphere may actually disable and criminalise children who are coping as best they can. All too often, policies and practices developed in the West function more in punitive than protective ways for Third World children – even in literal ways by being dispensed by the police, who in some Third World countries have been responsible for the murder of children in their custody.

Similarly, while the regulation of child labour is clearly important, attempts to abolish this in line with Western practice frequently ignore the extent to which families (and children) are dependent on the incomes children generate, and would therefore need to be compensated in order to let their children attend school. Further, the schooling which is on offer is often of varying quality, and may often take the form of enforced assimilation to a colonial language. The schooling experience may therefore be one which fails rather than enables children. The Western priority accorded to education may therefore be misplaced in the sense that this is unlikely to be organised around principles of personal development or enlightenment.

The undifferentiated, globalised model of childhood not only fails to address the varying cultural value and position of children (Zelizer, 1985), but also ignores gender as a structural issue in development (in both the senses of individual and economic development). Aid agencies are now being forced to recognise that specific priorities need to be set up for girls and women (e.g. Wallace and March, 1991), while the role of gendered meanings in structuring not only entirely different subjectivities and livelihoods, but actual nutrition and survival is gradually emerging through the efforts of women's organisations (Scheper-Hughes, 1989b; Batou, 1991).

In general, the concept of childhood on offer is a Western construction that is now being incorporated, as though it were universal, into aid and development policies (Burman, in press b). Associations between the development of the child and the development of the nation or State are familiar. Indeed many aid policy documents present their rationale for promoting child survival and development in terms of the future benefit to the State (e.g. Myers, 1992). But there are other resonances I want to mobilise here. Tim Morris opens his account of his experiences as an aid worker in the Middle East (in the extract I have positioned at the beginning of this chapter) with a critique of the cultural chauvinism, complacency and personal investments set up within aid work. Just as he is exposing the problems inherent in defining goals for societal development, so too do the same problems arise within the determination of the direction and endpoint of individual development. The notion of 'progress', whether of societies or through 'the life span', implies linear movement across history and between cultures. Comparison within these terms is now being recognised as increasingly untenable. In particular, the implication that there is a detached, disinterested set of devices or techniques for this purpose, such as developmental psychology purports to provide, illustrates the extent to which we have come to believe in the abstract disembodied psychological subject, and dismiss all it fails to address as merely either supplementary or inappropriate. In this regard, it should be noted that the focus within this book on literature and interpretations produced by researchers in Britain and especially the US, is not, or not merely, a reflection of my own parochialism. Anglo-US psychology extends its influence much further than its own linguistic and cultural domains through the dynamic of imperialism. Developmental psychology therefore functions as a tool of cultural imperialism through the reproduction of Western values and models within post-colonial societies.

DEVELOPMENTAL PSYCHOLOGY AND THE PRODUCTION OF CHILDHOOD

Closer to home, these issues arise in analogous ways within discussions of child abuse, in particular the recognition of child sexual abuse. Part of the reason why this issue commands such media attention lies in the challenge to the image of the safe, happy and protected child. Not only do the family, or trusted parental figures, no longer necessarily provide a safe, caring environment for children, but the model of the child as innocent can render the 'knowing' child as somehow culpable within her own abuse (Kitzinger, 1990). Issues of power that constitute the abuse are eclipsed within the effort to ward off children's agency and sexuality and maintain a romantic sentimental image of the passive, innocent child (Stainton Rogers and Stainton Rogers, 1992).

While developmental psychology plays a key role in the legitimation and perpetuation of these dangerously limited and sometimes plainly false conceptions of childhood, they mesh with dominant cultural imagery which glorifies and markets childhood as a commodity. In the green and caring 1990s, children signify as icons of simplicity and naturalness, the necessary accessory for any soap, shampoo and caring (especially male) figure. But according intrinsic, natural qualities to children gives rise to representations of gender and sexual orientation as somehow essential and inherent, as where child models are portrayed engaging in heterosexual dating postures as a means of selling clothes that are simply scaled-down versions of their parents' (Burman, 1991).

Discussions of the impact of developmental psychological knowledge often flounder on the issue of whether it reflects or produces the practices it describes. While it would be naive to accord too much significance to a minor arena of academic and popular culture, nevertheless the act of reproduction of both common-sense and technical-political understandings within the seemingly objective arena of scientific research functions to re-cycle existing historically and culturally specific ideas as legitimised, eternal knowledge. Models about children and child rearing achieve a reality in part because they comprise the fabric of both professional and everyday knowledge about ourselves and our relationships. We cannot easily get outside them since they have constituted our very subjectivities, and in that sense notions of 'reflection' and even 'production' fail to convey their reality within our lives.

Baker and Freebody (1987) discuss how a particular cultural form, in this case, children's first reading books, acts to 'constitute the child' by presenting a parti- cular, school-endorsed set of representations of child, family, school and social relations within the materials. While purporting to reflect the children's develop- ment, these function to organise it. They map out their school and personal careers and ambitions as pupils, boys and girls, with class positions (see also Rose, 1985), and relay sets of ideas about the positions and rights of adults and children. The consequences of this may even enter into the children's abilities to engage with educational processes. As they put it:

> Young readers, whose identities as children differ from the images embedded in the texts, may have particular difficulties in relating to these books. For all children there may exist the practical problems of knowing how to treat these images while taking part in a reading instruction based on them, in such a way as to appear to be concurring with school-endorsed portraits in the texts.
>
> (Baker and Freebody, 1987: 57)

MORALITY AND CHANGE

We have moved very fast in this chapter from a discussion of Piaget's work on morality to the role developmental psychology plays in the new world, and now the new world order. What developmental psychology all too often neglects, even when it studies morality, is its own moral status as a moral science, and its moral positions in the world. We have seen how developmental psychology has func- tioned as an instrument of classification and evaluation, as a tool for 'mental hygiene', a euphemism for the control and surveillance of populations deemed likely to be troublesome or burdensome – working-class children, single parents, minority groups and poor people the world over. Clothed in the rhetoric of scientific rigour and detachment, it has worked in very partial ways. The denial of moral-political assumptions underlying developmental psychology has merely worked to maintain reactionary practices. Now it is time to recognise that the 'science' of development is not separate from concerns of 'truth', and therefore of morality, politics and government.

This book started with an account of how developmental psychology arose, and the moral-political agendas it served and expressed. From the constitution of the isolated, individual 'child' as its unit of study, to an equivalent focus on families, mothers, and now fathers, developmental psychology functions as a key resource for legislating upon and distributing welfare interventions. Parts I and II of this book demonstrated how development is portrayed as either divorced from social and material circumstances, or within so over-simplified and sanitised a conception of the 'social' that it diverts and proscribes critical evaluation and colludes in the pathologisation of individuals and groups on the basis of their failure to reflect the Western, middle-class norms that have structured developmental psychological research. In Parts II and III we saw how these assumptions structure not only the explicit accounts of how to care for, and who should care for, children, but also enter in less direct but equally evaluative ways into accounts of language and learning. 'Sensitive' mothers are not only better mothers in the ways that they respond to and look after their charges, they also maximalise (Rose, 1990) their children's learning. We may claim, as the theories of cognitive development and education discussed in Part IV do, to deal with the 'whole child', but this child is endowed with a false unity conferred by its abstraction from social relations. These last chapters have argued that the rationality and individualism that 'he' is accorded construct an image of mental life that privileges cultural masculinity and mirrors market demands for skills and efficient functioning. The costs of accounting for 'mastery' and development in these ways are that, beneath the facade of the whole, adjusted and integrated self, the subject of developmental psychology is fragmented, alienated and split.

In over seven years of teaching a wide range of undergraduate and professional groups, within each group I have encountered two sorts of reactions to developmental psychology. One is that it is mystificatory and jargon-ridden, which creates some hostility on the grounds of its exclusivity and inaccessibility; the other is to dismiss it as simply common sense. And both reactions are correct. What should be clear from this book is that dressed up in its claims to present some particular expertise (of which it devotes considerable energy to maintaining sole control), developmental psychology (like the rest of psychology) imports ideological understandings into its theories that are incorporated into 'science'. As I have shown, the methodologies as well as the theories reflect these assumptions, but coded at a deeper level through the relation between science and modern States.

CONSTRUCTING AND DECONSTRUCTING

This book has attempted to identify and evaluate the central themes that structure contemporary developmental psychology. In part the journey has been a historical one, in aiming to understand the specific conditions that prompted the emergence of, and agenda for, what has come to be a central agency for the regulation and control of individual and family life. In other ways we have had to look beyond the theories to understand the cultural and political role that the academic practice of developmental psychology fulfils. Both home and school are informed by developmental psychology, and it enters into the ways we talk and reflect upon our feelings and intellect, and, more than this, produces 'us' in its image.

The process of delineating and commenting on these discourses is part of the process of deconstructing, of dismantling the power of this apparatus for the construction of subjects by which we are disciplined and constituted. We have seen how inequality and differential treatment on the basis of class, culture, gender, age and sexuality permeate the deep structure of developmental psychological practice. Developmental psychology therefore contributes to the maintenance of the social formation which gave rise to it.

I have been using the term deconstruction as a mode of analysis which invites scrutiny of the limits and presuppositions that have guided research. While deconstruction threatens to disallow absolute justification of any position (Burman, 1990) – including mine here – there nevertheless can be no fully practising deconstructor. Instead, the issue is to bring to light, acknowledge, the investment and hidden subjectivity that lie beneath the claims to disinterested, true knowledge. The impetus behind this book reflects Gayatri Chakravorty Spivak's (1990) characterisation of the 'corrective and critical' role of deconstruction:

> in one way or another academics are in the business of ideological production. . . . Our institutional responsibility is of course to offer a responsible critique of the structure of production of the knowledge we teach even as we teach it, but, in addition, we must go public as often as we can.
>
> (Spivak 1990: 103)

What is achieved by such a process of deconstruction? I would like to hope that at the very least some caution about the indiscriminate application of general models should follow. Ideas are tools for change, and they are certainly used to prevent change. The purpose of this deconstruction is to lay bare, to make public, the parameters by which our own change and development has been structured. The domain of developmental psychology is a modern, Western construction, which is itself contested and under revision, though currently often continually reinvented. Taking apart, challenging its scientific certainty and grip on common sense may help us to recognise other ways of talking about those issues that currently are dealt with within the terms of developmental psychology. Exploitation and oppression suffuse the structure of developmental psychology. Our task is to deconstruct it.

FURTHER READING

Boyden, J. (1990) 'Childhood and the policymakers: a comparative perspective on the globalization of childhood', in A. James and A. Prout (eds) *Constructing and Reconstructing Childhood*, Basingstoke, Hants: Falmer.
Rose, N. (1990) 'Psychology as a "social" science', in I. Parker and J. Shotter (eds) *Deconstructing Social Psychology*, London: Routledge.
Sampson, E. (1990) 'Social psychology and social control', in I. Parker and J. Shotter (eds) *Deconstructing Social Psychology*, London: Routledge.

SUGGESTED ACTIVITIES

1 Take any developmental psychology test or assessment task (whether of infant development scales, conservation tasks or child-rearing styles) and consider
   a) its claims to generality, and;
   b) the extent to which the categorisation of behaviours reflects or refers to specific cultural practices;
   c) the extent to which the definition of positive parenting behaviours addresses culturally specific understandings of children's qualities and corresponding models of caregiving activities.
2 Explore Boyden's (op cit.) notion of the 'globalization of childhood'. What are the dominant cultural images of childhood? Whose childhood do they reflect? Collect a corpus of images of children from all over the world and explore:
   a) whether the children are used to express the same or different sets of qualities;
   b) to what extent the children are represented within or as separate from their cultural and familial context. What implications can be drawn from this about i) models of development and ii) the symbolic functions played by images of children?

(Pat Holland's book *What is a Child? Popular Images of Children*, Virago, 1992, is a useful accompaniment to this exercise.)

References

Abbott, P. (1989) 'Family lifestyles and structures', in W. Stainton Rogers, D. Hevey and E. Ash (eds) *Child Abuse and Neglect: facing the challenge*, London: Batsford.

Abramovitch, R., Freedman, J.L., Thoden, K. and Nikolich, C. (1991) 'Children's capacity to consent to participation in psychological research: empirical findings', *Child Development*, 62: 1100–9.

Ainsworth, M.D.S., Bell, S.M. and Stayton, D.J. (1974) 'Infant–mother attachment and social development: "socialisation" as a product of reciprocal responsiveness to signals', in M.P.M. Richards (ed.) *The Integration of the Child into a Social World*, Cambridge: Cambridge University Press.

Ariès, P. (1962) *Centuries of Childhood*, Cape: London.

Arney, W.R. (1980) 'Maternal–infant bonding: the politics of falling in love with your child', *Feminist Studies, 6, 3*: 547–70.

Austin, J.L. (1962) *How to Do Things with Words*, London: Oxford University Press.

Avis, J. (1991) 'The strange fate of progressive education', in Education Group II, Cultural Studies University of Birmingham, *Education Limited: schooling and training and the new right since 1979*, London: Unwin Hyman.

Baetens Beardsmore, H. (1982) *Bilingualism: basic principles*, Avon: Multilingual Matters.

Baker, C.D. and Freebody, P. (1987) '"Constituting the child" in beginning school reading books', *British Journal of Sociology of Education, 8, 1*: 55–76.

Baltes, P.B., Reese, H.W. and Lipsett, L.P. (1980) 'Life-span developmental psychology', *Annual Review of Psychology, 23*: 611–26.

Barton, M. and Tomasello, M. (in press) 'The rest of the family: the role of father and siblings in early language development', in C. Galloway and B. Richards (eds) *Input and Interaction in Language Acquisition*, Cambridge: Cambridge University Press.

Bates, E., Camaioni, L. and Volyera, V. (1979) 'The acquisition of performatives prior to speech', in E. Ochs and B. Schieffelin (eds) *Developmental Pragmatics*, New York: Academic Press.

Batou, J. (1991) '100 million women are missing', *International Viewpoint, 206*: 26–8.

Beekman, D. (1979) *The Mechanical Baby: a popular history of the theory and practice of childraising*, London: Dobson.

Bell, R. and Harper, L. (1977) *Child Effects on Adults*, Hillsdale. NJ: Erlbaum.

Belsky, J. (1981) 'Early human experience: a family perspective', *Developmental Psychology, 17*: 3–23.

Belsky, J. and Rovine, M.J. (1988) 'Nonmaternal care in the first year of life and the security of infant–parent attachment', *Child Development, 59*: 157–67.

Bernstein, B. (1970) 'Education cannot compensate for society', *New Society, 26 February*: 344–7.

Bernstein, B. (ed.) (1973) *Class, Codes and Control*, Vol. 2, London: Roultedge & Kegan Paul.

Bettelheim, B. (1986) *Freud and Man's Soul*, Harmondsworth: Flamingo.

Billig, M., Condor, S., Edwards, D., Gane, M., Middleton, D. and Radley, A. (1988) *Ideological Dilemmas: a social psychology of everyday thinking*, London: Sage.

Blakemore, C. and Cooper, G.F. (1970) 'Development of the brain depends on the visual environment', *Nature, 228*: 477–8.

Blurton Jones, N. (1972) *Ethological Studies of Child Behaviour*, Cambridge: Cambridge University Press.

Bly, R. (1991) *Iron John: a book about men*, Shaftesbury: Element.

Boden, M. (1979) *Piaget*, London: Fontana.

Bohannen, J. and Hirsh-Pasek, K. (1984) 'Do children say as they're told? A new perspective on motherese', in L. Feagans, C. Garvey and R. Golinkoff (eds) *The Origins and Growth of Communication*, Norwood, NJ: Ablex.

Bohannen, J. and Marquis, A. (1977) 'Children's control of adult speech', *Child Development, 48*: 1002–8.

Boulton, M.G. (1983) *On Being a Mother: a study of women with pre-school children*, London: Tavistock.

Bower, T. (1966) 'The visual world of infants', *Scientific American, 215, 6*: 180–93.

Bower, T. (1977) 'Blind babies see with their ears', *New Scientist, 73*: 255–7.

Bower, T., Broughton, J. and Moore, M. (1970) 'Infant responses to approaching objects: an indication of response to distal variables', *Perception and Psychophysics, 8*: 51–3.

Bowers, J. (1990) 'All hail the great abstraction: star wars and the politics of cognitive psychology', in I. Parker and J. Shotter (eds) *Deconstructing Social Psychology*, London: Routledge.

Bowlby, J. (1951) *Maternal Care and Mental Health*, Geneva: World Health Organisation.

Bowlby, J., Figlio, K. and Young, R. (1986) 'An interview with John Bowlby on the origins and reception of his work', *Free Associations, 6*: 36–64.

Boyd, S. (1989) 'From gender specificity to gender neutrality? Ideologies in Canadian child custody law', in C. Smart and S. Sevenhuijsen (eds) *Child Custody and the Politics of Gender*, London: Routledge.

Boyden, J. (1990) 'Childhood and the policy makers: a comparative perspective on the globalization of childhood', in A. James and A. Prout (eds) *Constructing and Reconstructing Childhood: contemporary issues in the sociological study of childhood*, Basingstoke, Hants: Falmer.

Boyden, J. with Holden, P. (1991) *Children of the Cities*, London: Zed Books.

Boyden, J. and Hudson, A. (1985) *Children: rights and responsibilities*, London: Minority Rights Group.

Bradley, B.S. (1989) *Visions of Infancy*, Oxford: Polity/Blackwell.

Brainerd, C. (1973) 'Judgements and explanations as criteria for the process of cognitive structures', *Psychological Bulletin, 79, 3*: 172–9.

Brannen, J. and Moss, P. (1987) 'Fathers in dual-earner households – through mothers' eyes', in C. Lewis and M. O'Brian (eds) *Reassessing Fatherhood: new observations on fatherhood and the modern family*, London: Sage.

Brannen, J. and Wilson, G. (eds) (1987) *Give and Take in Families: studies in resource distribution*, London: Allen & Unwin.

Brazelton, T.B., Koslowski, B. and Main, M. (1974) 'The origins of reciprocity', in M. Lewis and L. Rosenblum (eds) *The Effect of the Infant on its Caregiver*, New York: Wiley.

Bremner, J.G. (1988) *Infancy*, Oxford: Blackwell.

Brice Heath, S. (1983) *Ways with Words*, Cambridge: Cambridge University Press.

Brice Heath, S. (1986) 'What no bedtime story means: narrative skills at home and at school', in B. Schieffelin and E. Ochs (eds) *Language Socialisation across Cultures*, Cambridge: Cambridge University Press.

Broughton, J. (1981a) 'Piaget's structural developmental psychology I: Piaget and structuralism', *Human Development, 24*: 78–109.

Broughton, J. (1981b) 'Piaget's structural developmental psychology III: logic and psycho- logy', *Human Development, 24*: 195–224.

Broughton, J. (1987) 'Introduction', in J. Broughton (ed.) *Critical Theories of Psychological Development*, New York: Plenum Press.

Broughton, J. (1988) 'The masculine authority of the cognitive', in B. Inhelder (ed.) *Piaget Today*, London: Erlbaum.

Brown, R. (1973) *A First Language*, Harmondsworth: Penguin.

Brown, R. and Hanlon, C. (1970) 'Derivational complexity and order of acquisition in child speech', in J.R. Hayes (ed.) *Cognition and the Development of Language*, New York: Wiley.

Browne, N. and France, P. (1985) '"Only cissies wear dresses": a look at sexist talk in the nursery', in G. Weiner (ed.) *Just a Bunch of Girls: feminist approaches to schooling*, Milton Keynes: Open University Press.

Bruner, J. (1975/6) 'From communication to language', *Cognition, 3*: 355–87.

Bruner, J. (1978) 'Learning how to do things with words', in J. Bruner and A. Garten (eds) *Human Growth and Development*, Oxford: Clarendon Press.

Bruner, J. (1983) *Child's Talk: learning to use language*, Oxford: Oxford University Press.

Buck-Morss, S. (1975) 'Socio-economic bias in Piaget's theory and its implications for cross-cultural studies', *Human Development, 18*: 35–45.

Bukatko, D. and Daehler, M. (1992) *Child Development: a topical approach*, Boston, Mass.: Houghton Mifflin.

Bullock, A. (1974) *A Language for Life: report of the committee of enquiry appointed by the Secretary of State for Education under the chairmanship of Sir Alan Bullock*, London: HMSO.

Burman, E. (1990) 'Differing with deconstruction: a feminist critique', in I. Parker and J. Shotter (eds) *Deconstructing Social Psychology*, London: Routledge.

Burman, E. (1991) 'Power, gender and developmental psychology', *Feminism and Psychology, 1, 1*: 141–54.

Burman, E. (1992a) 'Feminism and discourse in developmental psychology: power, subjectivity and interpretation', *Feminism and Psychology, 2, 1*: 45–60.

Burman, E. (1992b) 'Developmental psychology and the postmodern child', in J. Doherty, E. Graham and M. Malek (eds) *Postmodernism and the Social Sciences*, London: Macmillan.

Burman, E. (1993) 'Beyond discursive relativism: power and subjectivity in developmental psychology', in H. Stam, L. Moss, W. Thorngate and B. Caplan (eds) *Recent Trends in Theoretical Psychology*, Vol. III, New York: Springer Verlag.

Burman, E. (in press a) 'What is it? Masculinity and femininity in the cultural representation of childhood', in S. Wilkinson and C. Kitzinger (eds) *Feminism and Discourse*, London: Sage.

Burman, E. (in press b) 'Poor children: charity appeals and ideologies of childhood', *Changes: International Journal of Psychology and Psychotherapy*.

Burman, E. (1994) 'Prospects for old and new methodologies in developmental psychology', in preparation.

Burman, E. and Parker, I. (eds) (1993) *Discourse Analytic Research: repertoires and readings of texts in action*, London: Routledge.

Burns, R. (1986) *Child Development: a text for the caring professions*, Kent: Croom Helm.

Butterworth, G. (ed.) (1980) *Infancy and Epistemology: an evaluation of Piaget's theory*, Brighton: Harvester.

Camaioni, L. (1979) 'Child–adult and child–child conversations: an interactional approach', in E. Ochs and B. Schieffelin (eds) *Developmental Pragmatics*, New York: Academic Press.

Campbell, B. (1984) 'Women on the rock and roll', in *Wigan Pier Revisited*, London: Virago.

Caplan, P. (1985) 'Mother-blaming in major clinical journals', *American Journal of Orthopsychiatry, 55, 3*: 345–53.

Carter, A. (1978) 'From sensorimotor vocalizations to words: a case study in the evolution of attention-directing communication in the second year', in A. Lock (ed.) *Action, Gesture and Symbol*, London: Academic Press.

Cassidy, C. (1989) 'Worldview conflict and toddler malnutrition: changeagent dilemmas', in N. Scheper-Hughes (ed.) *Child Survival and Neglect*, Dordrecht: Reidel.

Chaika, E. (1982) *Language: the social mirror*, Rowley, Mass.: Newbury House.

Chomsky, N. (1959) 'A review of B.F. Skinner's *Verbal Behaviour*', *Language, 35*: 26–58.

Clancy, P. (1989) 'Form and function in the acquisition of Korean wh- questions', *Journal of Child Language, 16*: 323–47.

Clarizio, H., Craig, R. and Mehrens, W. (eds) *Contemporary Issues in Educational Psychology*, Boston, Mass.: Allyn & Bacon.

Clarke, A.M. and Clarke, A.D. (1976) *Early Experience: myth and evidence*, London: Open Books.

Clarke-Stewart, A. (1982) *Day Care*, London: Fontana.

Clarke-Stewart, K.A. (1988) 'The "effects" of infant day care reconsidered', *Early Childhood Research Quarterly, 3*: 293–18.

Cohen, C.B., Deloache, J.S. and Rissman, M.W. (1979) 'The effect of stimulus complexity on infant visual attention and habituation', *Child Development, 46*: 611–17.

Cohen, G. (ed.) (1987) *Social Change and the Life Course*, London: Tavistock.

Colby, A., Kohlberg, L., Gibbs, J. and Lieberman, M. (1983) 'A longitudinal study of moral judgement', *Monographs of the Society for Research in Child Development, 48, (1–2):* (no 200).

Cole, M. and Cole, S. (1989) *The Development of Children*, New York: Scientific American Books/Freeman.

Cole, M., Gay, J., Glick, J. and Sharp, D.W. (1971) *The Cultural Context of Learning and Thinking*, New York: Basic Books.

Condon, W. (1977) 'A primary phase in the organisation of infant responding behaviour', in H. Schaffer (ed.) *Studies in Mother–Infant Interaction*, London: Academic Press.

Conteh, J. (1992) 'Monolingual children and diversity: the space in the centre', *Multicultural Teaching, 11, 1*: 27–31.

Cooter, R. (ed.) (1992) *In the Name of the Child: health and welfare 1880–1940*, London: Routledge.

Council for Racial Equality (1992) *Set to Fail*, Oxford: Council for Racial Equality.

Cross, T. (1977) 'Mothers' speech adjustments: the contribution of selected child listener variables', in C. Snow and C. Ferguson (eds) *Talking to Children*, Cambridge: Cambridge University Press.

Dalley, G. (1988) *Ideologies of Caring: re-thinking community and collectivism*, Basingstoke: Macmillan Education.

Daniels, D. and Plomin, R. (1985) 'Differential experience of siblings in the same family', *Developmental Psychology, 21, 5*: 747–60.

Davies, B. and Harré, R. (1990) 'Positioning: the discursive production of selves', *Journal of the Theory of Social Behaviour, 20, 1*: 43–63.

Dingwall, R. (1989) 'Labelling children as abused or neglected', in W. Stainton Rogers, D. Hevey and E. Ash (eds) *Child Abuse and Neglect: facing the challenge*, London: Batsford.

Dingwall, R. and Eekelaar, J. (1986) 'Judgements of Solomon: developmental psychology and family law', in M. Richards and P. Light (eds) *Children of Social Worlds*, Oxford: Polity.

Dingwall, R., Eekelaar, J.M. and Murray, T. (1984) 'Childhood as a social problem: a survey of the history of legal regulation', *Journal of Law and Society, 11,* 2: 207–32.

Dinnerstein, D. (1978) *The Rocking of the Cradle and the Ruling of the World*, London: Souvenir Press.

DiPietro, J., Larson, S. and Porges, S. (1987) 'Behavioral and heart rate pattern differences between breast-fed and bottle-fed neonates', *Developmental Psychology, 23, 4*: 467–74.

Donaldson, M. (1978) *Children's Minds*, London: Fontana.

Dornbush, S. and Strober, M. (eds) (1988) *Feminism, Children and the New Families*, New York: Guilford Press.

Dunn, J. and Kendrick, C. (1982) *Siblings: love, envy and understanding*, London: Grant McIntyre.

Dunn, J., Brown, J., Slomkowski, E., Tesla, C. and Youngblade, L. (1991) 'Young children's understanding of other people's feelings and beliefs: individual differences and their antecedents', *Child Development, 62*: 1352–66.

Durham, M. (1991) *Sex and Politics: the family and morality in the Thatcher years*, London: Macmillan.

Durkin, K. (1987) 'Minds and language: social cognition, social interaction and the acquisition of language', *Mind and Language, 2*: 105–40.

Dworetzky, J. (1990) *Introduction to Child Development*, St Paul, MN: West.

Dworetzky, J. and Davis, N. (1989) *Human Development: a lifespan approach*, St Paul, MN: West.

Edwards, C.P. (1981) 'The comparative study of the development of moral judgement and reasoning', in R.H. Munroe, R.L. Munroe and B.B. Whiting (eds) *Handbook of Cross Cultural Human Development*, New York: Garland.

Edwards, D. and Mercer, N. (1987) *Common Knowledge: the development of understanding in the classroom*, London: Sage.

Egerton, J. (1991) 'The family way: Labour's policy on the family', *Trouble and Strife, 20*: 3–7.

Ennew, J. and Milne, B. (1989) *The Next Generation: lives of Third World children*, London: Zed Books.

Equal Opportunities Commission (1991) *Some Facts about Women 1991*, Manchester: EOC.

Ervin Tripp, S., O'Connor, M. and Rosenberg, J. (1984) 'Language and power in the family', in C. Kramerae, M. Schultz and W. O'Barr (eds) *Language and Power*, Beverly Hills, CA: Sage.

Fantz, R. (1961) 'The origin of form perception', *Scientific American, 204*: 66–72.

Farrar, M. (1990) 'Discourse and the acquisition of grammatical morphemes', *Journal of Child Language, 17*: 607–24.

Ferguson, C. (1977) 'Baby talk as a simplified register', in C. Snow and C. Ferguson (eds) *Talking to Children*, Cambridge: Cambridge University Press.

Fieldman, S. (1991) 'How a wedding ring separates bright mums from prize mugs', *Independent*, 21 September.

Finch, J. (1989) *Family Obligations and Social Change,* Cambridge: Polity.

Finch, J. and Groves, D. (1983) *A Labour of Love*, London: Routledge & Kegan Paul.

Fineman, M. (1989) 'The politics of custody and gender: child advocacy and the transformation of custody decision making in the USA', in C. Smart and S. Sevenhuijsen (eds) *Child Custody and the Politics of Gender*, London: Routledge.

Flavell, J. (1963) *The Developmental Psychology of Jean Piaget*, New York: Van Nostrand.

Fletcher, H. (1982) 'A social worker's view', in *No Accountability, No Redress: the powers of social workers and the rights of parents*, London: One Parent Families.

Fogel, A. (1991) *Infancy: infant, family and society*, St Paul, MN: West.

Fonagy, P., Steele, H. and Steele, M. (1991) 'Maternal representations of attachment during pregnancy predict the organisation of infant–mother attachment at one year of age', *Child Development, 62*: 891–905.

Ford, J. (1982) *Special Education and Social Control: invisible disasters*, London: Routledge & Kegan Paul.

Foucault, M. (1972) *The Archaeology of Knowledge*, London: Tavistock.

Freeman, M. (1989) 'Principles and processes of the law in child protection', in W. Stainton Rogers, D. Hevey and E. Ash (eds) *Child Abuse and Neglect: facing the challenge*, London: Batsford.

French, E.P. and Maclure, M. (eds) (1981) *Adult–Child Conversation*, London: Croom Helm.

Fuchs, E. (1973) 'How teachers learn to help children fail', in N. Keddie (ed.) *Tinker, Tailor . . . the Myth of Cultural Deprivation*, Harmondsworth: Penguin.

Gamsa, A. (1987) 'A note on the modification of the Parental Bonding Instrument', *British Journal of Medical Psychology, 69*: 291–4.

Gardner, H. (1982) *Developmental Psychology*, Boston, Mass.: Little, Brown.

Garland, C. and White, S. (1980) *Children and Day Nurseries*, London: Grant McIntyre.

Gesell, A. (1950) *The First Five Years of Life: a guide to the study of the pre-school child*, London: Methuen.

Geuter, U. (1987) 'German psychology during the Nazi period', in M. Ash and W. Woodwood (eds) *Psychology in Twentieth Century Thought and Society*, Cambridge, Mass.: Cambridge University Press.

Gibson, E. and Walk, R.D. (1960) 'The "visual cliff"', reprinted in T. Greenough (ed.) (1973) *The Nature and Nurture of Behavior: developmental psychobiology*, San Francisco: Freeman.

Gilligan, C. (1982) *In a Different Voice: psychological theory and women's development*, Cambridge, Mass.: Harvard University Press.

Ginsberg, H. and Opper, S. (1979) *Piaget's Theory of Intellectual* Development, Englewood Cliffs, NJ: Prentice-Hall.

Gittins, D. (1985) *The Family in Question*, London: Macmillan.

Glauser, B. (1990) 'Street children: deconstructing a construct', in A. James and A. Prout (eds) *Constructing and Reconstructing Childhood*, London: Falmer.

Goodnow, J. and Collins, W. (1990) *Development According to Parents: the nature, sources and consequences of parents' ideas*, Hove, E. Sussex: LEA.

Gopnik, A. and Choi, S. (1990) 'Do linguistic differences lead to cognitive differences? A cross-linguistic study of semantic and cognitive development', *First Language, 10*: 199–215.

Gould, S. (1984) *The Mismeasure of Man*, Harmondsworth: Penguin.

Graycar, R. (1989) 'Equal rights *versus* fathers' rights: the child custody debate in Australia', in C. Smart and S. Sevenhuijsen (eds) *Child Custody and the Politics of Gender*, London: Routledge.

Gruber, H. and Vonèche, J., (1977) *The Essential Piaget: an interpretive reference and guide*, London: Routledge & Kegan Paul.

Hakuta, K. (1986) *Mirror of Language: the debate on bilingualism*, New York: Basic Books.

Hall, D.M.B., Hill, P. and Elliman D. (1990) *Handbook of Child Surveillance*, Oxford: Radcliffe Medical.

Halliday, M.A.K. (1973) 'Foreword' to B. Bernstein (ed.) *Class, Codes and Control*, Vol. 2, London: Routledge & Kegan Paul.

Halliday, M.A.K. (1975) *Learning How to Mean: explorations in the development of language*, London: Arnold.

Hallpike, C. (1979) *The Foundations of Primitive Thought*, Cambridge: Cambridge University Press.

Handelman, D. (1989) 'Bureaucracy and the maltreatment of the child: interpretive and structural issues', in N. Scheper-Hughes (ed.) *Child Survival and Neglect: anthropological perspectives on the treatment and maltreatment of children*, Dordrecht: Reidel.

Haraway, D. (1989) 'Metaphors into hardware: Harry Harlow and the technology of love', in *Primate Visions: gender, race and nature in the world of modern science*, London: Verso.

Hardyment, C. (1983) *Dream Babies*, Oxford: Oxford University Press.

Harlow, H. (1959) 'Love in infant monkeys', reprinted in T. Greenough (ed.) (1973) *The Nature and Nurture of Behavior: developmental psychobiology*, San Francisco: Freeman.

Harlow, H., Harlow, M. and Suomi, S. (1971) 'From thought to therapy: lessons from a primate laboratory', *American Scientist, 659*: 538–49.

Harré, R. (1983) *Personal Being: a theory for individual psychology*, Oxford: Blackwell.

Harré, R. (1986) 'Steps towards social construction', in M. Richards and P. Light (eds) *Children of Social Worlds*, Oxford: Polity.

Harris, A. (1987) 'The rationalisation of infancy', in J. Broughton (ed.) *Critical Theories of Psychological Development*, New York: Plenum Press.

Hearnshaw, L.S. (1980) *Cyril Burt, Psychologist*, London: Hodder & Stoughton.

Hendrick, H. (1990) 'Constructions and reconstructions of British childhood: an interpretive survey, 1800 to the present', in A. James and A. Prout (eds) *Constructing and Reconstructing Childhood: contemporary issues in the sociological study of childhood*, Basingstoke, Hants: Falmer.

Hennessy, E., Martin, S., Moss, P. and Melhuish, E. (1992) *Children and Day Care: lessons from research*, London: Paul Chapman.

Henriques, J., Hollway, W., Urwin, C., Venn, C. and Walkerdine, V. (1984) *Changing the Subject: psychology, social regulation and subjectivity*, London: Methuen.

Hinde, R. (1983) 'Ethology and child development', in M.M. Haith and J.J. Campos (eds) *Infancy and Developmental Psychobiology*, New York: Wiley.

Hoff-Ginsberg, E. (1991) 'Mother–child conversation in different social classes and communicative settings', *Child Development, 63*: 782–96.

Hogen, R. (1975) 'Moral development and the structure of personality', in D. DePalma and J. Foley (eds) *Moral Development: current theory and research*, New York: LEA.

Holtrust, N., Sevenhuijsen, S. and Verbraken, A. (1989) 'Rights for fathers and the state: recent developments in custody politics in the Netherlands', in C. Smart and S. Sevenhuijsen (eds) *Child Custody and the Politics of Gender*, London: Routledge.

Homel, P., Palij, M. and Aaronson, D. (1987) 'Introduction', to *Childhood Bilingualism: aspects of linguistic, cognitive, and social development*, New York: LEA.

Horna, J. and Lupri, E. (1987) 'Fathers' participation in work, family life and leisure: a Canadian experience', in C. Lewis and M. O'Brian (eds) *Reassessing Fatherhood: new observations on fatherhood and the modern family*, London: Sage.

Hoyles, M. (1989) *The Politics of Childhood*, London: Journeyman.

Hunt, F. (ed.) (1985) *Lessons for Life*, Oxford: Blackwell.

Hunt, J. McV. and Uzgiris, I.C. (1964) 'Cathexis from recognitive familiarity: an exploratory study', paper presented at the Convention of the American Psychological Association, Los Angeles, California (September).

Hymes, J. (1955) *A Child Development Point of View*, Englewood Cliffs, NJ: Prentice-Hall.

Ingleby, D. (1985) 'Professionals as socializers: the "psy complex"', *Research in Law, Deviance and Social Control, 7*: 79–109.

Ingleby, D. (1989) 'Critical psychology in relation to political repression and violence', *International Journal of Mental Health, 17*: 16–24.

Izard, C.E., Haynes, O.M., Chisholm, G. and Baak, K. (1991) 'Emotional determinants of infant–mother attachments', *Child Development, 62*: 906–17.

Jones, D. (1987) 'The choice to breast feed or bottle feed and influences upon that choice: a survey of 1525 mothers', *Child Care, Health and Development, 13, 1*: 75–85.

Jones, K. (1989) *Right Turn: the conservative revolution in education*, London: Radius.

Joseph, G., Reddy, V. and Searle-Chatterjee, M. (1990) 'Eurocentrism in the social sciences', *Race and Class, 31, 4*: 1–26.

Kagan, J. (1984) *The Nature of the Child*, New York: Basic Books.

Kaplan, P. (1991) *A Child's Odyssey: child and adolescent development*, St Paul, MN: West.

Karmiloff Smith, A. (1979) *A Functional Approach to Child Language: a study of determiners and reference*, Cambridge: Cambridge University Press.

Kaye, K. (1982) *The Mental and Social Life of Babies: how parents make persons*, London: Methuen.

Kepler, K. and Randall, J. (1981) 'Individualization: the subversive of elementary schooling', in H. Clarizio, R. Craig and W.A. Mehrens (ed.) *Contemporary Issues in Educational Psychology*, Boston, Mass.: Allyn & Bacon.

Kershaw, A. (1991) 'How the new man became the new lad', *Independent on Sunday, 14 April*: 19.

Kitzinger, J. (1990) 'Who are you, kidding? Children, power and the struggle against sexual abuse', in A. James and A. Prout (eds) *Constructing and Reconstructing Childhood: contemporary issues in the sociological study of childhood*, Basingstoke, Hants: Falmer.

Klaus, M. and Kennell, J. (1976) *Maternal–Infant Bonding*, New York: Wiley.

Kohlberg, L. (1969a) 'The child as moral philosopher', in J. Sants (ed.) *Developmental Psychology*, Harmondsworth: Penguin.

Kohlberg, L. (1969b) 'Stage and sequence: the cognitive developmental approach', in D.A. Goslin (ed.) *The Handbook of Socialization Theory and Research*, Chicago: Rand McNally.

Kohlberg, L. (1976) 'Moral stages and moralisation', in T. Lickona (ed.) *Moral Development and Moral Behaviour: theory, research and social issues*, New York: Holt, Rinehart & Winston.

Konner, M. (1977) 'Infancy among the Kalahari desert San', in P.H. Leiderman, S.R. Tulkin and A. Rosenfeld (eds) *Culture and Infancy*, New York: Academic Press.

Lamb, M.E. (ed.) (1982) *Non-traditional Families: parenting and child development*, Hillsdale, NJ: Erlbaum.

Lamb, M.E. (1988) 'Social and emotional development in infancy', in M.H. Bornstein and M.E. Lamb (eds) *Social, Emotional and Personality Development*, Hillsdale, NJ: Erlbaum.

Lawrence, D.H. (1973) 'Education and sex in man, woman and child', in J. Williams and R. Williams (eds) *Lawrence on Education*, Harmondsworth: Penguin.

Leiser, D. and Gilliéron, C. (1990) *Cognitive Science and Genetic Epistemology: a case study of understanding*, New York: Plenum Press.

Levine, C., Kohlberg, L. and Hewer, A. (1985) 'The current formulation of Kohlberg's theory and a response to critics', *Human Development, 28*: 94–100.

Lewis, C. (1982) 'The observation of father–infant relationships: an "attachment" to outmoded concepts', in L. McKee and M. O'Brian (eds) *The Father Figure*, London: Tavistock.

Lewis, S. and Cooper, C. (1991) *Dual Earner Couples*, London: Unwin Hyman.

Licht, B. and Dweck, C. (1987) 'Sex differences in achievement orientations', in M. Arnot and G. Weiner (eds) *Gender and the Politics of Schooling*, London: Hutchinson.

Lichtman, R. (1987) 'The illusion of maturation in an age of decline', in J. Broughton (ed.) *Critical Theories of Psychological Development*, New York: Plenum Press.

Lieven, E. (1981) 'If it's natural we can't change it', in Cambridge Women's Studies, *Women In Society*, London: Virago.

Lieven, E. (1982) 'Context, process and progress in young children's speech', in M. Beveridge (ed.) *Children Thinking through Language*, London: Arnold.

Lieven, E. (1984) 'Interactional style and children's language learning', *Topics in Language Disorders*, September: 15–23.

Lieven, E. (in press) 'Crosslinguistic and crosscultural aspects of language addressed to children', in B. Richards and C. Galloway (eds) *Input and Interaction in Language Acquisition*, Cambridge: Cambridge University Press.

Lieven, E. and Pine, J. (1990) 'Review of E. Bates, I. Bretherton and L. Snyder, *From First Words to Grammar: individual differences and dissociable mechanisms*, C.U.P., 1988', *Journal of Child Language, 17*: 495–501.

Light, P. (1979) *The Development of Social Sensitivity*, London: Cambridge University Press.

Lock, A. (ed.) (1978) *Action, Gesture and Symbol*, London: Academic Press.

Lowe, N. (1982) 'The legal status of fathers: past and present', in L. McKee and M. O'Brian (eds) *The Father Figure*, London: Tavistock.

Lowenfeld, M. (1935) *Play in Childhood*, London: Gollancz.

Lubeck, S. (1986) *Sandbox Society: early education in black and white America – a comparative ethnography*, Lewes: Falmer.

Lumnis, T. (1982) 'The historical dimension of fatherhood', in L. McKee and M. O'Brian (eds) *The Father Figure*, London: Tavistock.

Lyon, C. (1989) 'The redefinition of parental rights – recent English developments relating to joint custodianship and adoption in England', *Journal of Social Welfare, 3*: 138–47.

McCabe, A. (1987) 'Failure in class inclusion reasoning in a university sample', *Journal of Psychology, 121, 4*: 351–8.

McDonald, L. and Pien, D. (1982) 'Mothers' conversational behaviour as a function of interactional intent', *Journal of Child Language, 8*: 337–58.

McGuire, J. (1991) 'Sons and daughters', in A. Phoenix, A. Woollett and E. Lloyd (eds) *Motherhood: meanings, practices and ideologies*, London: Sage.

McKee, L. (1982) 'Fathers' participation in infant care: a critique', in L. McKee and M. O'Brian (eds) *The Father Figure*, London: Tavistock.

McKee, L. and O'Brian, M. (1982) 'The father figure: some current orientations and historical perspectives', in L. McKee and M. O'Brian (eds) *The Father Figure*, London: Tavistock.

McLaughlin, B. (1984) *Second Language Acquisition in Childhood*, Vol. 1, Hillsdale, NJ: LEA.

McNally, D.W. (1974) *Piaget, Education and Teaching*, Sydney: New Educational Press.

McShane, J. (1980) *Learning to Talk*, Cambridge: Cambridge University Press.

Marks, D. (1993) 'Case conference analysis and action research', in E. Burman and I. Parker (eds) *Discourse Analytic Research: repertoires and readings of texts in action*, London: Routledge.

Marshall, H. (1991) 'The social construction of motherhood: an analysis of childcare and parenting manuals', in A. Phoenix, A. Woollett and E. Lloyd (eds) *Motherhood: meanings, practices and ideologies*, London: Sage.

Mearns, A.G. (1961) *The Whole Child*, London: National Children's Home.

Meltzoff, A. (1981) 'Imitation, intermodal co-ordination and representation in early infancy', in G. Butterworth (ed.) *Infancy and Epistemology*, Brighton: Harvester.

Meyer, P. (1983) *The Child and the State: the intervention of the state in the family*, Cambridge: Cambridge University Press.

Miller, S.A. (1976) 'Non-verbal assessment in Piagetian concepts', *Psychological Bulletin, 83*, 405–30.

Mitchell, P. (1992) *The Psychology of the Child*, London: Falmer.

Mitter, S. (1986) *Common Fate, Common Bond*, London: Pluto.

Moll, L. (ed.) (1990) *Vygotsky and Education: instructional implications and applications of sociohistorical psychology*, Cambridge: Cambridge University Press.

Moore, S. (1988) 'Getting a bit of the Other: the pimps of postmodernism', in R. Chapman and J. Rutherford (eds) *Male Order: unwrapping masculinity*, London: Lawrence & Wishart.

Morris, L. (1987) 'The no-longer working class', *New Society, 3 April*: 16–18.

Morris, T. (1992) *The Despairing Developer: diary of an aid worker in the Middle East*, London: IB Taurus.

Morss, J. (1990) *The Biologising of Childhood*, Hillsdale, NJ: Erlbaum.

Morss, J. (in press) *Going Critical: an introduction to the critical psychology of human development*, London: Routledge.

Moss, P. (1990) 'Work, family and the care of children: issues of equality and responsibility', *Children and Society, 4*, 2: 145–66.

Munn, P. (1991) 'Mothering more than one child', in A. Phoenix, A. Woollett and E. Lloyd (eds) *Motherhood: meanings, practices and ideologies*, London: Sage.

Murchison, C. (1933) 'Preface' to C. Murchison (ed.) *A Handbook of Child Psychology*, Worcester, Mass.: Clark University Press.

Myers, R. (1992) *The Twelve Who Survive: strengthening programmes of early childhood development in the Third World*, London: Routledge/UNESCO.

Nelson, K. (1973) 'Structure and strategy in learning to talk', *Monographs of the Society for Research in Child Development, 38*: 1–2, no. 149.

New, C. and David, M. (1985) *For the Children's Sake: making childcare more than women's business*, Harmondsworth: Penguin.

Newman, D., Griffin, P. and Cole, M. (1989) *The Construction Zone: working for cognitive change in school*, Cambridge: Cambridge University Press.

Newman, F. and Holzman, L. (1993) *Lev Vygotsky: revolutionary scientist*, London and New York: Routledge.

Newport, E., Gleitman, H. and Gleitman, L. (1977) 'Mother I'd rather do it myself: some effects and non-effects of maternal speech style', in C. Snow and C. Ferguson (eds) *Talking to Children*, Cambridge: Cambridge University Press.

Newson, J. and Newson, E. (1968) *Four Years Old in an Urban Community*, Harmondsworth: Penguin.

Newson, J. and Newson, E. (1974) 'Cultural aspects of childrearing in the English-speaking world', in M. Richards (ed.) *The Integration of the Child into a Social World*, London: Cambridge University Press.

Newson, J. and Shotter, J. (1974) 'How babies communicate', *New Society, 29*: 345–57.

Ninio, A. and Bruner, J. (1978) 'The achievement and antecedents of labelling', *Journal of Child Language, 5*: 1–15.

Oakley, A. (1980) *From Here to Maternity*, Harmondsworth: Penguin.

O'Brian, M. and Alldred, P. (1991) 'Children's representations of family life', paper presented to British Psychological Society Developmental Section conference, September.

O'Brian, M. and L. Mckee (1983) 'Interviewing men: "taking gender seriously"', in E. Garmarnikow, D. Morgan, J. Purvis and D. Taylorson (eds) *The Public and the Private*, London: Heinemann.

Ochs, E. (1983) 'Cultural dimensions of language acquisition', in E. Ochs and B. Schieffelin, *Acquiring Conversational Competence*, London: Routledge & Kegan Paul.

Ochs, E. (1986) 'Introduction', to B. Schieffelin and E. Ochs (eds) *Language Socialisation across Cultures*, Cambridge: Cambridge University Press.

O'Hagan, S. (1991) 'Is the New Lad a fitting model for the Nineties?', *Arena, Spring/ Summer*: 22–3.

O'Hara, M. (1991) 'The rights and wrongs of children', *Trouble and Strife, 20*: 28–33.

Olsson, M. (1991) 'Producing the truth about people: science and the cult of the individual in educational psychology', in J. Morss and T. Linzey (eds) *Growing up: the politics of human learning*, Auckland, New Zealand: Longman.

Papert, S. (1980) *Mindstorms: children, computers and powerful ideas*, Brighton: Harvester.

Parke, R.D. (1984) *Fathering*, London: Fontana.

Parke, R.D., MacDonald, K.B., Burks, V.M., Bhavnagri, N., Barth, J.M. and Beitel, A. (1989) 'Family and peer systems: in search of the linkages', in K. Krepner and R.M. Lerner (eds) *Family Systems and Lifespan Development*, Hillsdale, NJ: LEA.

Parker, G., Topling, H. and Brown, L. (1979) 'A parental bonding instrument', *British Journal of Medical Psychology, 52*: 1–10.

Parker, I. (1989) *The Crisis in Social Psychology and How to End It*, London: Routledge.

Parker, I. (1992a) *Discourse Dynamics*, London: Routledge.

Parker, I. (1992b) 'Wild men', paper presented at Psychoanalysis and the Public Sphere, 6th Annual Conference, University of East London, October.

Parker, I. (1993) 'Reflexive social psychology? Discourse analysis and psychoanalysis', *Free Associations, 28*.

Parker, I. and Shotter, J. (eds) (1990) *Deconstructing Social Psychology*, London: Routledge.

Parsons, B. (1983) *The Expectant Father: a practical guide to pregnancy and childbirth for the anxious man*, Middx: Quartermaine House.

Parton, N. (1991) *Governing the Family: child care, child protection and the state*, London: Macmillan.

Pedersen, F.A., Cairn, R. and Zaslow, M. (1982) 'Variation in infant experience associated with alternative family roles', in L. Laosa and L. Segal (eds) *The Family as a Learning Environment*, New York: Plenum Press.

Penn, H. (1990) 'Policy and structure for pre-school services in the European Community', unpublished paper.

Phoenix, A. (1987) 'Theories of gender and black families', in G. Weiner and M. Arnot (eds) *Gender under Scrutiny*, London: Hutchinson.

Phoenix, A. (1988) 'The Afro-Caribbean myth', *New Society, 4 March*: 10-13.

Phoenix, A. (1991) *Young Mothers?*, Oxford: Polity.

Phoenix, A. and Woollett, A. (1991) 'Motherhood: social construction, politics and psychology', in A. Phoenix, A. Woollett, and E. Lloyd (eds) *Motherhood: meanings, practices and ideologies*, London: Sage.

Phoenix, A., Woollett, A. and Lloyd, E. (eds) (1991) *Motherhood: meanings, practices and ideologies*, London: Sage.

Piaget, J. (1918a) 'Biology and war', reprinted in H. Gruber and J. Vonèche (eds) (1977) *The Essential Piaget*, London: Routledge & Kegan Paul.

Piaget, J. (1918b) 'Recherche', reprinted in H. Gruber and J. Vonèche (eds) (1977) *The Essential Piaget*, London: Routledge & Kegan Paul.

Piaget, J. (1919) 'La psychanalyse dans ses rapports avec la psychologie de l'enfant', *Bulletin Mensuel de la Société Alfred Binet*: 18–34, 41–58.

Piaget, J. (1926) *The Language and Thought of the Child*, London: Routledge & Kegan Paul.

Piaget, J. (1929) *The Child's Conception of the World*, London: Routledge & Kegan Paul.

Piaget, J. (1932) *The Moral Judgement of the Child*, London: Routledge & Kegan Paul.

Piaget, J. (1933) 'Social evolution and the new education', *Education Tomorrow, 4*: 3–25.

Piaget, J. (1950) *Etudes Sociologiques*, partial unpublished translation by Carol Sherrard.

Piaget, J. (1953) *The Origins of Intelligence in the Child*, London: Routledge & Kegan Paul.

Piaget, J. (1957) 'The child and modern physics', *Scientific American, 197*: 46–51.

Pine, J. (1992a) 'Maternal style at the early one-word stage: re-evaluating the stereotype of the directive mother', *First Language, 12, 2, 35: 169–86.*

Pine, J. (1992b) 'The functional basis of referentiality: evidence from children's spontaneous speech', *First Language, 12*: 39–55.

Pine, J. (in press) 'The language of primary caretakers', in B. Richards and C. Galloway (eds) *Input and Interaction in Language Acquisition,* Cambridge: Cambridge University Press.

Pine, J. and Lieven, E. (1990) 'Referential style at thirteen months: why age-defined cross-sectional measures are inappropriate for the study of strategy differences in early language development', *Journal of Child Language, 17*: 625–31.

Pintner, R. (1933) 'The feebleminded child', in C. Murchison (ed.) *A Handbook of Child Psychology,* Worcester, Mass.: Clark University Press.

Plowden Report (1967) *Children in their Primary Schools: a report of the central advisory council for education,* London: HMSO.

Pollack, S. and Vaughn, J. (1987) *Politics of the Heart: a lesbian parenting anthology,* Ithaca, NY: Firebrand Books.

Pollock, L. (1983) *Forgotten Children,* Cambridge: Cambridge University Press.

Ramirez, A. (1992) 'Honduras: the traffic in children', *Central America Report, 55*: 5.

Renvoize, J. (1985) *Going Solo: single mothers by choice,* London: Routledge & Kegan Paul.

Rich, A. (1983) 'Compulsory heterosexuality and lesbian existence', in A. Snitow, C. Stansell and S. Thompson (eds) *Desire: the politics of sexuality,* London: Virago.

Richards, M.P.M. (1974) 'First steps in becoming social', in M.P.M. Richards (ed.) *The Integration of the Child into a Social World,* London: Cambridge University Press.

Richards, M.P.M. (1981) 'The myth of bonding', unpublished paper.

Richards, M.P.M. (1982) 'How should we approach the study of fathers?', in L. McKee and M. O'Brian (eds) *The Father Figure,* London: Tavistock.

Riegel, K. (1976) 'The dialectics of human development', *American Psychologist,* 698–700.

Riley, D. (1983) *War in the Nursery: theories of child and mother,* London: Virago.

Roberts, C., Green, R., Williams, K. and Goodman, M. (1987) 'Boyhood gender identity development: a statistical contrast of two family groups', *Developmental Psychology, 23, 4*: 544–57.

Robertson, J. (1958) *Young Children in Hospital,* London: Tavistock.

Roche, J. (1989) 'Children's rights and the welfare of the child', in W. Stainton Rogers, D. Hevey and E. Ash (eds) *Child Abuse and Neglect: facing the challenge,* London: Batsford.

Rorty, R. (1980) *Philosophy and the Mirror of Nature,* Oxford: Blackwell.

Rose, N. (1985) *The Psychological Complex: psychology, politics and society in England 1869–1939,* London: Routledge & Kegan Paul.

Rose, N. (1990) *Governing the Soul: the shaping of the private self,* London: Routledge.

Rotman, B. (1978) *Jean Piaget: biologist of the real,* New York: Academic Press.

Russell, G. (1983) *The Changing Role of Fathers?,* St Lucia, Queensland: University of Queensland Press.

Russell, G. (1987) 'Problems in role-reversed families', in C. Lewis and M. O'Brian (eds) *Reassessing Fatherhood: new observations on fatherhood and the modern family,* London: Sage.

Russell, J. (1982) 'Propositional attitudes', in M. Beveridge (ed.) *Children Thinking through Language,* London: Edward Arnold.

Rutter, M. (1982) *Maternal Deprivation Reassessed,* Harmondsworth: Penguin.

Rutter, M., Maughan, B., Mortimore, P. and Ouston, J. (1979) *Fifteen Thousand Hours: secondary schools and their effects on children,* London: Open Books.

Rycroft, C. (1974) *A Critical Dictionary of Psychoanalysis*, Harmondsworth: Penguin.

Sacks, H. (1972) 'On the analyzability of stories by children', in J.J. Gumperz and D. Hymes (eds) *Directions in Sociolinguistics: the ethnography of communication*, New York: Holt, Rinehart & Winston.

Sampson, E. (1989) 'The deconstruction of self', in J. Shotter and K. Gergen (eds) *Texts of Identity*, London: Sage.

Sandkvist, K. (1987) 'Swedish family policy and the attempt to change paternal roles', in C. Lewis and M. O'Brian (eds) *Reassessing Fatherhood: new observations on fatherhood and the modern family*, London: Sage.

Sandler, L.W., Strchler, G., Burns, P. and Julia, H. (1970) 'Early mother–infant interaction and 24 hour patterns of activity and sleep', *Journal of American Academic Child Psychiatry, 9*: 103–23.

Santrock, J.W. (1989) *Life-span Development*, Dubuque, Iowa: Wm. C. Brown.

Savva, H. (1990) 'The rights of bilingual children', in R. Carter (ed.) *Knowledge about Language and the Curriculum*, London: Hodder & Stoughton.

Sayers, J. (1986) *Sexual Contradictions: feminism, psychology and psychoanalysis*, London: Tavistock.

Scaife, M. and Bruner, J. (1975) 'The capacity for joint visual attention in the infant', *Nature, 253 (5489)*: 265–6.

Schaffer, H.R.H. (1971) *The Growth of Sociability*, Harmondsworth: Penguin.

Schaffer, H.R.H. (1977) *Mothering*, London: Fontana.

Schaffer, H.R.H. and Emerson, P.E. (1964) 'The development of social attachments in infancy', *Monograph of the Society for Research in Child Development, 29, 3* (whole no. 94).

Scheper-Hughes, N. (1989a) 'The cultural politics of child survival', in N. Scheper-Hughes (ed.) *Child Survival: anthropological perspectives on the treatment and maltreatment of children*, Dordrecht: Reidel.

Scheper-Hughes, N. (1989b) 'Culture, scarcity and maternal thinking: motherlove and child death in Northeast Brazil', in N. Scheper-Hughes (ed.) *Child Survival: anthropological perspectives on the treatment and maltreatment of children*, Dordrecht: Reidel.

Scheper-Hughes, N. (ed.) (1989c) *Child Survival: anthropological perspectives on the treatment and maltreatment of children*, Dordrecht: Reidel.

Schieffelin, B. (1979) 'Getting it together: an ethnographic approach to the study of the development of communicative competence', in E. Ochs and B. Schieffelin (eds) *Developmental Pragmatics*, New York: Academic Press.

Schieffelin, B. (1983) 'Talking like birds: sound play in a cultural perspective', in E. Ochs and B. Schieffelin, *Acquiring Conversational Competence*, London: Routledge & Kegan Paul.

Schieffelin, B. (1990) *The Give and Take of Everyday Life: language socialisation of Kaluli children*, Cambridge: Cambridge University Press.

Schieffelin, B. and Ochs, E. (eds) (1986) *Language Socialisation across Cultures*, Cambridge: Cambridge University Press.

Searle, J. (1972) 'What is a speech act?', in P. Giglio (ed.) *Language and Social Context*, Harmondsworth: Penguin.

Segal, L. (1990) *Slow Change: changing masculinities and changing men*, London: Virago.

Seifert, K.L. and Hoffnung, R.J. (1987) *Child and Adolescent Development*, Boston, Mass.: Houghton Mifflin.

Shapiro, J. (1987) *A Child, Your Choice*, London: Pandora.

Sharp, R. and Green, A. (1975) *Education and Social Control*, London: Routledge & Kegan Paul.

Shatz, M. (1982) 'On the mechanisms of language development: can features of the communicative environment account for development', in E. Wanner and L. Gleitman (eds) *Language Acquisition: the state of the art*, Cambridge: Cambridge University Press.

Shinn, M. (1978) 'Father absence and children's cognitive development', *Psychological Bulletin, 85, 3:* 286–24.

Shotter, J. (1973) 'Acquired powers: the transformation of natural into personal powers', *Journal for the Theory of Social Behaviour, 3:* 141–56.

Siegel, L. (1978) 'The relationship of language and thought in the preoperational child: a reconsideration of non-verbal alternatives to Piagetian tasks', in L. Siegel and C. Brainerd (eds) *Alternatives to Piaget*, New York: Academic Press.

Silverstein, M. (1991) 'A funny thing happened on the way to the form: a functionalist critique of functionalist developmentalism', *First Language, 11:* 143–79.

Simpson, E. (1974) 'Moral development research: a case of scientific cultural bias', *Human Development, 17:* 81–106.

Singer, E. (1992) *Child-care and the Psychology of Development*, London: Routledge.

Sinha, C. (1989) *Language and Representation: a socio-naturalistic approach to human development*, Brighton: Harvester.

Skutnabb Kangas, T. (1981) *Bilingualism or Not: the education of minorities*, Avon: Multilingual Matters.

Skutnabb Kangas, T. (1988) 'Multilingualism and the education of minority children', in T. Skutnabb Kangas and J. Cummins (eds) *Minority Education: from shame to struggle*, Avon: Multilingual Matters.

Skutnabb Kangas, T. and Cummins, J. (eds) (1988) *Minority Education: from shame to struggle*, Avon: Multilingual Matters.

Slosberg Andersen, E. (1990) *Speaking with Style: the sociolinguistic skills of children*, London: Routledge.

Smart, C. (1989) 'Power and the politics of child custody', in C. Smart and S. Sevenhuijsen (eds) *Child Custody and the Politics of Gender*, London: Routledge.

Smith, D. and Tomlinson, S. (1989) *The School Effect: a study of multiracial comprehensives*, London: Policy Studies Institute.

Snarey, J.R. (1985) 'Cross cultural universality of social-moral development: a critical review of Kohlbergian research', *Psychological Bulletin, 97:* 202–32.

Snow, C. (1972) 'Mothers' speech to children learning language', *Child Development, 43:* 549–65.

Snow, C. (1977) 'Mothers' speech research: from input to interaction', in C. Snow and C. Ferguson (eds) *Talking to Children*, Cambridge: Cambridge University Press.

Solberg, A. (1990) 'Negotiating childhood: changing constructions of age for Norwegian children', in A. James and A. Prout (eds) *Constructing and Reconstructing Childhood: contemporary issues in the sociological study of childhood*, Basingstoke, Hants: Falmer.

Song, M.J., Smetana, J.G. and Kim, S.Y. (1987) 'Korean children's conceptions of moral and conventional transgressions', *Developmental Psychology, 23, 4:* 577–82.

Sorce, J.F., Emde, R.N., Campos, J. and Klinnert, M. (1985) 'Maternal emotional signalling: its effect on the visual cliff behaviour of one year olds', *Developmental Psychology, 21, 1:* 195–200.

Speekmann Klass, C. (1985) *The Autonomous Child: daycare and the transmission of values*, Lewes: Falmer.

Spivak, G.C. (1990) 'Practical politics of the open end', in S. Harasym (ed.) *The Postcolonial Critic: interviews, strategies, dialogues*, London: Routledge.

Sroufe, L.A. and Waters, E. (1976) 'The ontogenesis of smiling and laughter: a perspective on the organisation of development in infancy', *Psychological Review, 83:* 173–89.

Stainton Rogers, R. and Stainton Rogers, W. (1992) *Stories of Childhood: shifting agendas of child concern*, Hemel Hempstead: Harvester Wheatsheaf.

Stainton Rogers, W. (1989) 'Childrearing in a multicultural society', in W. Stainton Rogers, D. Hevey and E. Ash (eds) *Child Abuse and Neglect: facing the challenge*, London: Batsford.

Stallibrass, A. (1974) *The Self-respecting Child: a study of children's play and development*, London: Thames & Hudson.

Stanway, P. and Stanway, A. (1983) *Breast is Best: a commonsense approach to breast-feeding*, London: Pan.

Steedman, C. (1985) '"Listen how the caged bird sings": Amarjit's song', in C. Steedman, C. Urwin and V. Walkerdine (eds) *Language, Gender and Childhood*, London: Routlege & Kegan Paul.

Stein, N., Trabasso, T. and Garfin, D. (1979) 'Comprehending and remembering moral dilemmas', in S. Goldman (ed.) *Understanding Discourse: interactions between knowledge and process*, symposium presented to American Psychological Association, September.

Stern, D. (1977) *The First Relationship*, Fontana: London.

Stone, L., Smith, H.T. and Murphy, L.B. (eds) (1973) *The Competent Infant: research and commentary*, New York: Basic Books.

Strang, R. (1959) *An Introduction to Child Study*, New York: Macmillan.

Sullivan, E. (1977) 'A study of Kohlberg's structural theory of moral development: a critique of liberal social science ideology', *Human Development, 20*: 352–75.

Sutton Smith, B. and Kelly Byrne, D. (1984) 'The idealisation of play', in P. Smith (ed.) *Play in Animals and Humans*, Oxford: Blackwell.

Svejda, M.J., Campos, J.J. and Emde, R.R. (1980) 'Mother–infant bonding: a failure to generalise', *Child Development, 51*: 415–32.

Sylvester Bradley, B. (1983) 'The neglect of hatefulness in psychological studies of early infancy', unpublished ms.

Sylvester Bradley, B. (1985) 'Failure to distinguish between people and things in early infancy', *British Journal of Developmental Psychology, 3*: 281–92.

Thom, D. (1992) 'Wishes, anxieties, play and gestures: child guidance in inter-war England', in R. Cooter (ed.) *In the Name of the Child: health and welfare 1880–1940*, London: Routledge.

Thorne, B. (1987) 'Revisioning women and social change: where are the children?', *Gender and Society, 1, 1*: 85–109.

Tittnich, E., Bloom, L., Schomberg, R. and Szekeres, S. (1990) (eds) *Facilitating Children's Language: handbook for child-related professionals*, New York: Haworth Press.

Tizard, B. (1991) 'Employed mothers and the care of young mothers', in A. Phoenix, A. Woollett and E. Lloyd (eds) *Motherhood: meanings, practices and ideologies*, London: Sage.

Tizard, B. and Hughes, M. (1984) *Young Children Learning: talking and thinking at home and school*, London: Fontana.

Torres, P. (1992) 'Els Països Catalans, des del Sud', *Demà, Periòdic per la Revolta, 10*: 10–11.

Tosi, A. (1988) 'The jewel in the crown of the Modern Prince: the new approach to bilingualism in multicultural education in England', in T. Skutnabb Kangas and J. Cummins (eds) *Minority Education: from shame to struggle*, Avon: Multilingual Matters.

Trevarthen, C. (1977), 'Descriptive analyses of infant communicative behaviour', in H. Schaffer (ed.) *Studies in Mother–Infant Interaction*, London: Academic Press.

Turiel, E. (1983) *The Development of Social Knowledge: morality and convention*, Cambridge: Cambridge University Press.

Urwin, C. (1982) 'On the contribution of non-visual communication systems and language to knowing oneself', in M. Beveridge (ed.) *Children Thinking through Language*, London: Edward Arnold.

Urwin, C. (1984) 'Power relations and the emergence of language', in J. Henriques, W. Hollway, C. Venn, C. Urwin, V. Walkerdine, *Changing the Subject*, London: Methuen.

Urwin, C. (1985a) 'Constructing motherhood: the persuasion of normal development', in C. Steedman, C. Urwin and V. Walkerdine (eds) *Language, Gender and Childhood*, London: Routledge & Kegan Paul.

Urwin, C. (1985b) 'Review of *War in the Nursery* (D. Riley, Virago, 1983)', *Feminist Review, 19*: 95–100.

Urwin, C. (1986) 'Developmental psychology and psychoanalysis: splitting the difference', in M. Richards and P. Light (eds) *Children of Social Worlds*, Oxford: Polity/Blackwell.

Urwin, C. and Sharland, E. (1992) 'From bodies to minds in childcare literature: advice to parents in inter-war Britain', in R. Cooter (ed.) *In the Name of the Child: health and welfare 1880–1940*, London: Routledge.

Valentine, C. (1956) *The Normal Child and Some of his Abnormalities*, Harmondsworth: Penguin.

Valsiner, J. (1988) *Developmental Psychology in the Soviet Union*, Brighton: Harvester.

Van der Eyken, E. (1973) *Education, the Child and Society: a documentary history 1900–1973*, Harmondsworth: Penguin.

Van Every, J. (1992) 'Who is "the family"? The assumptions of British social policy', *Critical Social Policy, 33*: 62–75.

Venn, C. and Walkerdine, V. (1978) 'The acquisition and production of knowledge: Piaget's theory reconsidered', *Ideology and Consciousness, 3*: 67–94.

Vidal, F. (1987) 'Jean Piaget and the liberal protestant tradition', in M. Ash and M. Woodward (eds) *Psychology in Twentieth Century Thought and Society*, Cambridge: Cambridge University Press.

Vukelich, C. and Kumar, D.S. (1985) 'Mature and teenage mothers' infant growth expectation and use of child development sources', *Family Relations: Journal of Applied Family and Child Studies, 34*: 189–96.

Vuyk, R. (1982) *Overview and Critique of Piaget's Genetic Epistemology*, Vol. 1, New York: Academic Press.

Vygotsky, L.S. (1962) *Language and Thought*, Cambridge, Mass.: MIT Press.

Vygotsky, L.S. (1978a) *Mind in Society: the development of higher psychological processes*, Cambridge, Mass.: Harvard University Press.

Vygotsky, L.S. (1978b) 'Problems of method', in *Mind in Society: the development of higher psychological processes*, Cambridge, Mass.: Harvard University Press.

Wachs, T.D. and Gruen, G.E. (1982) *Early Experience and Human Development*, New York: Plenum Press.

Walker, L.J. (1989) 'A longitudinal study of moral reasoning', *Child Development, 60*: 157–66.

Walkerdine, V. (1981) 'Sex, power and pedagogy', *Screen Education, 38*: 14–21.

Walkerdine, V. (1984) 'Developmental psychology and the child-centred pedagogy', in J. Henriques, W. Hollway, C. Urwin, C. Venn and V. Walkerdine *Changing the Subject: psychology, social regulation and subjectivity*, London: Methuen.

Walkerdine, V. (1988) *The Mastery of Reason: cognitive development and the production of rationality*, London: Routledge.

Walkerdine, V. (1990) *Schoolgirl Fictions*, London: Verso.

Walkerdine, V. and the Girls and Mathematics Unit (1989) *Counting Girls Out*, London: Virago.

Walkerdine, V. and Lucey, H. (1989) *Democracy in the Kitchen: regulating mothers and socialising daughters*, London: Virago.

Wallace, T. and March, C. (1991) *Changing Perceptions: writings on gender and development*, Oxford: Oxfam.

Ware, V. (1992) *Beyond the Pale: white women, racism and history*, London: Verso.

Watson, J. (1973) 'Smiling, cooing and "the game"', *Merrill Palmer Quarterly, 18*: 323–39.

Wedge, P. and Prosser, H. (1973) *Born to Fail?*, London: Arrow Books.

Wells, G. and Robinson, W.P. (1982) 'The role of adult speech in language development', in C. Fraser and K. Scherer (eds) *The Social Psychology of Language*, Cambridge: Cambridge University press.

Wertsch, J. (1991) *Voices of the Mind: a sociocultural approach to mediated action*, Hemel Hempstead: Harvester.

Wexler, P. (1983) *Critical Social Psychology*, London: Routledge & Kegan Paul.

Wheelock, J. (1990) *Husbands at Home: the domestic economy in a post-industrial society*, London: Routledge.

Wheldall, K. and Poborca, B. (1980) 'Conservation without conversation? An alternative non-verbal paradigm for conservation of liquid quantity', *British Journal of Psychology, 71*: 117–34.

White, D. and Woollett, A. (1992) *Families: a context for development*, Basingstoke, Hants: Falmer.

Whiten, A. and Milner, P. (1986) 'The educational experiences of Nigerian infants', in H.V. Curran (ed.) *Nigerian Children: developmental perspectives*, London: Routledge & Kegan Paul.

Whitfield, R. (1980) *Education for Family Life: some new policies for child care*, London: Hodder & Stoughton.

Winnicott, D.W. (1958) 'Hate in the counter-transference', in *Collected Papers: through pediatrics to psychoanalysis*, London: Tavistock.

Wolfe, R. (1981) 'Maladjustment in the context of local authority decision making', in L. Barton and S. Tomlinson (eds) *Special Education: policy, practice and social issues*, London: Harper & Row.

Wolff, P.H. (1969) 'The natural history of crying and other vocalisations', in B. Foss (ed.) *Determinants of Infant Behaviour*, Vol. 4, London: Methuen.

Wolman, B. (ed.) (1982) *Handbook of Developmental Psychology*, Englewood Cliffs, NJ: Prentice-Hall.

Woodhead, M. (1988) 'When psychology informs public policy: the case of early childhood intervention', *American Psychologist, 43, 6*: 443–54.

Woodhead, M. (1990) 'Psychology and the cultural construction of children's needs', in A. James and A. Prout (eds) *Constructing and Reconstructing Childhood: contemporary issues in the sociological study of childhood*, Basingstoke, Hants: Falmer.

Woollett, A. (1986) 'The influence of older siblings on the language environment of young children', *British Journal of Developmental Psychology, 4*: 235–45.

Yarrow, L.J., Rubenstein, J.L. and Pedersen, F.A. (1975) *Infant and Environment: early emotional and motivational development*, Washington, DC: Hemisphere/Wiley.

Yonas, N. (1979) 'Studies of spatial perception in children', in A. Pick (ed.) *Perception and its Development*, New York: Wiley.

Yuval-Davis, N. and Anthias, F. (eds) (1989) *Woman-Nation-State*, London: Macmillan.

Zelizer, V.A. (1985) *Pricing the Priceless Child: the changing social value of children*, New York: Basic Books.

Name index

Abbott, P. 66
Abramovitch, R. 75
Ainsworth, M.D.S. 82
Alldred, P. 69
Anthias, F. 71
Ariès, P. 51
Arney, W.R. 90, 91
Aspel, M. 55
Austin, J.L. 111
Avis, J. 175

Baetens Beardsmore, H. 119
Baker, C.D. 186
Baltes, P.B. 9
Barton, M. 115
Bates, E. 111
Batou, J. 184
Beaumont, F. 138
Beekman, D. 52
Bell, R. 25
Belsky, J. 81, 84
Bernstein, B. 135, 136
Bettelheim, B. 85
Billig, M. 166, 176
Blake, W. 1
Blakemore, C. 26
Blurton Jones, N. 27
Bly, R. 94, 100
Boden, M. 153
Bohannen, J. 127
Boulton, M.G. 84
Bower, T. 27, 28, 32
Bowers, J. 27
Bowlby, J. 71, 78, 79, 80, 82, 85, 88, 89, 96
Boyd, S. 74
Boyden, J. 48, 49, 55, 56, 184, 189
Bradley, B. Sylvester 10, 33, 37, 99, 118, 146

Brainerd, C. 155
Brannen, J. 67, 101
Brazelton, T.B. 36
Bremner, J.G. 27, 28
Brice Heath, S. 133, 135
Broughton, J. 87, 152, 154
Brown, R. 119, 122
Browne, N. 134
Bruner, J. 39, 81, 115, 116, 122, 126, 158
Buck-Morss, S. 183
Bukatko, D. 56, 125, 135
Bullock, A. 124
Burman, E. 100, 102, 117, 144, 154, 157, 158, 186, 188
Burns, R. 152
Burt, C. 17, 20
Butterworth, G. 25

Camaioni, L. 136
Campbell, B. 96
Caplan, P. 81
Carroll, L. 138
Carter, A. 111
Cassidy, C. 184
Chaika, E. 119
Choi, S. 134
Chomsky, N. 109, 110, 112, 125
Clancy, P. 134
Clarizio, H. 162
Clarke, A.D. 80
Clarke, A.M. 80
Clarke-Stewart, A. 95, 96, 98
Clarke-Stewart, K.A. 83
Cohen, C.B. 38
Cohen, G. 69
Colby, A. 179
Cole, M. 112, 113, 114, 183
Cole, S. 112, 113, 114

Collins, W. 6
Condon, W. 36, 37, 39
Conteh, J. 120
Cooper, G.F. 26
Cooper, S. 101
Cooter, R. 20
Craig, R. 162
Cross, T. 125, 128
Cummins, J. 121, 123

Daehler, M. 56, 125, 135
Dalley, G. 71
Daniels, D. 69
Darwin, C. 10, 11
David, M. 78
Davies, B. 145
Davis, N. 50, 51, 56
Dawson, P. 172
Descartes, R. 1, 52, 53, 56, 117
Dewey, J. 164
Dingwall, R. 56, 68, 74, 76
Dinnerstein, D. 87, 95
DiPietro, J. 32, 33
Donaldson, M. 115, 155, 156
Dornbush, S. 70
Dunn, J. 45, 125
Durham, M. 70
Durkin, K. 116, 118, 126, 134
Dweck, C. 134
Dworetsky, J. 29, 49, 50, 51, 56

Edwards, C.P. 179, 182
Edwards, D. 166
Eekelaar, J. 74, 76
Egerton, J. 65
Emerson, P.E. 95
Ennew, J. 46, 51, 52
Ervin Tripp, S. 142

Fantz, R. 36, 38
Farrar, M. 128
Ferguson, C. 127, 131
Fieldman, S. 68
Finch, J. 71
Fineman, M. 74
Flavell, J. 112
Fletcher, H. 73
Fogel, A. 50
Fonagy, P. 83
Ford, J. 15, 176
Foucault, M. 139
Frailberg, M. 90

France, P. 134
Freebody, P. 186
Freeman, M. 73
French, E.P. 136
Freud, S. 11, 85
Froebel, F. 164
Fuchs, E. 170

Galton, F. 13, 18
Gamsa, A. 91
Gardner, H. 152
Garland, C. 174
Gergen, K. 108
Gesell, A. 16, 17, 36, 44, 80, 87, 170, 171
Geuter, U. 18
Gibson, E. 29, 30, 33
Gilliéron, C. 25
Gilligan, C. 87, 180, 181
Ginsberg, H. 152
Gittins, D. 66, 67
Glauser, B. 184
Goodnow, J. 6
Gopnick, A. 134
Gould, S. 27
Groves, D. 71
Graycar, R. 74
Green, A. 166, 167, 170, 176
Greenough, T. 33
Gruber, H. 153, 162
Gruen, G.E. 84

Hakuta, K. 119
Hall, D.M.B. 16
Hall, G.S. 11
Halliday, M. 135
Halliday, M.A.K. 111
Hallpike, C. 182
Handelman, D. 72
Haraway, D. 14, 77, 88, 89
Hardyment, C. 51
Harlow, H. 26, 87, 88, 89
Harper, L. 25
Harré, R. 47, 108, 114, 145
Harris, A. 19, 33
Hearnshaw, L.S. 17
Hendrick, H. 13, 53, 54
Hennessy, E. 81, 92
Henriques, J. 2, 4, 139, 145
Hinde, R. 27
Hirsh-Pasek, K. 127
Hoff-Ginsberg, E. 115, 116, 117, 119
Hoffnung, R.J. 29, 51, 56, 60

Hogen, R. 180
Holden, P. 56
Holland, P. 189
Holtrust, N. 74
Holzman, L. 47, 114
Homel, P. 119
Horna, J. 101
Hoyles, M. 54
Hudson, A. 48, 49, 55
Hughes, M. 84
Hunt, F. 13
Hunt, J.McV. 38
Hymes, J. 161, 163, 169

Ingleby, D. 18, 83
Isaacs, S. 164
Izard, C.E. 83

James, W. 24
Jolly, H. 61
Jones, D. 57
Jones, K. 175
Joseph, G. 182

Kagan, J. 180, 182
Kaplan, P. 29, 49, 50, 51, 56
Karmiloff Smith, A. 156
Kaye, K. 39, 40, 41, 42, 43, 44, 115
Kelly Byrne, D. 166
Kendrick, C. 45, 125
Kennell, J. 89
Kepler, K. 162, 167
Kershaw, A. 100
King, T. 52
Kitzinger, S. 53, 185
Klaus, M. 89
Kohlberg, L. 3, 179, 180, 181, 182, 183
Konner, M. 38
Kumar, D.S. 57

Lamb, M.E. 38, 70
Lawrence, D.H. 163
Leach, P. 61
Leiser, D. 25
Levine, C. 182
Lewis, C. 98
Lewis, S. 101
Licht, B. 134
Lichtman, R. 7
Lieven, E. 85, 115, 119, 122, 130, 132, 133, 137
Light, P. 38, 47, 84

Lock, A. 111
Locke, J. 24
Lowe, N. 73, 74
Lowenfield, M. 164, 166
Lubeck, S. 167
Lucey, H. 10, 80, 84, 117, 130, 137, 170, 171
Lumnis, T. 101
Lupri, E. 101
Lyon, C. 74

McCabe, A. 156
Mace, C.A. 15
McDonald, L. 129
McGuire, J. 119
McKee, L. 96, 97, 98, 101
McLaughlin, B. 119
Maclure, M. 136
McNally, D.W. 165
McShane, J. 117
March, C. 184
Marks, D. 75, 176
Marquis, A. 127
Marshall, H. 58
Mead, G.H. 114
Mearns, A.G. 172, 173
Mehrens, W. 162
Meltzoff, A. 28
Mercer, N. 167
Meyer, P. 13
Miller, S.A. 155
Milne, B. 46, 51, 52
Milner, P. 38
Mitchell, P. 29, 125
Mitter, S. 67
Moll, L. 167
Montessori, M. 164
Moore, S. 97
Morris, L. 100
Morris, T. 177, 185
Morss, J. 11
Moss, P. 71, 101
Munn, P. 69
Murchison, C. 9, 12
Murdock, R. 67
Murphy, L. 34
Myers, R. 171, 185

Nelson, K. 128
New, C. 78
Newman, D. 114
Newman, F. 47

Newport, E. 131
Newson, E. 51, 57, 58, 84
Newson, J. 25, 51, 52, 57, 58, 84
Ninio, A. 116, 126

Oakley, A. 97
O'Brian, M. 69, 96, 97, 98, 101
Ochs, E. 131, 132, 133, 148
O'Hagan, S. 100
O'Hara, M. 74
Olsson, M. 18
Opper, S. 152

Papert, S. 153
Parke, R.D. 84, 96
Parker, G. 91
Parker, I. 2, 4, 108, 117, 139, 145
Parsons, B. 67, 99
Parton, N. 72, 73
Pearson, K. 18
Pedersen, F.A. 99
Penn, H. 81
Pestalozzi, J. 164
Phoenix, A. 56, 68, 69, 71, 96
Piaget, J. 3, 6, 11, 110, 112, 113, 114,
    151, 152, 153, 154, 155, 156, 157, 158,
    159, 160, 161, 163, 164, 165, 167, 175,
    177, 178, 179, 180, 181, 183, 186
Pien, D. 129
Pine, J. 127, 128, 129, 130, 137
Pintner, R. 14
Plomin, R. 69
Poborca, B. 155
Pollack, S. 70
Pollock, L. 51
Preyer, W. 11
Prosser, H. 172

Ramirez, A. 55
Randall, J. 162, 167
Renvoize, J. 96
Rich, A. 144
Richards, M.P.M. 36, 47, 90, 99, 102
Riegel, K. 154
Riley, D. 10, 11, 12, 17, 46, 78, 94, 157
Roberts, C. 98
Robertson, J. 79
Robinson, W.P. 128
Roche, J. 75
Rorty, R. 158
Rose, N. 10, 13, 14, 15, 18, 20, 52, 73,
    78, 130, 186, 187

Rotman, B. 112
Rousseau, J.-J. 53, 164
Rovine, M.J. 81
Russell, G. 98, 100
Russell, J. 156
Rutter, M. 80, 89, 170
Rycroft, C. 19

Sacks, H. 140, 141, 147
St Vincent Millay, E. 48
Sampson, E. 183
Sander, L.W. 36, 37, 39
Sandkvist, K. 100
Sandler, L.W. 33
Santrock, J.W. 51
Savva, H. 120
Sayers, J. 181
Scaife, M. 115
Schaffer, H.R.H. 36, 94, 95
Scheper-Hughes, N. 66, 77, 85, 86, 184
Schieffelin, B. 131, 132, 133, 134, 148
Searle, J. 111
Segal, L. 97
Seifert, K.L. 29, 51, 56, 60
Shapiro, J. 96
Sharland, E. 17, 78
Sharp, R. 166, 167, 170, 176
Shatz, M. 126
Shinn, M. 98
Shotter, J. 2, 25, 108, 114, 145
Siegel, L. 155
Silverstein, M. 109, 110, 112
Simpson, E. 183
Singer, E. 70, 80, 81, 92, 164
Sinha, C. 110
Skinner, B.F. 109
Skutnabb Kangas, T. 120, 121, 123
Slosberg Andersen, E. 142
Smart, C. 74
Smith, D. 170
Smith, H. 34
Snarey, J.R. 182
Snow, C. 115, 125, 128, 131, 137
Solberg, A. 60
Song, M.J. 180
Sorce, J.F. 31, 43, 58
Speekman Klass, C. 167
Spivak, G.C. 188
Spock, B. 61
Sroufe, L.A. 38
Stainton Rogers R. 53, 185
Stainton Rogers, W. 53, 68, 185

Stallibrass, A. 169
Stanway, A. 59
Stanway, P. 59
Stein, N. 180
Stern, D. 95
Stone, L. 24, 33, 77, 88
Strang, R. 171
Strober, M. 70
Sullivan, E. 183
Sully, J. 10, 11, 12
Sutton Smith, B. 166
Svejda, M.J. 90
Sylvester Bradley, B. 10, 33, 37, 99, 118, 146

Taine, J. 11
Tedlock, D. 148
Tennyson, A. 35
Terman, L. 18
Thom, D. 78
Thorne, B. 59
Tittnich, E. 116, 119, 135
Tizard, B. 80, 81, 82, 84
Tomasello, M. 115
Tomlinson, S. 170
Torres, P. 121
Tosi, A. 120
Trevarthen, C. 37
Turiel, E. 180

Urwin, C. 13, 17, 58, 78, 118, 122, 136, 146
Uzgiris, I.C. 38

Valentine, C.W. 15
Valsiner, J. 6, 114
Van Every, J. 65, 68
Van der Eyken, E. 20
Vaughn, J. 70
Venn, C. 153, 154, 175
Vidal, F. 159

Vonèche, J. 153, 162
Vukelich, C. 57
Vygotsky, L.S. 11, 112, 113, 114, 115, 151, 155

Wachs, T.D. 84
Walk, R.D. 29, 30, 33
Walker, L.J. 179
Walkerdine, V. 4, 10, 13, 17, 80, 84, 87, 117, 130, 134, 137, 143, 144, 145, 153, 154, 157, 164, 166, 170, 171, 175
Wallace, T. 184
Ware, V. 70, 71
Waters, E. 38
Watson, J. 38, 52
Wedge, P. 172
Wertsch, J. 114
Wesley, J. 51
Wesley, S. 51
West, R. 1
Wexler, P. 79
Wheelock, J. 100
Wheldall, K. 155
White, D. 69, 83, 84, 90
White, S. 174
Whiten, A. 38
Whitfield, R. 65
Wilson, G. 67
Winnicott, D.W. 57, 78, 86
Wolfe, R. 75
Wolff, P.H. 35
Wolman, B. 30
Woodhead, M. 53, 92
Woollett, A. 68, 69, 70, 71, 83, 84, 90
Wordsworth, W. 23

Yarrow, L.J. 38, 65
Yuval-Davis, N. 71

Zelizer, V.A. 184

Subject index

adaptation 35–6, 41–2, 152, 157, 158
adult development: and infancy 26, 27–9
Ainsworth Strange Situation Test 83
artificial intelligence 27, 153
attachment theory 4, 35, 77–93, 94, 98, 124
attribution: adult 39–41
autonomy: and education 167–8, 183

behaviourism 18, 24, 25–6, 37, 39, 52, 152, 153, 164
bilingualism 119–22
biology: and philosophy 152; role of 4, 10, 11, 12–13, 24, 35–6, 37, 38, 39, 41, 42–3, 45–6, 51, 85, 98, 112, 114
black oppression 70; *see also* culture, imperialism, multilingualism, oppression, racism
bonding 89–91
breast-feeding 32–3, 41, 58–9

child 2, 3, 4–5, 7; advocates 74–5; best interest of 5, 74; -centred approach 130, 154, 158, 159, 163–76, 184; development 9, 14–15, 16–17, 24–5, 164–5, 171, 173–4, 183, 184; -directed speech 125–30; image of 53–4; and intentionality 39; labour 54, 55–6, 60, 184; and language 3, 107–23, 124–37, 138–48; and law 73–5, 102; protection 72; rearing 43, 49, 65, 71, 168–9, 171, 173–4, 183, 184; *see also* childhood, children, infancy
child abuse 53, 56, 65–6, 72–3, 85, 86, 97, 185
child sexual abuse 72, 97, 185
child study movement 10–11, 12, 17, 19, 24

childcare 4, 71, 77, 78–82, 92, 95, 97, 99, 100, 103, 134, 187; advice 51–3, 57–60
childhood 2, 6, 7, 11; and class 54–5; conceptions of 2, 184–5; and culture 185–6; depiction of 48–61, 183, 184; history of 51–6; model of 163; obesity 56
children 2, 4, 6; and morality 177–80; rights of 73–4, 102; *see also* child, childhood
Children Act (1989) 73
class 4, 45, 57, 59, 69, 84, 85, 101, 183, 186, 187; and childhood 54–5; and education 166, 167, 171; and language development 115, 118–19, 121, 125, 130, 133, 135–6, 188; oppression 4
cognitive development 3, 51, 134, 151, 180, 183
cognitive psychology 24
cognitivism 25, 26, 36
colonialism 10, 55, 70, 121
communication 3, 39; parent–child 108; *see also* language
constructionist approach 39, 44–5
conversation analysis 140, 141
crying 38
culture 2, 3, 4, 6–7, 10–11, 38, 43, 44, 46, 49–51, 56, 58–60, 83, 85, 92, 122, 153–5, 160–1, 167–8, 170, 183, 185, 188; and childhood 185–6; and context 152; and the family 66–7, 71, 75, 98, 100, 170; and language development 114, 115, 119–22, 125, 130, 131–5, 135–6, 145; and moral development 177, 179, 182–5

day-care provision 81, 92, 167; *see also* childcare

degeneracy 13–14
democracy: and education 168–70, 171, 176
demography 66, 69
deprivation: cycle of 135; maternal 26, 72, 78, 79–81, 82; sensory 26; social 91
depth: perception of 29–30
development: conceptions of 2, 3, 5, 6, 7, 9, 10–11, 12–13, 14, 15, 16–17, 19, 24–6, 27–9, 33, 35, 42, 43–4, 48–56, 58, 59–60, 80, 91, 107, 108, 113–14, 152–3, 173–4, 187; child 9, 14–15, 16–17, 24–5, 164–5, 171, 173–4, 183, 184; moral 177–89; regulation of 16–17; social 2, 3, 35–47, 107, 133; see also Piagetian theory
developmental psychology: function of 185, 186–7; goals of 177; history of 9–20, 35–47; impact of 2, 3; key issues of 3–4, 5, 7; and morality 177–89; political role of 188; status of 9
disability 58; see also handicap

education 3, 4, 5, 12, 13, 17, 18, 52, 54, 81, 135, 152, 159, 170, 172, 184; and achievement 170; and autonomy 167–8, 183; child-centred 158, 159, 163–76; and class 166, 167, 171; compensatory 158, 170; and democracy 168–70, 171, 176; and individualism 167–8, 176; and inequality 107, 135, 170, 172; parental 171; and Piaget 159, 161, 163–76; and power relations 44, 102; pre-school 81, 92, 174; 'progressive' 164–6, 175; special 15
educational policy 163
educational psychological services 75, 139
elaborated code 135
environmental influence 10, 18, 24, 25, 26, 32, 33, 42, 65, 69, 80, 81, 114, 153, 157
epistemology see genetic epistemology, knowledge
ethology 83, 85, 87, 90, 98
eugenic movement 18
evolutionary influence 4, 9, 17, 24, 26–7, 28, 29, 30, 35, 41, 42, 43, 45, 85, 90, 103, 112, 152
experimenter: role of 155

families 2, 3, 4, 6, 18, 43, 57, 60, 65–76,

79, 98, 100, 104, 169–70, 171–2, 173, 184, 187, 188; and culture 66–7, 71, 75, 98, 100, 170; and economic context 66–7, 75; and historical context 66–7, 75; and language development 119, 121; and research 69–70; single-parent 96, 97, 186; and the State 67–8, 70–5, 91; see also siblings
fatherhood 94–104; see also fathers
fathers 2, 3, 11–12, 57, 69, 70, 74, 82, 84, 92, 94–104, 187; see also parenting, parents
feminism 7, 78
functionalism 67, 107, 110, 111–12

games: children's 177–9; see also play
gay men 68, 70, 98; see also homosexuality
gender 5, 10, 11–13, 45, 67, 86, 87, 88, 95, 97, 98, 100, 101–2, 134, 143, 145, 157–8, 161, 167, 173, 183, 184, 186, 188; and morality 181; oppression 4; relations 59
genetic determinism 153
genetic epistemology 152, 153, 157
Guardianship of Infants Act (1925) 74

handicap: child 13–14, 28; visual 28; see also education
health visiting 5, 139
heredity 17, 24, 173
hermeneutics 25
heterosexism 43–4, 49, 68, 70
heterosexuality 58, 67, 68, 69, 158, 186; compulsory 144; see also heterosexism, sexual orientation
historical background 2, 3, 9–20, 35–47, 51–6, 66–7, 75, 78, 152, 154, 160, 183; of infancy research 23–33
home: and school 170–3; see also families, fathers, mothers
homosexuality 173; see also gay men, lesbians, sexual orientation

imperialism 10, 55, 70, 182, 183, 185
individualism 182, 187; and education 167–8, 176
inequality: and child-centred education 169; and education 107, 135, 170, 172; social 107, 135, 163, 164, 167–8, 170, 172, 175–6, 188
infancy 7; research 2, 23–33, 36, 39, 114;

see also child, childhood
Infant Custody Act (1839) 74
infertility 68
intentionality: and child behaviour 39
interviewing 101–2, 153, 155; *see also* researcher

knowledge 10, 11, 12, 13, 18, 23–4, 25, 26, 29, 30, 32, 60, 88, 138, 152, 153, 154, 155, 156, 175; sensory 28

labelling 116–19
language 2, 107–23, 155; and adult–child interaction 115, 116, 118, 124–37; child 3; and class 115, 118–19, 121, 125, 130, 133, 135–6, 188; and contexts 124–37; and culture 114, 115, 119–22, 125, 130, 131–5, 145; development 3, 4, 39, 107–23; and families 119, 121; and mother's role 124–37; and power 138–48; research 107–23, 124–37; and siblings' role 115–16, 125, 131–2; and social control 121, 136; and turn taking 115, 140, 144
law 5, 97; and the child 73–5, 102
lesbians 68, 70; *see also* homosexuality, sexual orientation
liberalism: and Piaget 159–60, 175
'life-span' development 7, 9, 50, 185

marriage 66
maternal deprivation 26, 78, 79–81, 82, 87–8
measurement 3, 9–10
medicine 12; and childbirth 90
methodology 3, 32, 90, 91, 97–9, 101, 119, 124, 127, 129–30, 134, 183, 187; and moral development 180, 182; and Piaget 153, 154, 156, 161
moral development: models of 177
moral reasoning 179, 180
morality 1, 3, 158–9, 177–89; and children 177–80
motherhood 58, 69, 78, 79
mothering 3, 6, 33, 69, 70, 81, 97, 99, 117, 130; sensitive 128–30
mothers 2, 3, 4, 6, 12, 38, 43–5, 46, 57, 58, 65, 67, 69, 70, 71, 74, 75–6, 77–93, 94, 95, 102, 103, 104, 117, 118, 143, 147, 172, 187; black 69; and infant interaction 36, 40, 43, 129–30, 133; and language development 124–37; *see*

also maternal deprivation, motherhood, mothering, parenting, parents, women
multilingualism 119–22

nature/nurture 13, 29, 30, 42, 49
normalisation 15

oppression 4, 117; black 70; class 4; gender 4, 10–12, 124, 181; racial 4, 68, 70–1, 135; *see also* black oppression, class, culture, gender, heterosexism, imperialism, mothers, multilingualism, racism, social regulation

parenting 33, 45, 53, 57, 71; and education 171; and power 136; *see also* mothers, fathers
parents 2, 4, 6, 176; and child interaction 39; and child relationship 7, 77; gay 70; lesbian 70; role of 24, 102; *see also* mothers, fathers
Piagetian theory 3, 25, 151–62, 163–76
play 52, 116, 118, 130, 157–8, 165, 166; and rules 177–9
Plowden Report (1967) 163
political motivations 1, 5, 17, 177, 188
positivist psychology 108
post-structuralism 7–8
poverty 85–6, 104, 184
power relations 44, 102; and child abuse 185; and education 166–7; and language 136, 138–48
pregnancy 57
pre-school education 81, 92, 174
psychoanalysis 4, 13, 19, 52, 83, 84, 85, 87, 94, 104, 151
psychology: comparative 26

racism 69, 70–1, 88, 115, 119, 120, 184; *see also* oppression
rationalisation *see* psychoanalysis
rationality 3, 10, 12–13, 19, 87, 158; as gendered 11–12, 87; *see also* psychoanalysis
reading 116, 186
recapitulationism 11
regulation *see* social regulation
research 3, 5, 7, 10; application of 26; and attachment 78, 83–4; and culture 167; and the family 69–70; and fathering 97–9, 101–2; impact of 5; and infancy 2, 23–33, 36, 39, 114; and interviewing

101–2, 153, 155; and language 107–23,
124–37; and mothers 69; observational
98, 102, 116; and political influences 5;
and power 136, 138–47; role of 5; and
social influences 5; and social policy 1;
and survey methods 101; *see also* child
study movement
researcher: role of 101, 153, 155, 182, 183
residential care 79, 82
restricted code 135–6
rules: and children 177–9; *see also* games

school organisation 170
science 10, 11, 15, 18, 24–5, 156, 157,
158–9, 161; as gendered 10, 11–12, 43,
69, 78, 79–85, 87–9, 94, 95–6, 97–8,
99–102, 157; *see also* psychoanalysis,
rationality
sensorimotor period 25, 110
sexual orientation 173, 186, 188; *see also*
gay men, heterosexuality,
homosexuality, lesbians
siblings 45, 115–16, 125, 131–2
single mothers 65, 68, 98
single-parent family 96, 97, 186
smiling 38–9
social constructionism 108, 110, 114
social control 13–14, 15, 19, 171, 174;
and language 121, 136; *see also* social
regulation
social Darwinism 10–11, 13, 158
social development 2, 3, 35–47, 107; and
biology 35; and language 133; *see also*
socialisation
social factors 5, 9–10, 13–14, 32, 33
social pathology 16, 68, 170, 175, 187
social policy: and childcare 19, 77, 78;
and childhood 53–4, 55, 56; and

education 163; and the family 65–8,
75; and research 1
social psychology 108, 145
social regulation 15, 108, 117, 156,
171–2, 174, 175, 188; *see also* social
control
social relationships 139, 155, 175
social structure relations 44
social work 5, 71–4, 139
socialisation: and child development
35–47; and the family 71
socio-cultural context 153–4; *see also*
culture
standardisation 15; *see also* testing
state: and the child 53–4, 56, 59, 60; and
the family 67–8, 70–5, 91; intervention
2
structuralism 152
survey methods 101
systems theory 83

teachers: and patterns of interaction
167–8; and power 166–7; role of
165–6, 170; women 164
teaching methods 164
technology: role of 24–5
teenage pregnancy 56
teenage suicide 56
testing 14–15, 16, 18, 19, 83, 153, 154;
and the social situation 31
Third World 55–6, 60, 86, 184

welfare 5, 12, 71, 152, 187; policies 2, 16
women 3–4, 12, 58, 59, 66, 67, 70, 71,
74, 75, 96, 117, 130, 181; black 68;
and child study 10; and childcare 158;
headed households 68; teachers 164;
see also mothers